COURTROOM
WARRIOR

Books by Richard O'Connor

Fiction

GUNS OF CHICKAMAUGA

COMPANY Q

OFFICERS AND LADIES

THE VANDAL

Non-fiction

THOMAS: ROCK OF CHICKAMAUGA

HOOD: CAVALIER GENERAL

SHERIDAN THE INEVITABLE

HIGH JINKS ON THE KLONDIKE

BAT MASTERSON

JOHNSTOWN: THE DAY THE DAM BROKE

HELL'S KITCHEN

WILD BILL HICKOK

PAT GARRETT

BLACK JACK PERSHING

GOULD'S MILLIONS

THE SCANDALOUS MR. BENNETT

COURTROOM WARRIOR: THE COMBATIVE
CAREER OF WILLIAM TRAVERS JEROME

COURTROOM WARRIOR

The Combative Career of William Travers Jerome

RICHARD O'CONNOR

With Photographs

LITTLE, BROWN AND COMPANY · BOSTON · TORONTO

Published simultaneously in Canada
by Little, Brown & Company (Canada) Limited

PRINTED IN THE UNITED STATES OF AMERICA

Contents

Contents

Illustrations

COURTROOM
WARRIOR

1

"Hardly Any Sense of Sin"

A CENTURY AGO it was exceptional for any right-thinking American male to concern himself unduly just because his wife was giving birth. Far from pacing the delivery room, disheveled and distraught, he held himself aloof and awaited the outcome with dignity. All the fuss over childbirth was "women's business," which was not an admiring phrase. A man had to beware of giving his womenfolk any undue sense of their importance, already the silly creatures were demanding their "rights" and campaigning for the "single standard." Only when the infant assumed a recognizable human shape did the American male begin to consider it worthy of his attention.

On the evening of April 18, 1859,* when Mrs. Catherine Hall Jerome was delivered of a male child at her home at 33 West Nineteenth Street, in Manhattan, her husband naturally absented himself from the small crowd of female relations, friends, neighbors, doctor and midwife in attendance. The only male on the scene, aside from the newborn child, was the doctor. Mrs. Jerome was thirty-six years old and this was her fourth son, her fourth and final child.

Her husband, Lawrence Jerome, social, sporting and political

* The front-page news that day concerned the trial of Dan Sickles for the murder of Philip Barton Key in Washington, D.C., perhaps the most famous American murder trial until the Thaw case, which the infant born that day was to prosecute.

figure, Wall Street operator, wit, clubman in New York, boulevardier in Paris, and a blithe spirit wherever he was, was sensibly
dining at Delmonico's when his last son was born.

With him was his dearest friend, William Travers, celebrated
as the "stammering wit of Wall Street," which did not always
appreciate his humor. (At a yacht race in Newport the names
of the winning skippers were announced. Every one of them,
like Travers himself, was a wealthy stockbroker. "And where,"
demanded Mr. Travers, "are the customers' yachts?" Flippancies
of that sort convinced his more serious-minded colleagues that
Mr. Travers wasn't half respectful enough of the sacerdotal
mysteries of high finance.)

Mr. Jerome and Mr. Travers had just finished their oysters
and steak when a waiter brought word to their table that Mrs.
Jerome had given birth to a son. He whispered the news to Mr.
Jerome, who looked pleased and said, "Bring champagne."

Mr. Travers raised his brows inquiringly.

"It's a boy, Billy," his friend told him.

"Wh-what's his n-name?"

Mr. Jerome's large pink face was suffused by a sudden inspiration. He and Mrs. Jerome had not consulted on a name for
their forthcoming child, but he felt quite capable of deciding
the matter over the foaming bottle of champagne the waiter was
opening at their table. Who better deserved the honor than his
companion? Finally he announced:

"His name is William . . . Travers . . . Jerome!"

Mr. Travers was so overcome by the gesture that, for once,
he was caught without an appropriate remark.

2

THE INFANT, whose health and prospects his father and god-
father toasted in champagne, was to resemble them only in
his most social aspect. He also possessed a sense of humor, a
liking for various alcoholic beverages, a taste for conversation

and conviviality, and a talent for friendship. But there he parted
company with those two estimable gentlemen, those two middle-
aged playboys who prolonged their adolescence, deliberately and
amiably, to the verge of senescence. The senior Mr. Jerome and
his friend found nothing in life worth taking seriously; the infant
they gave so impromptu a christening grew up to make the name
William Travers Jerome synonymous with political reform and
the stern pursuit of justice, to become "St. George of Manhattan" slaying the dragons of the underworld, to gain the respect
of his profession as the master of ruthless cross-examinations and
incisive summations. Yet thanks to that infusion of his father's
blood with its tolerance and amiability he never became a self-
righteous bluenose. That inherited sense of proportion was not
the least of his legacies from the Jerome side of the house.

When he was seized by the moral and intellectual necessity for
reforming a corrupt metropolis, William Travers Jerome had to
foreswear practically everything the preceding generation of
Jeromes stood for. If they had any sense of dedication, it was to
wine, women, song and sport. One of their more serious endeavors was to promote thoroughbred horse racing in the United
States.* If they believed in anything, it was style, behaving like a
gentleman under all circumstances. Even when they made fortunes in Wall Street, they did so lightheartedly; to them pursuing
wealth grimly or greedily, like a Jay Gould or a Daniel Drew,
was simply a violation of form, graceless and therefore contempti-
ble. You had to have the light touch; you never censured or
preached, and you never explained or apologized. The Union
Club was your home. If you were faithful to your wife or
possessed any of the other humdrum virtues, you did not preen
yourself over it. You refused to pay lip service to the Puritan ideals

* An endeavor in which William Travers joined wholeheartedly. The
$75,000 Travers Stakes is the oldest such race for thoroughbreds in the
United States. It is run annually at Saratoga. First run in 1864, it is ante-
dated on this continent only by the Queen's Plate in Canada.

which, until the years of demoralization following the Civil War, supposedly governed the more privileged classes.

From their ease of manner, it might have seemed that the Jeromes inherited their wealth and position in New York society. Actually, and it was all the more a credit to their innate aplomb, they were one-generation aristocrats, descended from tillers of the upstate soil, craftsmen and artisans.

The three Jerome brothers who made such a fine splash in metropolitan society — Addison, Leonard and Lawrence — were born on a farm at Pompey Hill, near Syracuse, in Onondaga County. They had six brothers and one sister who survived infancy. Their mother was the former Aurora Murray, of Scottish descent, while their father, Isaac, came of a sturdy and durable Huguenot family. The first Jerome known to genealogy was Timothy, a Protestant who fled France in 1710 after the revocation of the Edict of Nantes, settled on the Isle of Wight for seven years and migrated in 1717 to the American colonies. He and his English wife Abigail established themselves at Meriden, Connecticut, where he followed his clockmaker's trade with fair success. Some of their descendants began farming around Stockbridge, Massachusetts, where Isaac Jerome was born. Isaac moved to New York State early in manhood and cleared the ground at Pompey Hill, where he and Aurora raised their lively brood.

A Scottish Presbyterian–French Huguenot background was practically a guarantee of a somber, if not dour outlook on life, reinforced by the exigencies of working a hardscrabble farm. In later years Lawrence Jerome recalled that his mother educated her sons by reading to them and disciplining them sternly, and he frequently said that he owed her "everything but my ill health." Addison, Leonard and Lawrence, of the nine sons, were determined to find wider horizons. Addison, the oldest of the three, worked his way through two years of Princeton, then quit school to make his fortune in New York City.

Leonard, who was born in 1818, and Lawrence, two years

younger, made their way to Rochester, where their uncle Hiram K. Jerome was appointed judge in 1842. Uncle Hiram also established a law firm, which Leonard joined as a junior partner and Lawrence as a clerk. The fortunes of the brothers Jerome were improved considerably in 1845 when Lawrence married Miss Catherine Hall, whom the newspapers identified as "an heiress of Palmyra." Catherine, a dark-eyed, serious and rather intense young woman, was one of three orphaned sisters raised by elderly and severe maiden aunts in Palmyra. All that is known of their meeting, courtship and marriage is that the aunts opposed any union with an amiable but impecunious law clerk. The various sources of family history agree that Catherine Hall's father was of English descent and her mother was half Iroquois. Some members of the present generation of Jeromes are inclined to doubt romantic tales of their great-grandmother's Indian blood, but the Churchill branch of the family in England embraces them with enthusiasm.* Thus Catherine's sons could boast of a volatile mixture of racial strains, Anglo-Saxon, Gaelic and Gallic, with a one-eighth dash of Indian blood.

Catherine's inheritance enabled Lawrence, with his brother Leonard as a partner, to buy a substantial interest in the Rochester *American*, a Whig organ. Newspapers, as mid-century approached, were beginning to be a profitable investment with population and literacy increasing. The *American* prospered, and Lawrence, as one historian recorded, "endeared himself to many Rochestrians" with his "blithe spirits and love of practical jokes." The Jerome brothers published the *American* for five years until

* Including Anita Leslie, a Jerome descendant, in her compassionate but clear-sighted *The Remarkable Mr. Jerome*, a biography of Leonard Jerome. William Travers Jerome's daughter-in-law, Mrs. John Sloane, says that many of the Hall sisters' descendants show more than a trace of Indian blood in their features. And John Spencer Churchill, painter-nephew of Sir Winston, said recently at the beginning of an American lecture tour: "I have 20 to 25 talks, but the one they all want to hear is 'Redskins and Blue Bloods.' The redskin branch of our family is through Sir Winston's American mother, Jennie Jerome." New York *Post*, February 18, 1962.

it was possible to dispose of their interests at a handsome profit.

In the meantime, Catherine's sister Clara, a gayer and more sprightly girl, succumbed to the formidable charm of Leonard Jerome on her frequent visits to the house at 63 South Fitzhugh Street, which he shared with his brother and sister-in-law. Clara and Leonard were married in 1849, thus twice confounding the Hall sisters' disapproving aunts, and both families shared the house on Fitzhugh Street.

After the brothers disposed of their interest in the *American*, the clannish household broke up temporarily, and Leonard and his wife left Rochester. Lawrence stayed on to be elected alderman from the third ward, 1850–1851, then deputy collector of customs until a Whig defeat in 1853 deprived him of office. When the Whig party was dissolved, both Jerome brothers became Democrats. For a year or so Lawrence worked as a traveling agent for the Michigan Southern Railroad, then decided to join Leonard and Addison in New York, where they had invaded Wall Street with some success and formed a brokerage with William Travers as their partner. Lawrence and his family moved in with Leonard's at 33 West Nineteenth Street, where William Travers Jerome was born.

Lawrence Jerome opened his own brokerage and cooperated with his brothers and Travers in various financial maneuvers which, for almost a score of years, were attended by a considerable prosperity. Looking upon Wall Street as a gigantic gaming den, they plunged into speculation, particularly in the risky field of railroad and steamship financing, with more verve than discretion.

To the lofty and acerb lawyer-diarist George Templeton Strong the Jeromes were fair samples of the high-living "Belmont Clique." Their particular friends, aside from William Travers, were Henry Clews, a broker descended from the English gentry, and August Belmont, who was born in the Rhenish Palatinate, was apprenticed to the Rothschilds' bank in Frankfort and in

1837 was sent to the United States as the banking family's first American agent.

In his gossipy history of the financial district, *Fifty Years in Wall Street*, Henry Clews characterized his friend Lawrence Jerome thus: "He is the prince of metropolitan wags. His friends are legion. The great, genial, warm-hearted Larry Jerome, as his friends love to call him is literally a man without an enemy." Lawrence's sense of humor was so infectious that one of his friends said he wanted Larry brought to him when he was dying so he could "laugh the thing off." One newspaper characterized him as "the most popular man on the Stock Exchange."* August Belmont recalled of him that "he could scarcely ever be serious."

After his brother's three daughters married into aristocratic English families, he began a speech before the American Jockey Club: "Many years ago, before I had any blue blood in my veins . . ."

His prime companion in waggery and practical joking, William Travers, specialized in puncturing bores, a sport just a touch too bloody for the amiable Larry. One dullard who had been monopolizing the conversation at a dinner party finally turned to Travers and asked him, in the course of a long dissertation on the natural history of bivalves, if he believed that oysters had brains. "Well, y-yes," Travers replied. "Just enough to keep their mouths shut."

Larry and Billy, in tandem, seemed to their contemporaries more interested in hell-raising than money-making. One of their favorite pranks when mellow with wine was to board a horse-car, jostle each other and pretend to become embroiled in an argument, shouting, "You unmannerly oaf!" "How dare you, sir?" "I'll thrash the daylights out of you!" "Put down that cane, sir!" and other pleasantries until the whole car was in an uproar. At their demand the car would be halted "so we can settle our differences." Then, while the other passengers waited with delight

* New York *Times*, August 13, 1888.

for the bloodshed to begin, Billy and Larry would link arms and stroll off laughing.

Happy-go-lucky though the methods of Travers and the Jeromes seemed, "mingling ruthlessness with frivolity," as Anita Leslie has observed, they managed to make (and lose) several fortunes between them. Addison Jerome was "a gigantic operator," Henry Clews recorded, but he "went beyond his depth and disaster followed" when he attempted to corner the stock of the Lake Shore Railroad. He made and lost approximately ten million dollars before his death in 1861, Clews estimated.

Leonard Jerome meanwhile was forming a profitable business and personal relationship with Commodore Vanderbilt, then engaged in his enormously successful organization of the New York Central. The Commodore's sulphurous speech and his uninhibited pursuit of sightly females made him unacceptable in the more polite and dignified circles of society, but Leonard Jerome cultivated him and joined profitably in his schemes. Lawrence Jerome was brought into these maneuvers, of course, and prospered accordingly. The Jeromes necessarily allied themselves, as good Democrats and lively opportunists, with Boss Tweed, the Grand Sachem of Tammany Hall, and with John Morissey, ex-pugilist, professional gambler and leader of the Dead Rabbits gang which was notably efficient in getting out the Irish vote on election day. The way financiers then operated — manipulating and watering the stocks of various companies, to their private advantage and the ordinary investor's great loss — they needed the cooperation of the politicians and the more shadowy underworld figures who kept them in power. Rich and powerful as he was, Commodore Vanderbilt also took Tweed and Morissey to his bosom, and through them controlled several judges who protected him whenever outraged stockholders tried to curb his greed. It was a rankly corrupt situation, which flowered most brilliantly when Jim Fisk and Jay Gould used the same system to loot the Erie Railroad of millions of dollars.

Thanks to their politico-financial alliances, the Jeromes managed to operate profitably in the roiled and muddy backwaters of the economy — and think none the less of themselves for it. Their morality was that of the times. Personal honesty, in post-Civil War society as a whole, was at a premium. "This community is devoid of moral sense," as George Templeton Strong confided to his diary. "It has proclaimed an extra Beatitude of greater influence than all the others put together, namely, 'Blessed are the smart.' "

The Jeromes were among the smart and the blessed, at least until their luck ran out.

A fair sample of the piratical behavior of the Wall Street "insider" of that day was the knavery committed by their friend Travers and another broker named Addison Cammack. Their chosen victim was Jay Gould, the highly successful lone wolf whom everyone abominated, mostly because he was bolder and cleverer than any of his fellow predators. Travers and Cammack struck at Gould during a spring storm when all the telegraph lines were down and Gould had to rely on messengers to carry his buying and selling orders downtown from his home at 579 Fifth Avenue. They kidnaped one of his messengers and substituted a youth in their employ, then established themselves at the Windsor Hotel across the street from the Gould mansion. Their hireling brought them Gould's orders, which they read before sending them on their way, and thus they were enabled to inflict losses estimated at more than a hundred thousand dollars on Gould before he uncovered their scheme. For a trick which in later days would have earned them stiff prison sentences, Travers and Cammack were heartily congratulated by their friends and associates.

3

It was in the social and sporting worlds where Leonard and Lawrence Jerome really shone and where their judgment on such

matters as food, wine, fast horses, swift boats and lovely women
was really valued. As financiers and speculators, they had attained
a respectable amount of success — Leonard in particular — but as
connoisseurs of high living and arbiters of gentlemanly form they
were unrivaled, except, possibly, by August Belmont. In the highly
febrile society, inhabited in great part by the people enriched by
the Civil War, which flourished in the Flash Age (1865–1873),
they were the leaders of fashion, the pacesetters, the latterday
Beau Brummels.

"One rode better, sailed better, banqueted better when Mr.
Jerome was one of the company," Anita Leslie quotes a member
of the Belmont Clique as saying. He was referring to Leonard
Jerome, as was another contemporary who remarked that he
"outdid all others bent on cutting a figure." Lawrence Jerome
traveled along in his older and more successful brother's wake.
As for the genial but tough-minded August Belmont, whose financial resources were superior, he also found himself following
Leonard's lead. No one else had quite his originality, verve and
style. Everyone envied his success with women, and even more,
perhaps, his success in keeping his wife from open rebellion
while he chased various lovely ladies of society, theater and the
opera. Every day, according to that impeccable chronicler Ward
McAllister, he sallied forth — while Clara Jerome sat at home
with her three daughters — "with his drag or coach loaded with
beautiful women, and drove to every desirable little country inn"
in the rustic areas of the Bronx and Westchester, making a gay
spectacle "driving up Broadway with the ease and skill of a
veteran whip, which he was." Even the more resentful pro-
letariat couldn't help raising a cheer, it was said, when Leonard
Jerome, gorgeously turned out with a whole bouquet in the
buttonhole of his bright green coat, took a corner full tilt with
his lady friends shrieking and giggling behind him.

It was Leonard Jerome who revived the sport of coaching and
with Delancey Kane, James Gordon Bennett, Jr., August Bel-

mont and other lively spirits organized the Coaching Club, which every swell in New York yearned to join.

Another celebrated social and sporting institution organized by Leonard and Lawrence Jerome, with August Belmont quickly joining in, was the American Jockey Club. Its guiding principles, so the founders proclaimed, were to "promote the improvement of horses, to elevate the public taste in sports of the turf, and to become an authority on racing matters in the country." In brief, the Jeromes intended to keep horse racing a sport for gentlemen. They took over the old Bathgate Estate in the Fordham section, built a grandstand seating eight thousand spectators and held their first meeting in September, 1866. Many of the leading personalities of the Flash Age were present — Jim Fisk, Boss Tweed, John Morissey (who was now "political agent" at Albany for Commodore Vanderbilt and Leonard Jerome in their Harlem Railroad venture), and some even less reputable people. The star attraction, however, was Lieutenant General Ulysses S. Grant, whose coming Presidential administration was to epitomize politically what the Flash Age meant socially.

That same year, when his youngest son was seven years old, Lawrence Jerome risked life and limb as a member of the crew of James Gordon Bennett, Jr.'s *Henrietta* in the first transAtlantic yacht race with Pierre Lorillard's *Vesta* and Frank Osgood's *Fleetwing* for a $90,000 purse. Lawrence was then fortyfive years old but he signed on as a member of young Bennett's crew when professional sailors backed out of the dangerous midwinter race across the Atlantic to the Needles off the south coast of England. After almost fourteen days of bucking the Atlantic storms, in which *Fleetwing* lost six crew members, Bennett's *Henrietta* crossed the line a winner; it is still regarded as one of the great feats in yachting history. Bennett, Jerome and their comrades were royally feted in England and France.

In those years, when insiders could make money on Wall Street without half trying, before Boss Tweed was sent to prison and the panic of '73 smashed so many carefree speculators and drained off so much easy money, Larry Jerome led a splendidly sybaritic life, bounded on one side by sporting interests, on a second side by a busy social life on both sides of the Atlantic, and finally and offhandedly by a few hours daily at his brokerage and on the Exchange. With so many lively distractions, the lovable Larry could spare little time for his role as head of a growing family. His wife was a spoilsport, with Puritanical inhibitions, a ridiculous yearning for dignity and respectability and a ready frown for anything that smacked of bawdy or irreverent wit. There was a chill over the house of Jerome that repelled her fun-loving husband's deepest instincts, which urged him to enjoy life at all costs. Naturally he was more attracted to the jolly good fellowship of the Union Club and other haunts. His four sons had to get along without much paternal guidance, which, in Larry Jerome's book, was a crashing bore to both the giver and the recipient.

In his middle years he was a stout, ruddy-faced, Pickwickian fellow, according to his friend Henry Clews, whose sunny outlook was clouded only by the bitter disapproval of his wife, so unlike her complaisant sister. He was obviously going to end his days as an elderly playboy, purple-veined complexion and all. It was hardly surprising that Catherine Hall Jerome did not encourage her sons to follow in their father's footsteps.

Her pithiest comment on the Jerome way of life, with which many were inclined to agree, was that "The Jeromes seem to have so much sense of honor and hardly any sense of *sin*." She was insistent that her sons be something more than urbane gentlemen who cut a fine figure in society. The Jeromes, no less disapproving of what they considered her provincial and excessively grim attitude, referred to her as "the plague." A photograph taken of her in her later years shows a woman with a very firm jaw, chilly and austere eyes, a rigid and forceful face in every aspect. Neither wit nor cajolery could persuade her to take a more relaxed view of life, and she did not hesitate to express her opinion of drinking even at Leonard Jerome's sophisticated board. Leonard once tried to straighten her out on the subject of alcohol, citing evidence that Christ Himself looked upon wine without moral disapproval. "In that case," was Catherine Jerome's dour comment, "our Lord showed poor judgment."

Even more alarming from her point of view was her husband's association with the wild young publisher of the New York *Herald*, James Gordon Bennett, Jr., both before and after he was forced to exile himself to Paris. Young Mr. Bennett had committed an unforgivable breach of manners at a New Year's party given by his fiancée's family, which resulted in a broken engagement and a bloodless duel with one of her brothers. The Belmont Clique was bad enough, but she was convinced, and rightly, that her aging husband's valiant efforts to keep up with Bennett's pace in Paris would shorten his life. No doubt she agreed with an open letter Jay Gould, not entirely suited to the role of public moralist, addressed to Bennett in the newspapers: "Your private life has been a succession of debauches and scandal . . . Not a gentleman in New York, as you well know, would allow you to cross the threshold of his residence where virtue and family honor are held sacred." Bennett was not welcomed across Catherine Jerome's threshold either, of course, but he found various ways of luring her husband beyond her ken, one of which was a midnight summons to a Paris bordello on the pretext that he had been seriously injured in an accident.

During the sinking spells suffered by the stock market in the late sixties and early seventies, Larry Jerome lost a good deal of the money accumulated in happier times when the Jerome brothers were allowed to function as pilot fish for Commodore Vanderbilt. He was "badly crippled" in the speculation surrounding the Pacific Mail steamship line."* Finally, according to Henry Clews, he was forced to withdraw from the Street, sold

* New York *Herald*, August 13, 1888.

his seat on the Stock Exchange for about $30,000 and bought an annuity paying him $4,000 a year for life. "This, with other income, places him in easy circumstances and preserves his naturally cheerful disposition, rendering him one of the most companionable men in the city . . ." The "other income" presumably referred to his wife's inheritance.

Clews put a good face on Larry Jerome's comeuppance but both he and Leonard Jerome had had their wings clipped to the nub, and while they still comported themselves in gentlemanly style, their highflying and fashion-setting days were over.

By way of further consolation, Boss Tweed saw to it that Lawrence was elected to the Board of Aldermen in 1870 and was appointed to the Committee of Arts and Sciences as its chairman, "a most honourable though not very busy post." When Tweed was driven from office and deposited in the Ludlow Street jail, Lawrence Jerome was "known as one of the two honest men" on the Board of Aldermen.* He was a close friend of President Chester Arthur and Senator Roscoe Conkling, but he failed in a subsequent attempt to be elected to Congress. His opponent was General Anson McCook, and Civil War service was still a potent influence on the electorate. Joviality, he learned, could carry a man just so far in politics as in finance.

4

LAWRENCE and Catherine Jerome's youngest son found himself caught between his father's easygoing attitude toward public and private morality and his mother's stern, unsparing code of behavior. It would be oversimplifying to suggest that he rejected his father's way of life and was influenced toward his mother's more rigorous and purposeful outlook. Yet all his life, as he later told his daughter-in-law, he was subject to fears that there was a hereditary disposition toward loose living on his father's side of the house, an inclination he suspected would be passed along to

* New York *Times*, August 13, 1888.

his own descendants. The fact that one brother drank himself to death and another eloped with a servant only reinforced this deep-rooted fear, which did not, however, prevent him from indulging in the drinking, gambling and other amenities of club life his father and uncles so thoroughly enjoyed. His own indulgences ran parallel, and without noticeable conflict, with his driving ambition and his relentless crusading against corruption and lawlessness.

Travers, as the family called him, was some years younger than his brothers and cousins; his childhood was one long series of illnesses, and the fact that he came along too late to share in the luxuries and privileges available to the others, before the family fortunes declined, also embittered him. All these factors contributed to a sense of isolation in his boyhood, encouraged a fondness for working things out independently, and saved him from the curse of sentimentality.

In the transplanted English tradition, he was placed in a boarding school early in boyhood, but illness forced his parents to bring him home. Later, while they sojourned in Paris and London and on the Riviera, he was left in a school at Loney, Switzerland. For the most part, however, his primary education was placed in the hands of a tutor. From then until early manhood his health kept breaking down, perhaps because his mother kept him surrounded with such a grim and precise solicitude. His three brothers were much older, and Catherine Jerome could not help but cling to him in desperation; her two oldest sons had gone West and were leading hazardous lives and the third son was away at college. She thought it only fair that at least one of her four sons should be kept at her side.

He was the sort of small boy who was always suffering from catarrh, asthma and a hacking cough, nausea, dizzy spells and a constantly alarming pallor — all symptoms which might now be catalogued as psychosomatic and diagnosed by an amateur psychiatrist as evidence of his reaction to Mrs. Jerome's overly protective attitude, and possibly to the disharmony between his high-living father and puritanical mother. He had a "weak chest" and a "delicate stomach" and must not be allowed to play in the streets with the young ruffians down the block. He must be guarded against the night air. He must be dosed with calomel regularly, as well as the other tenderly regarded specifics of the Victorian medicine chest. Young Travers was so smothered in maternal and medical devotion that it was no wonder he had difficulty in breathing.

It was probably a great relief when the domestic bonds were loosened slightly and he was permitted to enter the Williston Preparatory School at Easthampton, Massachusetts, in his middle teens, and with a rather late start, to prepare himself for college.

This was about the time that his three beautiful cousins, the daughters of his Uncle Leonard and Aunt Clara, began making their series of brilliant marriages overseas.

In 1874, Jennie Jerome married Lord Randolph Churchill, an event privately troublesome to her father who, a year after the panic of '73, was hard pressed to provide the $10,000 annually he promised the couple in a pre-nuptial agreement. Leonard agreed to the *dot* only after long and sometimes rancorous negotiations. As his celebrated grandson was to describe the delicate situation later, "Mr. Jerome had strong and, it would seem, not unreasonable views, suggested by American usage, about married women's property . . ." There was "embarrassing discussion" about the matter and "negotiations had already extended over seven months" before "a satisfactory treaty was ratified."*

Leonard's reluctance to supply a dowry was dictated not so much by paternal pride or an American aversion to helping support a son-in-law as financial stringency. All he now owned was a Manhattan town house at Twenty-sixth Street and Madison Square, which had been rented first to the Union League Club and then to the Manhattan Club. Now it stood vacant. His

* Winston Churchill's *Lord Randolph Churchill*.

friends in New York, including Colonel Lawrence Kip, Pierre Lorillard and James R. Keene, decided to come to Leonard's rescue by renting the premises for a private gaming club. Baccarat and poker were played there, and the race results from Paris and London were chalked up on a large blackboard. "Gambling was high there," one patron recalled, "so extravagant that after a few years the club went out of existence."* By then, however, the $25,000 annual rent paid Leonard enabled his daughter to become Lady Churchill and produce a red-haired son named Winston.

Travers's other two cousins also came off well in the trans-Atlantic matrimonial sweepstakes, Clara marrying the well-born Morton Frewen and Leonie a Guards officer named John Leslie. Leonard Jerome's daughters, in fact, did much better for themselves and their family than most American heiresses, if they could be called heiresses in view of their father's dwindling finances, and with the least expenditure of patrimony.

These cousinly triumphs were of little interest to young Travers at the moment, for the hero of his adolescence was, by all odds, his eldest brother. Lovell Hall Jerome had become an army officer, and Travers would have liked to emulate him if people hadn't kept telling him that he was much too delicate for anything but a sedentary career.

Lovell, ten years older than Travers, was graduated from West Point in 1870 and immediately assigned to the frontier army. Twice cited for gallantry in various cavalry actions, he was serving with Major John Gibbons's column when it marched from Fort Ellis to join with other converging forces, including Custer's Seventh Cavalry, in a campaign against the Sioux and their allies. Gibbons's column arrived on the Little Big Horn two days after Custer and his troopers had been massacred; all they could do was bury the victims of Custer's rash miscalculations and send

---

* E. Berry Wall in *Neither Pest Nor Puritan.*

their commander's body back East for a questionable hero's fare-well.

Lieutenant Jerome distinguished himself in the various subsequent actions designed to avenge the Seventh Cavalry's misadventure. A year later he led a mounted charge against Chief Lame Deer, one of Sitting Bull's lieutenants, on the Big Muddy. He was recommended for the Congressional Medal of Honor. Later, in 1877, after the battle of Bear Paw Mountain, he volunteered to enter Chief Joseph's camp as a hostage while the valiant chieftain came to brigade headquarters to discuss the terms of surrender after his people's long and futile exodus northward. It was said to have been the only exchange of hostages between the United States Army and the dissident tribes during the long history of Indian warfare. Later Lovell recalled that White Bird, Chief Joseph's second-in-command, told him, "Joseph no come back, Miles [General Nelson A. Miles who commanded the pursuing forces] hurt Joseph, me kill you. Savvy?"* Lovell was returned safely to his own camp when negotiations were completed. He retired from the army in 1879 and was appointed collector of customs at Corpus Christi by President Arthur, a friend of his father's. Later he returned to New York and, like many men trained for a military career, found it difficult to establish himself in civilian life. Travers's hero worship did not survive closer acquaintance with his older brother. Close up, Lovell seemed ineffectual and unheroic as he struggled for a foothold outside the certainties of a military career, and the two brothers were never on very friendly terms until the last years of their lives.

Travers's other two brothers, Roswell Hart and Lawrence Roscoe Jerome, conducted themselves in such a way as to con-

---

* From a manuscript included in the Jerome family scrapbook kept by Mrs. John Sloane. Many years later Lovell held a reunion with Chief Joseph in New York, when the latter was appearing in Buffalo Bill's Wild West show. The chief gave Lovell his old hunting shirt, which Lovell presented to the museum at West Point.

vince their younger brother that there was an hereditary flaw
in the Jeromes, the consequences of which he feared all his life.
Roswell studied for the law and was appointed an assistant district attorney in the Tammany-dominated regime of Samuel E.
Garvin, but died soon thereafter, in February of 1872, at the
age of twenty-three. His death was attributed to excessive drinking.

Lawrence was a wayward, undisciplined youth who eloped
with his mother's cook while in his early twenties, went West to
seek his fortune and was never seen again by any member of the
family. A letter was sent after him declaring that he was disinherited and was never to cross the threshold of the Jerome
house again. Doubtless it was his Spartan mother who wrote that
letter of excommunication. Lawrence enlisted as a private in the
regular army and served in the campaigns against Geronimo.
Later, as his family informed the newspapers at the time of his
father's death, he was reportedly "managing a large cattle ranch
in the West." None of the Jeromes ever heard from him again.*

Spurred on by a determination to "get away from home" and
its oppressive memories, as he later told his daughter-in-law,
Travers proceeded with his education at a ruinous pace. He was
nineteen when he entered Amherst, a year or two older than
most of his classmates, and he committed himself to making up
for time lost during his sickly childhood. He was also determined
to scourge from his system whatever it was that drove one
brother to drink and another to reckless adventure in the West.
Forswearing the horseplay and mandolin-strumming of the
fraternity houses, he assumed a heavy schedule of studies and
in addition took over as assistant instructor in chemistry in his
second year.

---

* In her will, Catherine Jerome noted that Lawrence had been formally
disinherited "on account of his unfilial conduct." She left an estate of
$45,000 in real estate and $25,000 in personal property, half of which went
to Travers and the income of the balance to Lovell.

In his junior year, however, his health broke down completely under the work load he was carrying. He had to quit school. His mother, hopeful of the tensile strength of the silver cord attaching her to one son at least, insisted that he come back home.

Travers now had to make one of the fateful choices of his life, to return to the iron solicitude of the house in Nineteenth Street or strike out on his own. He chose the latter course, went upstate, and worked on a farm until his health slowly returned.

Those hard and lonely months undoubtedly were the making of the man; they contributed to his lifelong obsession with physical and mental toughness. By the time he had completed his self-imposed regimen, he was still gaunt and weedy but the appearance of frailty was deceptive. Actually he was as tough and as flexible as a buggy whip, and in later years could boast that he was immune to illness, despite a forthright addiction to cigarettes, whiskey, hard work and late hours.

Once his health was restored he resumed his education. He had decided on a legal career and entered Columbia, from which he emerged in 1884 with a law degree, a continuing urge to make up for lost time, a sizable amount of ambition, and enough kinetic energy, it seemed, to light up Manhattan from the Battery to the Bronx.

2

Stirrings of Conscience

SOCIAL HISTORIANS refer to the decade in which Travers Jerome entered manhood and began his career as the Elegant Eighties. It was perhaps the most tranquil decade in American history, midway between wars, comparatively serene domestically, with the Indians finally driven at gunpoint into reservations, no serious depressions, no great issues in the balance. It was as good a time to be alive as any in the past century — but elegant? Perhaps for a few: the Vanderbilts finally rising to the crest of social prominence, the costumed dandies and their ladies dancing at Mrs. Astor's cotillions, and the new industrial and financial magnates lording it over their estates in Tuxedo Park, Newport and Bar Harbor.

For the submerged ninety-nine one-hundredths of the populace, it was a simple and much more brutal life, largely consumed by work for subsistence wages, the constant struggle to keep even with the landlord, and an occasional seidel at the corner saloon by way of recreation. The ordinary person caught only distant glimpses of that legendary elegance. The most he hoped for was a debt-free death.

People worked a twelve-hour day, a six-day week, and ten dollars a week wasn't a bad wage — many had to work longer hours for less. Poverty was so close to most people's daily lives that it is inconceivable today; there was no form of public relief, no workmen's compensation, no old-age pensions, and private charity was tightfisted and humiliating; a week's illness was a disaster, and the death of a breadwinner simply scattered the family in orphanages or, more likely, dumped the children on the streets.

In New York, the melting pot was constantly threatening to boil over rather than amalgamate. Of the city's 2,000,000 population, nearly half a million couldn't speak English. The slums were still filled from Mulberry Bend to Hell's Kitchen with the giant waves of Irish and German immigration; even so, and with a violent resentment, they were elbowed by thousands of newcomers from Italy, Greece and other parts of central and eastern Europe. Violence stemming from crime and racial differences was so prevalent that the authorities could only hope to contain it in certain sections of the Lower East Side and the midtown section west of Eighth Avenue, where the police ventured only in riot-squad strength. You could get away with murder on Tenth Avenue or in the Bowery, but any thug who showed his face on Fifth Avenue or in the financial district was hustled off for a beating in the backroom of the nearest station house.

Juvenile delinquency has never been so unchecked as then, with some of the street gangs numbering from five hundred to one thousand members, most of them armed with knives, revolvers and blackjacks. The adolescent fascination with violence was then blamed on the evil influence of Beadle's Dime Library and Nick Carter's detective stories.

Manhattan was a city of two-, three- and four-story structures with brownstone or red-brick fronts. Only a few skyscrapers were tentatively thrusting their towers, all of ten or twelve stories high, downtown on Park Row and in the financial district. The theater district was centered around Fourteenth and Broadway but was slowly moving uptown toward Dodge Place (soon to be Herald Square) and Longacre Square (now Times Square).

Harlem, far to the north, was a quiet residential district with a surburban atmosphere and the Bronx was largely countryside.

Old prints, woodcuts and photographs testify to what now seems a delightfully picturesque time so charmingly recaptured in the songs about the sidewalks of New York, hokeypokey men, organ-grinders, strolling bands, waltz-filled Sunday afternoons and dashing exploits on bicycles. A modern man afflicted with a severe case of nostalgia, however, would probably be put off by its actual discomforts and inconveniences. There was a wooden Indian in front of every cigar store and the little horse-cars clanged happily, but there was no electricity and illumination was provided by kerosene lamps or gas fixtures. Offices, stores and homes were heated by the potbellied stoves called Base Burners. Brimstone matches gave off poisonous fumes. Transportation was limited to hansom cabs, omnibuses, horse-drawn streetcars (slowly giving way to cable lines) and the elevated railways which roared overhead and showered pedestrians with soot and ashes — the subway wasn't built until 1900. Men wore scratchy paper collars and cuffs, and women were encased in so many layers of cloth and whalebone they could hardly breathe.

Millionaires were playing polo and living it up on their steam yachts, but there were few sports in which poorer folk could interest themselves, if they had the time and energy to spare from their work. Baseball was denounced from the pulpit and in the press as a game played by oafs and watched only by "ill-mannered persons" who raised their voices and threw things when they were displeased.

Cycling became all the rage with the invention of the low-wheeled safety bicycle. Preachers inveighed against it as conductive to immorality, but they could do little to stop the craze. From early in the spring to late in the fall, Riverside Drive at night was a firefly stream of headlamps. On thoroughfares favored by cyclists cobblestones were replaced by asphalt paving, and every Sunday they pedaled by the thousands along the country roads in the Bronx and Queens. Even the upper classes took up the sport. The young Duke of Marlborough, a member of the Churchill family and an intimate of Lawrence Jerome's, who had come over to press his eventually successful suit for the hand of Consuelo Vanderbilt, a mismatch which cost her family an estimated ten million dollars, was arrested on Riverside Drive for "scorching" — fast and reckless cycling. The Duke protested that pursuing an American heiress was hard work and he was entitled to some sort of relaxation from his efforts, but he was hauled off to court and fined just the same.

For those less appreciative of fresh air and outdoor exercise, those who yearned for forbidden delights and heady pleasures denied them back in the old home town, there was always the brownstone Babylon west of Sixth Avenue known as the Tenderloin, a district that will be more thoroughly explored later.

Perhaps the most succinct description of the ethical state of the New York bar when Travers Jerome began practicing was provided by George W. Alger, himself a prominent attorney. "The grievance committee of the bar association was not functioning," he noted, "and a lawyer could do pretty nearly anything he wanted. Most of them did."

The leading trial lawyers included John R. Dos Passos, the father of the novelist; DeLancey Nicoll, whose aristocratic birth did not prevent him from becoming, as district attorney, one of Tammany Hall's more persuasive advocates; William Bartlett, who had represented Boss Tweed during some of the more critical moments of his career in the previous decade; Roger Pryor, George Gordon Battle, and Abraham Levy, who was known as "The Last Hope" for his willingness to take on apparently hopeless cases.

By all odds the most successful firm specializing in criminal law was Howe and Hummel, whose offices at 89 Centre Street, opposite the Tombs, were Mecca, before and after commission

of a crime, to every well-heeled hoodlum, bookmaker and
policy shop operator. As mouthpieces for the underworld,
William F. Howe and Abe Hummel have never been equaled in
skill and efficiency, not even by such a later virtuoso as William
Fallon. Between 1869, when the partnership was formed, and
1907, by which time Howe was dead and Hummel disbarred,
they defended more than a thousand persons charged with
murder or manslaughter. In addition to acting as general counsel
of the Tenderloin, they were expert at rigging up breach of
promise cases. "Seduction under promise of marriage," as they
phrased it, enriched the firm, kept many a young woman in
finery, and bedeviled the city's wealthier womanizers. Howe
and Hummel may not have invented the breach of promise
suit but they developed it to the point where it was a more
effective deterrent to stage-struck husbands than wifely tirades
or hell-fire sermonizing. Almost any morning their waiting
room contained several charmers from the theatrical district
eager to discuss how their activities of the night before could be
converted into ready cash.

Howe was an English-born ex-convict whose ability to sway
juries with his ready tears, organ-toned voice and pleas on
bended knee won him a striking percentage of acquittals. A
large fat man, he fitted himself out in purple suits with diamonds
glittering on fingers, cuffs and shirtfronts, "a gaily bedecked
elephant," as David Graham Phillips described him, "careening
across the sky." Howe was generally regarded as the flamboyant
front man who spoke the lines in court while owlish little Abe
Hummel did the firm's brainwork and conniving behind the
scenes. Not all their colleagues agreed with the view of Howe
as simply the brazen mouthpiece with Hummel pulling the
stops, but as one contemporary wrote, "Who could, at the
beckoning of his little finger, summon to his dungeon-like offices
the most eminent of citizens? — surely none but Abe Hummel. A
whisper from Hummel was enough to make the dry bones of

many a powerful and ostensibly respectable official rattle and his tongue cleave to the roof of his mouth in terror." Their biographer, Richard Rovere, has deprecated Hummel's evil-genius publicity, however, picturing him as "a cheerful and rather gracious little man" who luxuriated in racetrack and theatrical society while Howe was "a very queer tick indeed . . . whose interest in violent death always seemed excessive even for a murder lawyer."

An indication of the discretion with which Howe and Hummel operated was their abhorrence of the written, and therefore potentially incriminating, word. They kept no records, no account books, no files; all the firm's business was conducted ad-lib and on the spot. Every evening the partners met in Pontin's Restaurant, the rendezous favored by lawyers and judges and their hangers-on, emptied their pockets and split the day's take evenly. All communication, between themselves, their associates and their clients, was by word of mouth.

Until they came on the scene, the criminal bar was regarded as an unprofitable field which for many years had been worked over haphazardly by drunkards, unfrocked priests, former police magistrates and other riffraff. For more than thirty years Howe and Hummel were to dominate this raffish milieu, until the surviving partner was finally eliminated through the efforts of the young lawyer who hung out his shingle in the fall of 1884. Travers Jerome was then twenty-five years old and still running hard to catch up with his contemporaries.

Shortly after graduation from Columbia with a law degree, and a brief apprenticeship with an established firm, Jerome entered into a partnership with another young lawyer named Daniel Nason, and together they struggled to work up a clientele that would keep them going on something more substantial than hope. But lawyers were plentiful, and not many clients found their way to the offices of Nason and Jerome with such celebrated practitioners of corporate law as Elihu Root, Charles Evans Hughes, Joseph Choate and Chauncey Depew available. Nason and Jerome did not specialize in corporate law, or in any particular phase of their profession; they specialized in anything they could get.

It may have seemed that Travers Jerome was born with a silver spoon in his mouth, but by the mid-eighties it was plated rather than sterling. Among his assets — aside from such personal qualities as a quick intelligence, a bear-trap tenacity and a driving ambition — were: (1) his family's social connections, and (2) the Jeromes' long support of and intimacy with the leaders of Tammany Hall, dating back to Boss Tweed's days and including the present grand sachem, Dick Croker. The problem of how to convert these assets into a profitable law practice was to engage Jerome for four years after he left law school. The solution eluded him. He simply couldn't go around, hat in hand, to the various nabobs, whose office doors would have swung open to him on the strength of his name, and ask for a piece of their legal business. It would be a handout, if extended, and Jerome had his full share of the family pride.

During those years, his father's health was declining. Cheerful as ever, he was afflicted by the first of a series of strokes while on a fishing trip in Maine. The Duke of Marlborough, a member of the party, was on his way home when he received a telegram at the station reporting that Larry Jerome had been stricken. The Duke, who was not the brightest offshoot of the Churchill clan, grinned and commented, "Another of Larry's jokes," and continued on his way.

Lawrence Jerome's best friend, William Travers, died in 1887 while vacationing in Bermuda. Travers's fortunes, like those of the Jeromes, had also suffered from the depredations of the Wall Street wolf pack, but he was survived by a considerable body of humorous legend. One of his two-liners traveled the vaudeville circuits for many years after his death. Returning home at the crack of dawn, he was creeping into the bedroom when his wife suddenly awakened. "Is that you, Bill?" she called out. "Y-yes," he stammered. "Wh-who did you expect?"

Catherine Hall Jerome was still as vinegary and self-contained as ever, and as defiant of the amiable sophistication which ruled the male side of the Jerome clan. One of her triumphs over Jerome easygoingness involved the family-founded race track, Jerome Park, although she had undoubtedly disapproved of that enterprise. Her husband and his brother Leonard had contributed heavily to the construction of a broad, tree-lined avenue leading to the track. Mrs. Jerome, who yearned for some mark of civic recognition for the family, was outraged when she learned that an alderman named Murphy had arranged to have the thoroughfare named for himself. Her husband and brother-in-law were inclined to shrug it off, but Mrs. Jerome had new street signs made, hired a crew of workmen, and saw to it that Murphy Avenue underwent an overnight transformation to Jerome Avenue — and the alderman did not dare contest the matter. So it remains today, in a much less glamorous setting.

On August 10, 1888, less than a year after the death of his friend Travers, Larry Jerome was stricken with another cerebral hemorrhage while the Jeromes were staying at the country home in Sharon, Connecticut. He sank into a coma, and the New York *Sun* headline recorded: "The Prince of Good Fellows Slowly Gives Up the Fight."

In the New York *Herald*, his old friend James Gordon Bennett's paper, an editorial mourned that "the merriest spirit in all the world goes when Lawrence Jerome crosses the dark river." On August 12, with his wife and his son Travers at his bedside, Larry Jerome died without regaining consciousness. Many great and sterner figures of his era were missed a lot less when they, too, crossed the dark river.*

---

* His widow died ten years later, in February, 1898, just when her youngest son was beginning to win the sort of civic renown she had always hoped would accrue to the family.

"A Jovial Spirit Passes," Bennett's *Herald* mourned in its headline, with the obituary beneath recording that he was the "subject of more anecdotes than any other society or business man in New York." He was buried in the family vault at Greenwood Cemetery in Brooklyn.

One dubious legacy Larry Jerome managed to leave his youngest son — a job obtained, lamentably enough in view of his later activities, through pull with Tammany Hall.

Shortly before his father's final illness, Travers expressed a desire to leave private practice after four painful years of waiting for clients to beat a path to his door, and find more gainful employment.

These years were made all the more painful by a broken love affair. He had fallen in love with a socially prominent young lady and hoped to marry her, but she discarded him in the belief that it would be many more years before he would be able to support a wife in any kind of style.

The fairly predictable result was that, "on the rebound," he become involved with another young woman totally unlike her predecessor.

Eager to obliterate all traces of his first love and its bitter aftermath, he became engaged to Miss Lavinia Taylor Howe, of Elizabeth, New Jersey. The daughter of Augustus and Ann Massie Howe, she was descended on her mother's side from officers who had served with honor in the Revolutionary War. Miss Howe was an attractive, patient and retiring — almost withdrawn — young woman, seldom assertive, rarely demanding, with a strong distaste for Manhattan society. She seemed a perfect antidote. Travers was determined to marry her as soon as possible. Aside from the fact that he had already lost one girl who refused to play patient Griselda, he was conscious of the delicate problem of their ages: Lavinia was almost five years older, and in a day of early marriages could almost be said to be beyond the ordinary marriageable age. Travers himself was then twenty-nine. There were other differences between them more critical than age, but these were not yet startlingly apparent.

Travers wanted a job with salary attached. His late brother had served in the district attorney's office, and at this point he had no pronounced aversion to Tammany Hall. His father took him to meet Grand Sachem Dick Croker, a reticent and hard-bitten type, who looked the young man over, nodded, and uttered the magic words: "All right, he's in."

Travers was sent to District Attorney John R. Fellows at the Criminal Courts Building with instructions that he be added to the staff. He was appointed an assistant district attorney, Lavinia became his wife, and both Tammany Hall and Jerome himself soon had cause to regret the bargain they had made.

Unable to establish their own home, Travers and Lavinia moved in with his parents at the house on Nineteenth Street, which his brother Lovell and his wife were also occupying. This, of course, was in the clannish Jerome tradition; his father and his brothers had lived amicably under one roof with their families, under that same roof, in fact. But it didn't work out for Travers and Lovell. Travers secretly resented the fact that Lovell had absorbed more than his share of the patrimony in an effort to convert himself into a successful civilian. After this period, in fact, they were virtually estranged for many years. Worse yet, their wives disliked each other intensely. Mrs. Lovell Jerome, the former Anita Gilbert, was "very social," with aspirations Lavinia considered ridiculous. Lavinia, to her sister-in-law, was unforgivably dowdy and anti-social. The young woman quarreled, and Travers found the situation so "intolerable" that as soon as they were financially able, and immediately after the birth of their son, they moved uptown to a house in 116th Street, in peaceful and sedate Harlem.*

* Details of his early married life were supplied by his daughter-in-law and confidante, Mrs. John Sloane. Diaries expressing his resentment against

2

YOUNG MR. JEROME's fellow servants of justice in the district attorney's office were largely time-servers and paper-shufflers, in-laws and lackluster cousins of Tammany leaders, and lawyers who couldn't make the grade in private practice. It was a bee-hive populated by drones who weren't expected to do much more than draw their salaries, demonstrate loyalty to The Organization and keep their mouths shut. The crimes they might have prosecuted, after all, were being committed by people under the protection of their own patrons. The office was described by Arthur Train as "somewhat resembling a home for aged, infirm and jobless men."*

Members of the staff, as Mr. Train described them, uniformly wore tall silk hats, frock coats and high stiff collars which made them look as though rigor mortis was setting in. All smoked large black cigars and referred constantly to the brother-in-law or second-cousin-once-removed who provided their job security. All gave ten percent of their salaries to the omnipotent Organization. Inertia, wrote Mr. Train, hung over the place "like a pall."

Just how a complaint was treated depended on the complainant and what his connections were. Anyone without sponsorship was likely to have a hard time having his grievance considered, and harder still obtaining prosecution. Someone with the proper Tammany connections would be much more sympathetically received. As Mr. Train recalled, the complainant would be introduced by his Tammany patron as follows: "This is Mr. Dudd. He's a friend of Senator Grady's. Tom Foley sent him down here. Look out for him. Mr. Dudd, shake hands with the district attorney."

If the assistant to whom the matter was referred for investi-

---

his family and his feeling that he had been "cheated" of any residual patrimony were destroyed by Mrs. Sloane, who felt that they were "unworthy" of the mature man.
* *From the District Attorney's Office.*

gation and possible action did not agree that the hypothetical
Mr. Dudd has a case, he would for all time alienate both the
affections and political support of (1) Mr. Grady, (2) Mr.
Foley, (3) the gentleman making the actual verbal introduction,
and (4) Mr. Dudd himself. Therefore he would frequently decide, irrespective of the weight of the evidence, that there was
"a case," and so inform the indictment clerk, who would "shoot
it in" to the grand jury, with the result that an indictment
would follow. The defendant would thereupon be arrested on
a bench warrant, be cast into the Tombs, and languish there
until tried or, if fortunate, bailed out.

Having started the ball rolling as a favor to Mr. Foley, or
to Mr. Dudd, it now became necessary to keep the ball rolling,
in order to retain their regard. It would not do to let any one
of them suppose the evidence insufficient, since that would
argue legal incompetency in the first instance or lack of proper
enthusiasm later. On the contrary, Mr. Dudd had to be slapped
on the back and filled with encouragement lest he should
complain to someone higher up. The deputy was committed
to the case, yet the case was no good! The first false step, taken
out of a mistaken geniality, now came of necessity to involve
a dozen others, at a large cost to the county and to Mr. Dudd,
of both time and money. Cases would come up on the trial
calendar as many as twenty or thirty times, with the complainant
and his witnesses sitting expectantly in court, when the trial
assistant knew he wouldn't try the case, couldn't try it, and
had no thought of trying it. And all to please Mr. Grady, Mr.
Foley, and the unfortunate Mr. Dudd himself! Of course, in
time — after a year or so — the complainant died or got tired
out, or his witnesses moved to New Jersey — and the indictment
was dismissed on the application of the very man who had
asked the grand jury to find it.

In this morass of inefficiency, nepotism and political favoritism,
William Travers Jerome, as a very junior assistant district at-

torney at the bottom of the official totem pole, felt his way cautiously and kept his own counsel. If he was repelled by what he saw and heard, and even perhaps by what he was forced to do, he kept it to himself. He knew that he was lucky to have obtained the appointment, that it was a testimony to his family's past connivance with Tammany Hall rather than any recognition of his own merits. The necessity of supporting a wife, and soon their first and only child, William Travers Jerome, Jr., kept his sense of outrage from boiling over. His niche on the county payroll was all that mattered for the time being.

For almost two years the wiry, energetic young man, a passionate intensity only occasionally flashing in his blue eyes, seethed inwardly but held his tongue. New Yorkers, he recognized, have a built-in tolerance for graft and corruption. His own livelihood at the moment depended on his going along with the system. But gradually that cynical acceptance of what has always been and always will be, the easy rationalization that a great metropolis and a world port will always breed more than its share of evil, began to wear thin with him.

Jerome, of course, had a vantage point few others enjoyed in observing how the collaboration between crooked police officials, the underworld and the politicians worked. The police department was rotten from top to bottom, and gambling and prostitution thrived as never before. Human termites had burrowed into the municipal and county offices to the extent that they operated under the *mordita* or little-bite system familiar to banana republics and other less enlightened parts of the world; bribery was required for the smallest service a citizen might ask of the bureaucrats whose salaries he was paying. Almost everyone on the public payroll had his hand out.

Personally honest though he was, Jerome could not keep denying to himself that he was a part of this corruption, that his silence was a form of acquiescence. He recognized his moment of truth early in 1890, after he had been a member of the district attorney's staff for slightly less than two years. His first step toward purging himself was to prosecute the owner of a police-protected policy shop in which a clerk had lost several thousand dollars of his employer's funds. He risked the censure of his superiors by prosecuting simply because he was fed up with being a tame tabby in the Tammany zoo, with bartering his personal integrity for enough money to pay the rent and grocery bills.

His opportunity to break with Tammany and do it a little damage in the process came when he was assigned to prosecute an assault case against James Barker, the Tammany leader in the thirteenth assembly district. As the New York *Times* of May 20, 1890 described the case: "Barker, a big, burly ruffian, attacked [James] Hernan, who was a much smaller and weaker man, in a barroom, knocked him down and kicked and pounded him so that he had to pass eight months in a hospital, and was left with injuries from which he can never fully recover." Barker, as the *Times* pointed out editorially, was "a man of power and influence" in the "system of saloon politics which is potent in this city." It was necessary for the district attorney's office to go through the motions of obtaining an indictment against Barker and bringing him to trial because of the considerable amount of newspaper publicity attracted to the case. Apparently District Attorney Fellows's confidence in Jerome's discretion had some-how been restored, otherwise he would hardly have been en-trusted with a matter of such delicacy. He was expected to present the case in such a light that Barker would be quickly acquitted.

Instead Jerome crossed up his superiors and his party leaders by conducting the case with a forthright objectivity. So much newspaper attention was focused on the court proceedings that it was too late to remove Jerome as the trial assistant and sub-stitute someone else.

Much to the rage and dismay of Barker and his patrons, the

ready-fisted district leader was convicted in the Court of General Sessions.*

Leonard Jerome, bursting with pride over his nephew's triumph in the courtroom, wrote his wife, "Travers has just made a great hit by the conduct of a case and an hour's speech in court as Assistant District Attorney. He fought a great Tammany leader on a brutal assault and got him convicted and sentenced to one year's imprisonment and a $500 fine."**

After that, of course, there was nothing for Travers to do but resign. He had the satisfaction of making a sensational exit, plus a sheaf of newspaper clippings, but little else.

His defiance of Tammany made him the natural subject for recruitment by a pioneering reformist group, the People's Municipal League, which bravely but futilely campaigned for "clean government" in 1890. He could see that the beginnings of a great popular movement had been made; it would become politically important when another severe depression came along and stripped people of their complacency. The pricklings of conscience which drove Jerome to defy his superiors eventually determined the course of his career, which waited only upon the propitious moment.

Meanwhile he returned to private practice with Daniel Nason again his partner for another four years. The only time he came to public attention was when he defended a young medical student named Carlyle Harris on a charge of poisoning his wife. His knowledge of chemistry, gained as a student and instructor at Amherst, "astonished the legal profession," made the case a

* Jerome was replaced by another assistant district attorney shortly thereafter, according to the *Times* (June 4, 1890). His substitute quickly approved of $15,000 bail for Barker and did not oppose a stay of execution granted by Judge O'Brien in Supreme Court. Nor was a subsequent reduction of sentence opposed, after Jerome had been removed from the case.

** Leonard Jerome died less than a year later, in March, 1891, leaving little more than one of the Gilded Age's most glamorous legends — and, of course, that English grandson.

brief newspaper sensation and though his client was convicted won him much favorable attention.

3

> Hear, see and say nothin',
> Eat, drink and pay nothin'.
> — Police Chief Bill Devery's
> advice to the constabulary.

TWENTY-FIVE THOUSAND prostitutes were estimated to be working on and off the streets of New York, particularly around the Bowery and in the Tenderloin. No other city on earth — not even Port Said, the Marseilles waterfront, San Francisco's Barbary Coast, New Orleans's French Quarter or the Casbah of Algiers — could boast of so much wickedness per square mile. Every whore, pimp and madam operated virtually under license of the New York Police Department. No one could live in New York for a week without becoming aware of the fact that female flesh was the most readily obtainable merchandise in that huge market place. Yet except for an occasional sin-killing preacher, few were outraged and fewer protested. Respectable people were merely disgusted and repelled when a young free-lance journalist named Stephen Crane ventured to describe such conditions in his first novel, *Maggie: A Girl of the Streets*, written in 1891 and published three years later, a work said to have been inspired by an incident witnessed by Crane: a young street-walker being beaten to her knees by a beefy cop in the Broadway Gardens, a Tenderloin deadfall, with hardly an eyebrow raised by the patrons.

The Tenderloin is now depicted in song and story — recently, in particular, by a rollicking Broadway musical so titled — as a place bursting with picturesque merriment, full of quaint and harmless revelry. Actually it was the heart of a city's tragedy. The girls who walked its streets, in preference to working in sweatshops for eight dollars a week, were driven there by such pressures as that which formed the tragedy of Crane's Maggie; "the sordid squabbles of a besotted tenement family become titanic struggles and mud puddles are magnified into measureless oceans."

Every day a score of Maggies slipped away from their tenement homes, went "on the turf," and were never seen again by their families until — a year or two later, perhaps — their bodies were grappled out of the East River.

Lower East Side girls naturally gravitated to the Bowery nearby, while the slum children of Chelsea and Hell's Kitchen, on the West Side, found themselves quickly recruited for the Tenderloin. In the last decade of the century, the Tenderloin had become the larger and gaudier of the two as vice followed more respectable business uptown. The Tenderloin, located along Sixth Avenue and the streets radiating from it between Forty-second and Twenty-third, was a vast harlotville of dance halls, barrooms, concert saloons and red-light houses catering to every conceivable fancy. Long before Krafft–Ebing, Freud or Kinsey published their discoveries on the variety of sexual experience, any enthusiastic amateur investigator could have compiled equally eye-opening documentary evidence after a few weeks in the Tenderloin, whose specialized resorts catered to homosexuals, sadists, voyeurs, masochists, miscenegators (The House of All Nations was a leading attraction) and the whole catalogue of wayward desires. These attractions were to be found in establishments ranging from two-dollar whorehouses and houses of assignation to palatial parlor houses like those of the Seven Sisters — seven New England spinsters who operated a row of brownstones on West Twenty-fifth Street — where patrons were not admitted unless they wore full evening dress, brought bouquets and treated the inmates in the most decorous manner.

The girls who wandered into this "Satan's Circus," as a preacher named it, generally walked the streets on their own

for a night or two until a cop or a pimp — morally there was
little difference between the two — straightened them out on the
facts of life in the Tenderloin. Free-lancing streetwalkers were
strictly discouraged. They were required to enlist under the
"slave system," indenturing themselves to a pimp or madam who
owned them body and soul and who saw to it that the police
received their cut every time the girl turned a trick.

Most girls drifted into prostitution and "the system," which
held them in bondage until their earning powers diminished, out
of desperation, but some were forcibly recruited. Gangs of
"cadets" specialized in snatching comely girls off the streets,
drugging them or beating them up until they submitted to
the routine of a bordello. Allen Churchill (*Park Row*) has cited
the case of a girl, whose father was a prominent rabbi, kidnaped
in broad daylight and placed in a brothel. The newspapers kicked
up a tremendous fuss but "so strong were vice interests that no
paper suggested the possibility of getting the girl out of the
brothel in which she had been placed. This was known to be
utterly impossible, and the girl was left to her life of shame."

Hardly a tenement in New York did not shelter some family
whose secret shame was "the picture turned to the wall," as
the lachrymose ballad had it, the daughter who had "disappeared" — perhaps only a few blocks away.

O. Henry in his wanderings often noted the curiously bitter
and defiant look in the eyes of a young girl about to consign
herself to a whore's life. "It is a look of silent but contemptuous
revolt against cheated womanhood; of sad prophecy of the
vengeance to come. When she laughs her loudest the look is still
there. The same look can be seen in the eyes of Russian peasants;
and those of us left will see it some day on Gabriel's face when
he comes to blow us up . . ."

One place that O. Henry's typical shopgirl meditating revolt
might wind up, particularly if she were prettier than most, was
the Haymarket at Sixth Avenue and Thirtieth Street, the

most celebrated of all the Tenderloin resorts. It was a huge dance hall with private rooms and up to five hundred girls waiting to entertain the customers. John Sloan and other artists and writers have immortalized its bawdy revels and riotous color. The noise of its blaring bands, its shrieking girls and drunken men could be heard for blocks away, above the noise of the el overhead. Often it cost a man up to a hundred dollars to buy champagne for the girl of his choice; it was the glamor spot of the Tenderloin, and supposedly the best run. The girls had to observe the owners' regulations. Rule number one was that no man who fell for them was to be robbed on the premises. Rule number two was that if they stole from a patron after taking him elsewhere, and the man put in a rap against them with the police, then they had to pay the money back to calm the patron and save the police from undue embarrassment. The Haymarket, as a matter of fact, was the police department's showcase, to which they pointed proudly as an example of how a "clean house" should be run; it also provided five hundred dollars a month in payoffs to police officials from the commissioner on down. But the girls who enlisted at the comparatively "classy" Haymarket were as surely doomed as those working the "hot bed" traps along the side streets. Reporters covering the violent death of a young girl, even a suicide, used to say by way of consolation, "At least she'll never wind up at the Haymarket."

Even less happy, generally, was the fate of the girls who ended up at the Tivoli, the Broadway Gardens, the Bohemia, the Heart of Maryland, the Cairo, the Tuxedo, the Buckingham Palace, the Star and Garter, Sailors Hall, Dan the Dude's, Paddy the Pig's, the Pig's Head, the Burnt Rag, the Cremorne or the French Madame's. The only one of these squalid resorts that was ever closed down — despite the brawls, murders, robberies and other outrages which contributed to the lurid charm of the Tenderloin — was Charlie Ackron's Tivoli. State Senator John

Ford showed up there one night incognito, got in a row with a sticky-fingered waiter and was thrown out on Ackron's orders. The senator raised such a ruckus that the Tivoli was finally padlocked, much to the distress of the police officials who had a piece of the action.

Occasionally Police Superintendent Thomas F. Byrnes would announce that he was "cleaning up the Tenderloin," which simply meant that every establishment had to come up with another five hundred dollars "initiation fee" for the captain shifted to that precinct. Often, too, the brass hats at Police Headquarters would declare themselves a dividend by ordering raids on brothels and increasing their payoffs. The bail monopoly was held by a Tammany district leader who received five dollars for every prostitute he bailed out.

It got so the proprietors of bawdyhouses and other protected enterprises were being taxed to death by the police. They were also enslaved by "the system," and many were beaten by the police when they protested against higher payoffs. When this saturation point was reached, an explosion of some sort was inevitable. Given half a chance, the divekeepers would turn on their protectors; any alliance between the police and the underworld works only so long as there is enough profit to keep both parties satisfied.

Into this potentially explosive situation stepped the myopic, unworldly figure of Dr. Charles H. Parkhurst, pastor of the Madison Square Presbyterian Church, who would have been the man voted least likely to succeed as the head of any reformist movement. On February 14, 1892, the frail minister launched his famous broadsides at Boss Croker, Mayor Hugh J. Grant and others he considered responsible for protecting organized prostitution, gambling and other rackets, a jeremiad possibly inspired by the New York *Mail and Express'* revelations of a week earlier that there were 250 faro banks, 720 policy games (now known as the numbers racket), hundreds of houses of prostitution, and 600 saloons which were brazenly violating the 1 A.M. closing law. Dr. Parkhurst raised his reedy voice to declare that "Every effort to make men respectable, honest, temperate, and sexually clean is a direct blow between the eyes of the Mayor and his whole gang of drunken and lecherous subordinates . . . while we fight iniquity they shield or patronize it; while we try to convert criminals they manufacture them; and they have a hundred dollars invested in manufacturing machinery to our one invested in converting machinery."

Oddly enough, the first reaction to Dr. Parkhurst's strongly worded sermon was a great tut-tutting against "so violent an outburst of vituperation from the pulpit"; Tammany spokesmen christened him "Saint Billingsgate," and the New York *Sun* suggested that he be removed from his pastorate.

It was demanded that he "put up or shut up." Boss Croker and his lieutenants simply couldn't imagine a man of Parkhurst's apparent frailty and timidity going out and getting proof of his charges. Yet that turned out to be a recklessly indiscreet challenge: the Reverend Parkhurst and two companions, flimsily disguised as roistering out-of-towners, toured the deadfalls of the Bowery and the Tenderloin. They secured evidence of openly merchandised sex in all sorts of packages from a nude leapfrog game at Hattie Adams's to a "French circus" at Marie Andrea's. Dr. Parkhurst's subsequent revelations attracted so much publicity that the authorities had no alternative but to prosecute, confident that with Howe and Hummel representing Madam Adams the Parkhurst testimony would be blown sky-high. Not even the loudest bellows of Counsellor Howe could shake the star witness, nor did he flinch when Howe assailed him as a lecher in ministerial broadcloth. Both madams were convicted. Now the political tides started running against Tammany, and a sizable reform movement began to take shape.

There was nothing new about this except its vigor and scope. Anti-machine movements sprang into formal being in

1863, when the Citizens Association was formed, and in 1871 when the Council of Political Reform was organized to combat the misrule of Boss Tweed, but none showed any permanence. Political reform lasts about as long as the burst of civic indignation which brings it forth.

Now the League for Political Education and the City Club were clamoring for a house-cleaning. Many of those who threw in their lot with the clean-up forces were young professional men who, in addition to whatever idealism and disgust with the status quo motivated them, had less to lose by openly opposing the city's political masters. They were nominally members of both the Republican and Democratic parties, but locally they were independent of both political machines and visualized the kind of fusion program that seems to become necessary in New York at regular intervals, roughly on an average of once a decade.

By reason of his spectacular defiance of Tammany as an assistant district attorney, William Travers Jerome occupied a prominent place among the groups stirring up a citywide demand for reform. His ebullient optimism was one of his greatest assets, as expressed in a speech before the League for Political Education:

"My own opinion is that crime may be stamped out by rational means, just as smallpox and fever, which were considered necessary evils a few years ago, are now practically unknown in civilized countries. The power that is going to stamp it out is education and occupation. The vast system of blackmail in this city is known by everyone but the District Attorneys, who have never done anything to root it out. When you have in that position a man who is aggressively honest, and who does not sit and wait for crime to rub against him, you may look for revelations and reforms where you little think it now."*

* A copy of this speech was found in a bound collection in the possession of William Travers Jerome, III.

His work in the vanguard of civic reform, carried on as an unpaid sideline to a struggling law practice, was so highly regarded that Amherst conferred an honorary Master of Arts degree upon him in 1892.

His prestige among the reform-minded was greatly increased early in 1893 when he joined John W. Goff and Frank Moss, two other attorneys of the same persuasion, in defending Charles Gardner against what they charged was a police department frame up. Gardner, a hulking young private detective, was one of the two men who accompanied Dr. Parkhurst on his tours of the brothels and all-night saloons.

Gardner was arrested on December 4, 1892, shortly after his testimony helped to convict Madams Adams and Andrea, on charges that he had tried to shake down Lillie Clifton, operator of a whorehouse on West Fifty-fourth Street, three other madams and a saloonkeeper.

These alleged victims all took the stand to testify that Gardner had indeed extorted money from them, promising that he would protect them against police raids.

Despite a vigorous defense by Jerome, Goff and Moss, who protested in vain when Recorder Frederick Smyth prompted Mrs. Clifton from the bench when she faltered in her testimony, Gardner was convicted and sentenced to two years in jail.

Jerome and his associates refused to give up. They leaned on Madam Clifton until she confessed that she had perjured herself on orders from the police. The State Supreme Court reversed the conviction, and Gardner was free to produce his curious, and often comic memoir, *The Doctor and the Devil, or Midnight Adventures of Dr. Parkhurst.* A greater result than this, however, was the fact that the Gardner frame up revealed just how vicious and stupid were the higher officials of the New York Police Department.

The Goff–Jerome–Moss team was to perform again, soon after the Gardner trial, when the state legislature began its

inquiry into the New York Police Department and its connections with Tammany Hall and the underworld. Public opinion
was now running so strongly in favor of a clean-up — urged
along as it was by the sobering influence of the severe depression which had begun the previous year — that Albany, reading
the political barometer with its usual accuracy, pushed along the
investigation at top speed. Less than a month after it was ordered
into action by the legislature, with State Senator Clarence E.
Lexow as its chairman, the investigating committee had con-
vened in New York City and begun taking evidence. Goff was
appointed counsel for the committee, and in turn named Jerome
and Moss as his assistants; District Attorney DeLancey Nicoll,
most of whose time was now given up to defending Tammany
and its recently maladroit works, appeared as counsel for the
police department.

Out went the word that this investigation was on the level,
and people with dangerous truths to tell had best skip town.
First to get the wind up was Boss Croker himself, who departed
for his estate in England with more haste than dignity, not at
all comforted by the philosophy of an East Side politician: "These
reform movements are like queen hornets. They sting you once,
and then they die." Tenderloin business leaders scattered like
quail sensing a storm; a whole colony of madams moved to
Chicago en masse and set themselves up in business there until
it was safe to return, and the celebrated "French Madam," Mrs.
Mathilda Hermann, who fancied large plumed hats, fled to
Canada, then to Chicago, where the committee's subpoena was
handed her. Her testimony was regarded as so important that
a gang of hoodlums tried to kidnap her from the custody of
the Lexow committee's detectives in Jersey City when she was
being returned to New York. The thugs were repulsed after a
bareknuckle brawl in the railroad station.

From June 29 to October 18, 1894, the committee took the
testimony of every Tenderloin figure they could lay hands on,

the published report of its proceedings running to almost 5,800 pages. It is an amazing record, containing the definitive evidence of just how a corrupt political machine, working with an equally subverted police department and an underworld which tamely submitted to having most of its profits drained away by greedy protectors, could squeeze enormous profits from crime and vice organized on a businesslike basis.

Travers Jerome's role was largely that of a silent partner; he laid the groundwork, directed the efforts of the committee's investigators and stage-managed the parade of witnesses, while Goff and Moss conducted the questioning.

To the observant Lincoln Steffens, it appeared that Jerome, largely hush-hush though his operations were, acted as the mainspring of the committee's investigative machinery. Jerome impressed him as a man of a "great dash, vigor and courage," who "knew conditions like an insider," a knowledge gained at bedrock level during his two years as a Tammany appointee to the district attorney's office. Steffens, then a young police reporter, deduced that it was Jerome's insight and knowledge of how the underworld-police-Tammany combination worked, and his ruthless application of them, that kept the investigation steamrolling over obstacles.

"He bargained with his witnesses . . . used police methods . . . He could send them to prison, he could let them go, he could compromise, according as they told the truth and gave away the system and their colleagues," Steffens wrote in his autobiography. "So he threatened, he traded; he fought, as I afterwards saw other investigators 'fight the devil with fire.' Evidently he had to fight both the enemy before him and his friends behind . . ."

One who attacked from the rear, having ruefully discovered how discomforting a runaway investigation could be, was Republican Boss Tom Platt, who was as alarmed as Tammany

Boss Dick Croker by the way the hearings were branching out.

Offstage and *sotto voce* though most of his work was, Jerome undoubtedly learned much from the Lexow investigation, particularly from John Goff's relentless, almost savage style of cross-examination. Goff ripping into a hostile witness was a spectacle to recall one of the bloodier programs at the Roman circus.

Jerome's subsequent manner in the legal arena, his feline approach to the witness stand, his ruthless marshaling and presentation of evidence, his method of ensnaring a witness in his own lies and evasions, owed much to his education at Goff's side. The white bearded and saintly looking Goff, an Irish immigrant who won admission to the bar after studying as a law clerk, had served in the district attorney's office at the same time as Jerome and similarly, but less spectacularly, had resigned in disgust. Before that, he had distinguished himself as a leader of the Fenian party in New York, which labored to free Ireland from British rule, and gained a reputation defending Irish patriots who got themselves in trouble with the American law. The most quixotic venture of his career was the organization of Goff's Irish Rescue Party, which chartered a New Bedford whaler and plotted an invasion of Ireland to snatch away a number of Fenians held by the British authorities for deportation to Australia. The courage of Irish patriots is matched only by their fecklessness, and the scheme was aborted long before sailing time. After the Lexow investigation, Jerome's mentor served as a Recorder (judge) of the Court of General Sessions, and in 1906 was elected to the State Supreme Court. Defense lawyers who lost their cases claimed that when Goff charged a jury all they could hear of his soft, low-pitched voice was, "Buzz-buzz . . . buzz-buzz-buzz . . . find the defendant guilty," but convictions in his court were generally sustained on appeal.

Goff and his two young associates, operating generally on hostile or intimidated witnesses, drew from them a lurid picture of the intimacy of the New York Police Department, at every level, with the smallest detail of the Tenderloin's nightly activities.

Madam Hermann was a particularly enlightening witness, revealing that she had paid $20,000 to the police in the past two years and was known to them as "the French gold mine" until she balked at paying any further protection. Then, she said, she was beaten with a night stick, arrested and robbed of her diamond earrings.

Almost hysterical with fear, Madam Evelyn Bell, a pale woman who affected flowing lavender gowns, admitted that she paid fifty dollars a month for police protection. The night following her appearance before the committee she disappeared from the city. Several months later she returned while the committee was still in session, was served with another subpoena, and promptly slashed her throat with a razor. Committee investigators removed her to a New Jersey sanitarium for safekeeping, but she was never called to testify again. Her stark fear of retribution from her former protectors was testimony enough.

Captain Max Schmittberger, a beefy and genial fellow whose precinct included the Tenderloin, was the soul of cooperation, in return for which he was allowed to remain on the force and eventually rise to the rank of chief inspector. Schmittberger testified that he collected an average one thousand dollars a month from brothels, gambling houses and saloons in the Tenderloin. Two hundred dollars of this, he said, went to his immediate superior, Inspector Alexander "Clubber" Williams, who was credited with first having called the honky-tonk district the Tenderloin.

Williams faced Goff's cross-examination with a massive self-assurance only slightly diminished when he was forced to admit that he owned a seventeen-room mansion at Cos Cob, a racing stable and a fair-sized yacht. He denied that he was worth half a million dollars, and that he had ever received a dollar of the squeeze collected by Captain Schmittberger. Why, then, did he permit the brothels to operate? Goff inquired. "Because," Williams blandly replied, "they were kind of fashionable at the time."

Police Superintendent Thomas F. Byrnes was trapped into admitting that he was worth $350,000 but was ready with an explanation. The late financier, Jay Gould, for whom he provided twenty-four-hour police protection, and other Wall Street figures grateful for his solicitude had given him tips on the market. Byrnes soon retired from the force and prospered in the insurance business, while Inspector Williams was dismissed "for the good of the service."

Other disclosures before the Lexow Committee included that fact that from 1891 to 1893 thousands of fraudulent ballots were cast with the active connivance of the police. Those especially adept at helping to rig elections were given the first chance at promotion. Others bought their way up the ladder. Thus Schmittberger, with the payment of $12,000, obtained his promotion to captain. Another officer paid $15,000 for his captaincy. Patrolmen obtained their appointment for an average $300 paid into Tammany's coffers.

Captain Schmittberger, recalled as a witness, dolefully testified that his share of the graft now amounted to only $200 a month.

"What is the world coming to?" Goff inquired sympathetically. "Only $200 a month in the Tenderloin? The golden days have passed."

"Yes, sir," Schmittberger solemnly replied.

Perhaps the most shocking bit of testimony, from the public standpoint, came with the appearance of the Reverend Cornelius Praetori, pastor of the St. Francis Roman Catholic Church on West Thirty-first Street, which was bounded on both sides by whorehouses. As a specification in the charges against the police department later read, the inmates of these houses had no respect for the cloth, and "lewd women continually insult and solicit him as he passes in the street — priest though he be — and have even done so without clothing upon them." Father Praetori also complained that "the young ladies of my church are especially subjected to insult and indignities by the men who come to patronize these houses."

He said that when he demanded of Inspector Williams that the bawdyhouses be closed down, the latter piously replied, "Oh, it would be too bad to drive the inmates out in the cold of winter."

The only house in the Tenderloin exempt from paying tribute was the "very quiet" establishment operated by Mrs. Georgianna Hastings, which was patronized by various wealthy citizens, judges, city officials and others who needed guarantees of discretion when they relaxed. When a Lexow Committee investigator appeared at Mrs. Hastings's place, in fact, a judge of the criminal courts who happened to be disporting himself on the premises prevented execution of the warrant demanding her presence before the committee.

The cooperative Captain Schmittberger told about another place that was under the direct protection of his superiors. Schmittberger sent a patrolman to Mrs. Sadie West's house to investigate complaints of her neighbors. Next day Schmittberger was summoned to Police Commissioner J. J. Martin's office, told to "lay off" Mrs. West's place and ordered to tender her his apologies for the inconvenience caused by his patrolman's visit . . .

None of this testimony should have shocked any knowledgeable New Yorker of adult years. The situation had been tolerated so long that it was almost legalized. Yet now, with the facts laid before them in the cold type of their newspapers, the metropolis seethed with indignation. Somehow, in print, it all looked so much worse; the city had its nose rubbed in the mire and was made to feel responsible for the fact that, as Goff summed it up, "every source of blackmail and extortion was utilized and formulated into a system so that the trail of graft was traceable through nearly every channel of municipal life and activity." Tom Platt, the state Republican boss, had encouraged the investigation in the hope that election frauds would be uncovered and Tammany would be given a black eye, but the thing had gotten out of hand and spilled too many applecarts. The public, it was noted, was in a "hyper-excited mood." Furthermore, to Boss Platt's dismay, the Republican member of the bi-partisan Board of Police Commissioners was besmirched along with the Democrats. Too much reform, as any experienced politician knew, was a damned bad thing. Any sort of uncontrollable amateur might ride into power with the tail wind whipped up by the Lexow investigation.

Even before the committee stopped taking testimony, only a few weeks before the fall election, Travers Jerome was working strenuously to bring about that result.

3

Dragon-Slayer on the Bench

AT THE AGE of thirty-five, having surmounted more handicaps
than usually confronted a young man of position and
influence, William Travers Jerome was finally on his way. His
renown as a fighter of corruption had placed him in the front
ranks of the young men who, like himself, were endeavoring to
bring about a middle-class revolution in municipal politics.

Until recent years the men of Jerome's background and aspirations had been content to allow the old-line politicians to have
their way; politics was a dirty business, best left to the cigar-
chewing vulgarians who would keep at least a decent minimum
of law and order in return for the privileges of graft. There had
been sporadic, short-lived reform movements as far back as the
Civil War, in which such civic-minded men as Peter Cooper,
Carl Schurz, George William Curtis (editor of *Harper's Weekly*)
and E. L. Godkin (editor of *The Nation* and later of the New
York *Evening Post*), John Jay Chapman (also a man of letters),
and William Jay Schieffelin, Chapman's cousin and inheritor of
the family drug company, had worked with varying success.
The City Club and the Good Government Club (sardonically
called the "Goo-Goos" by the New York *Sun*, which had little
patience with amateur politicians), were both established in 1892
to keep an eye on the city government, watch the polls on
election day, coax the working classes away from Tammany and

educate the citizenry to its responsibilities. The City Club's trustees subsequently formed the Citizens Union as a separate party which would nominate reform-minded candidates in city elections, a movement in which Elihu Root and other prominent Republicans joined.

Reform, civic decency, clean government, anti-corruption crusade and other such verbal banners had been raised in the past without rallying any considerable support. Reformers, from the mild-mannered Reverend Dr. Parkhurst to the fanatical Anthony Comstock, were regarded as spoilsports and bluenoses. Now reform was becoming socially acceptable, even glamorous, the avocation of young men on the rise who had not yet been able to acquire a steam yacht or a country estate.

Jerome, moving toward a leading position in the effort to make municipal politics respectable and respectable people more political, had come along at a fortunate time. His appearance, character and personality were well adapted to the role he assumed. First of all, he had inherited the Jerome sense of style. Even while lashing out at the forces of evil, he eschewed the eye-rolling, sin-killing evangelism which would have repelled a generation which regarded pleasure with a tolerant gaze but was sensible enough to want it kept in bounds. His approach was practical rather than moralistic, factual rather than hyperbolic.

He could rouse an audience, even a barely literate one, but it was always with a blunt statement of facts rather than gassy platitudes. Orotundity was going out of fashion, and the type of public speaker who modeled himself after the steam calliope was already becoming faintly ridiculous, particularly in the big cities. (William Jennings Bryan, the Beamish Boy of nineteenth century oratory, appealed to the rural and pineywood masses and seemed a trifle quaint, with his magnificent organ tones and windmill gestures, in the dryer climate of the eastern cities.) Political crusaders might still fulminate under torchlight, but they were expected to make sense, first, and appeal to the emotions, if necessary, secondly.

A. L. Hodder, a young novelist (*The Powers That Prey*) who subsequently joined the reformist movement, described Jerome's style on the platform as devoid of all the expected grace notes of the old-school orator. "He does not deal in striking metaphors or stately verbiage . . . His voice is harsh; his speech is blunt, to the verge at times of downright rudeness; and his gestures come as God pleases."*

In dress as well as manner he avoided every lineament of the political caricature — the portly figure with aldermanic belly and Percheron haunches encased in funereal broadcloth or Prince Albert, with leonine mane and full mustache or burnsides, with eyeglasses attached to a black ribbon manipulated with statesmanlike gestures. Jerome wore glasses, of necessity, but they were clamped to his nose (the *pince-nez* then favored by professional men). He wore his hair short and his mustache was closely trimmed. Instead of clawhammer coats he was partial to natty business suits, a trifle sportive for more conventional members of the bar. Defiant of the tradition that political wisdom should be well larded, his figure was as trim and wiry as any halfback's. He was handsome, approximating the magazine-cover ideal captured by Charles Dana Gibson, with regular features, a full head of blondish hair, and eyes which flashed, when he was aroused, with a warrior light that would have been recognizable to any putative Iroquois in his ancestry.

Worn fine by his exertions during the Lexow inquiry, he appeared deceptively frail to political wiseacres who held to the belief that the public wouldn't trust any office seeker who wasn't at least fifty pounds overweight. "Why," said Big Tim Sullivan, who was filling in for Boss Croker at Tammany Hall, "that feller couldn't strike a blow that would knock a hole through a pound of butter."

* *A Fight for the City*, published in 1903.

His ease of manner, in contrast to the overly hearty back-slapping and hand-pumping of the old-line politicians, also appealed to the young men who were interesting themselves in politics and who were making the word "reformist" almost as attractive a label, in a more constricted sense, as "socially conscious" was in the 1930's. He was a political Carrie Nation, it was observed, "who drank highballs at the corner bar and cussed when he felt like it." The fat cigar which jutted out of most politicians' faces and dribbled ashes on their bulging vests was replaced, in Jerome's case, by an omnipresent cigarette. This, too, was a badge of independence in a day when cigarettes were referred to as "pimp weeds" and the yellowed forefinger was a symptom of depravity. He was not at all affronted by his nickname of "Cigarette Willie."

But it was his immense vigor, plain in every word and action, which so impressed his contemporaries. The Jerome vitality, blazing up from a sickly and overprotected childhood, burned as fiercely as the flame from a blowtorch.

If he nonchalantly displayed a "cavalier exterior," complete with highball in one hand and cigarette in the other, as Hodder noted, it was also apparent that burning beneath it was "the wrath of a Hebrew prophet."

2

ONE OF THE SEEDBEDS of reform in the nineties was the University Club, to which young business and professional men hastened late in the day to plot ways of combatting Tammany over drinks and the pipes they'd learned to smoke on Fraternity Row. It was as unlikely a place for political conspiracy as the conspirators themselves were, clean-cut young fellows who hardly knew a ward heeler from a district leader, who were so ignorant of practical politics they believed that they could successfully oppos a party machine which for many decades had managed to drag the vote out of all sorts of dark places in the city.

At their bull sessions Jerome and his friends formed the Committee of Seventy to find an honest man they could run for mayor in the fall of 1894 against Hugh J. Grant, an ex-mayor whom Tammany had dredged up to run "on his record." His record, of course, was that of an amiable stooge.

Jerome was appointed counsel to the committee, which proceeded to nominate Colonel William L. Strong, a wealthy merchant and nominally a Republican, to head a Fusion ticket. Strong immediately chose Jerome as his campaign manager. Thus the latter had to wind up his Lexow Committee activities and simultaneously start Strong's campaign rolling, all within a few weeks, a task that burned off even his phenomenal energy. Fortunately he had plenty of eager helpers, not only the idealistic amateurs of the Committee of Seventy but a conglomeration of Tammany haters with some experience in the field and a certain amount of organizing ability. The Committee allied itself with such political reform organizations as the City Club and the Citizens Union, the Reverend Parkhurst's Society for the Prevention of Crime, various independent Republicans and anti-Tammany Democrats . . . the whole nonpartisan rainbow which appears over the Manhattan skyline in a vintage year for Fusion.

Tom Platt, the Republican boss, could have helped immensely but he preferred to sit out the election on the sidelines. He was as troubled by the turn of events as Tammany's Sullivan and Croker, whose strategic retreat to an English estate was not the easiest thing to explain away. The Fusionists' argument that Strong was a registered Republican and therefore deserved his support failed to sway Mr. Platt, who knew that Strong was an *independent* Republican and that the Fusionists were denouncing the spoils system and beating the drums for Civil Service reform. Furthermore Mr. Platt was still annoyed at the way the Lexow investigation had gotten out of hand and paved the way for the Fusion movement. He was not at all interested in sin-killing or moral crusades, having had "private experiences" with sin, the revelation of which by his political opponents, "who had climbed up to a window in the Delevan House in Albany to make their investigations, had caused him some embarrassment."* Seeing no political profit in fusing with do-gooders who would probably turn on him in evangelistic fervor the moment he asked a favor, Platt stayed aloof throughout the campaign, silently praying, perhaps, that the Tammany professionals would prevail over the unwelcome intrusion of the Fusionists.

It was just as well, undoubtedly, that the nonpartisan aspect of Fusion was maintained and its crusading fervor was uninhibited by the purse-lipped considerations of practical politics. Because they went at it with a novel enthusiasm and a virginal innocence, Fusion campaigners stirred the imagination of the electorate and made it believe that decent government was possible.

Jerome whirled around the town in a hack, speaking half a dozen times nightly, under torchlight and to increasingly exuberant street throngs, in the final two weeks of the campaign. Daytimes he spent planning speeches and strategy with Strong and other Fusion leaders. Together they generated so much zeal for the cause that campaign headquarters was swamped with volunteer workers who wanted to help throw the rascals out.

The tide began running strongly against Tammany. At a Committee of Seventy rally on October 24 at the Cooper Union, the speakers were constantly interrupted by cries of "Down with Tammany's misrule" and "Let the Tiger's pelt be taken," according to the anti-Tammany New York *Times*. That quavering echo from the Civil War, Carl Schurz, was stumping the town to line up the German vote, and even the Irish were turning against Tammany. Members of the Catholic hierarchy indicated in pastoral letters that they expected their flocks to stay loyal to

*M. R. Werner in *Tammany Hall*.

Tammany, but Father Ducey of St. Leo's Church in East Twenty-eighth Street and other priests defied their superiors to campaign for the Fusion ticket. "Not an Irishman in New York," Father Ducey would shout from the platform, "will vote again for Tammany Hall!"

By November 1, the atmosphere under the Wigwam was so apprehensive that Tammany's executive committee, according to the *Times* report, held the longest meeting in its history. More money was poured into the final phase of the campaign, and Tammany's battalions, it was observed, "went into battle with well-drilled precision," but the stanchest brave could not deny that there was a rush for the Fusion bandwagon going on all over town.

On election day, November 6, even people who rarely, if ever, voted were rushing to the polls by the thousands. The testimony given at the Lexow hearings had penetrated to many minds hitherto closed against municipal politics. As always in New York, the issue would depend upon Democrats turning against the regular organization. "Throughout the middle and upper classes," Lothrop Stoddard has written, "party lines melted in the heat of emotional contagion, and the tenement districts were affected as well."

Early on election night it became obvious that the city was going to receive its first real reform administration. Jerome, hoarse but happy, read out the bulletins at the Committee of Seventy's headquarters at 39 East Twenty-third Street. Before the night was out, Fusion was in, by a healthy majority of 45,187 votes.

"The Tammany tiger has been flayed alive," exulted the New York *Times*, which on its editorial page more soberly pointed out that the victory could only have been won by a switch in Democratic votes to the Fusion ticket, a support that could fade as quickly as it had been offered. "There should be no illusions about the causes . . . it was due mainly to the arousing of the moral sense of the people by the revelations of police corruption . . ."

John Goff was elected Recorder of the Court of General Sessions in the Fusion landslide; now some sort of reward had to be bestowed on Jerome as the stage manager of that victory. Some months before, with another attorney named Lewis Delafield, he had been commissioned to draw up a statute creating a Court of Special Sessions, which would handle appeals from the police courts and also try misdemeanor cases. In judicial majesty, it would be a cut above the Magistrates Courts, a step below the Court of General Sessions.

Mayor Strong appointed Jerome to this bench, a reward which, as the new appointee made plain, was hardly overwhelming in its magnificence. For the next half-dozen years he would be condemned to sitting on this minor bench, his ambitions and resentments simmering, his career pulled up to a full stop.

Afterward Jerome always referred to Special Sessions as "a little squirt of a court," unmindful of the fact that he had drawn up the terms creating it.

Eventually he found a way of using the Special Sessions bench as a springboard to more spectacular endeavors than sentencing North River longshoremen for brawling on the piers, but until the final year of his service as a judge, unsuited as it was to his temperament, his ambitions, his political goals, he was a disappointed and frustrated man. The victory of 1894, he believed, was a heady foretaste of future triumphs. Somehow he had to break out of the confines of the minor judiciary and return to the partisan arena, where fortunes were made. Until he seized the opportunity for a breakthrough, he could only watch in disgust as the city's first reform administration, which he had done so much to bring about, stumbled into the situation celebrated by the pro-Tammany street song:

> Well, well, well,
> Reform has gone to hell.

3

AT THE OUTSET the Strong administration delivered on its promises to provide an honest and efficient city government. A new police commission, headed by Theodore Roosevelt, reorganized the department and cracked down on organized gambling and prostitution. With Roosevelt in command of the police "graft kept coyly under cover," as Lothrop Stoddard has written, "and gambling, vice and 'blind tigers' bowed their diminished heads." New schools, parks and playgrounds were planned and built, with a minimum of graft larding the contracts.

For the first time in its history, the city even had clean streets, thanks to a bone-rattling shake-up in the Sanitation Department. The vigorous Colonel George E. Waring, Jr. was placed in charge of this department and immediately eliminated the padded contracts and soft jobs reserved for faithful party workers. All street cleaners had to wear conspicuous white uniforms (and thus were known as "Waring's White Wings") so that the moment one of them leaned against his broom too long or lingered over a schooner of beer in a nearby saloon he could be reported and cashiered.

New York was being decently governed, everything considered; yet within a year of taking office the Strong administration was widely unpopular. The city was disenchanted with the reformers, and the reformers with each other. It wasn't that the citizenry didn't appreciate better schools and cleaner streets, but these advantages were more than balanced, from the viewpoint of the ordinary man, by what were regarded as infringements on personal liberty.

Once the reformers got in power, they quickly fell out among themselves. Every Fusion movement carries within itself the seeds of its own disintegration, being necessarily a combination of highly diverse individuals initially held together by idealistic zeal but with little to hold them together once they have achieved power, when jealousy and internal dissension quickly crop up. Thus no reform administration in New York ever succeeded itself until the dynamic years of Fiorello La Guardia. There was no one like La Guardia to hold Strong's administration together, and soon enough Republicans became Republicans again, and Democrats began having second thoughts about straying from the regular organization, and the simon-pure, YMCA-secretary types who had followed the Reverend Parkhurst into the hurly-burly found that crusading against evil was more fun than supplanting it. Lincoln Steffens, who was just beginning his journalistic career, was surprised to learn that many supposedly respectable men preferred Tammany to the newcomers in City Hall and quoted Dick Croker as saying, "Sure, your reformer friends talk about business, but the businessmen who have business with the city government and so know about the Tammany administration — they are with us."

Some of the shrewdest observations on the failure of reform to work out its internal problems were recorded by an Englishman, Sydney Brooks, writing in the *Fortnightly Review* of London, who noted that reformers in power had developed no sense of team-play.

> The heads of various departments work far too independently of each other; they are too much like a company of star actors; they quarrel with one another and criticize each other's conduct with a publicity and freedom quite destructive of any real unity.

> All this the public sees. It is amusing and piquant enough for a time; but amusement ends by passing into boredom, and finally into disgust. There comes at last a period when to the ordinary citizen Tammany seems preferable to the discord and din of this jangling jealousy. Tammany has at least the precious healing gift of working in silence . . .

> The reformers were unable to conquer that social distrust of "gentlemen" which one encounters so often and so unexpectedly in American, and especially in city politics. The average New Yorker dislikes

to be governed by men of refinement, independent means, superior position. At a time of strong moral excitement he may vote for them; but he quickly wearies of their aloofness, exaggerates their detachment from the "plain people," and comes in the end to resent their pretense and activity as a sort of affront to democracy.

Popular as Theodore Roosevelt was in the muscular role of monitoring the constabulary, his strict enforcement of the Sunday drinking laws, in particular, aroused the resentment of the city's masses. In brief, it "got between the people and their beer." The sizable proportion of German voters, whose weight at the polls had been a decisive factor in Tammany's overthrow, were especially indignant at being deprived of their great pleasure in life, a Sunday afternoon in the beer gardens of Yorkville. Not only the Germans were outraged by Roosevelt's letter-of-the-law enforcement but the bulk of the working class, to whom it appeared that the ambitious young man had much too large a sense of his own righteousness. Roosevelt and his roundsmen were never more unpopular than when, having supposedly slain the larger monsters of vice, they moved on smaller game. Thus he "became a terror to pinochle players in the back rooms of saloons. The small joys began to disappear from daily life, and their place was taken by that abstract ghost, The Law, which, try as hard as they could, people who liked sex, beer, and cards could neither see, taste, nor touch."*

The neo-Puritans in City Hall and Police Headquarters simply didn't know when to call a halt to their reforming.

Nobody outside Tammany Hall watched Roosevelt's much-publicized maneuvers with less sympathy than Judge Jerome of Special Sessions. The men who wanted a drink or two on Sunday, he indicated, had all his sympathy, personal and professional. As he was to demonstrate in the district attorney's office, Jerome detested hounding people for petty infractions of the law. He

* M. R. Werner, *Tammany Hall.*

believed that reform would defeat itself and alienate the electorate with such tactics.

And furthermore Roosevelt himself, in Jerome's opinion, was a partisan Republican and a johnny-come-lately to the reform movement, who was grabbing all the laurels as head of the Police Commission while worthier reformists, with long records of fighting corruption, were relegated to obscurity. According to Arthur Train, who knew him as well as anyone, Jerome "disliked Theodore Roosevelt and was, I think, intensely jealous of his success." Almost from the beginning of their edgy association, there was a strong sense of rivalry between the two men; both aimed at the highest goals, and both recognized a potentially serious rival in the other. As Colonel Archibald B. Roosevelt recalls, his father and Jerome had a wary mutual respect for each other. They should have been friends, having much the same outlook, but their relations with each other were never "easy or free of tension."

Both men came of gilt-edged social backgrounds, both had suffered almost identical boyhood illnesses and conquered them by the same self-reliant means, both were boiling over with energy and ideas, both had divined that the reformist tendency in politics was running as strongly as the tides in the Bay of Fundy — and unfortunately both had the same ambitions, and there was room in the field for only one of them. As will be seen later, both men seldom passed up an opportunity to needle each other in a politely ferocious manner.

When Jerome was running for district attorney — by which time Roosevelt had climbed far above him, moving rapidly from the Police Commission to assistant secretary of the navy, to second-in-command of the Rough Riders, to Governor of New York, to the vice presidency, and finally to the White House when President McKinley was assassinated — people in his audiences had the irksome habit of shouting up at him, "You are Teddy Number Two!"

Jerome always winced a little when he heard that shouting, having no wish to be number two in anything.

Once he replied to the dubious compliment by saying: "President Roosevelt is a sterling man right down to the ground, and he always rings true, but as police commissioner he enforced the law in an unwise way and in a way that his oath of office did not call for."

Whatever the degree of unwisdom with which he shut off the workingman's Sunday beer and his privilege of gambling a few cents on policy games, Roosevelt escaped the political consequences by quitting the Police Commission before the election of 1897 and taking the post in the Navy Department.

That election was disastrous for the reform element. Its portents were so plain that Dick Croker returned from England in September, 1897, confident that New York was thoroughly disillusioned by its three-year experience of clean, but overly strict government. Newspaper cartoonists greeted this event as "The Return from Elba," but there was to be no Waterloo in November for the boss of Tammany Hall. Tammany chose an obscure judge named Robert A. Van Wyck to run for mayor against the Citizens Union and other reform groups' candidate, Seth Low, the president of Columbia University and a former mayor of Brooklyn. The Labor Party nominated Henry George, author of *Progress and Poverty*. And the Republican boss, Tom Platt, seized his opportunity to knife reform in unsubtle fashion. Instead of backing Low, Platt insisted that the Republicans would field their own candidate, Benjamin F. Tracy, who hadn't the slightest chance of winning but who would make Low's defeat inevitable.

Colonel Asa Bird Gardiner, Tammany's candidate for district attorney, sounded the keynote of the campaign when he shouted from the platform, "To hell with reform!" — and the crowds cheered wildly.

The most stinging riposte of reform campaigners was to ring

the changes on Croker's flight to England, charging that "He spent his time consorting with the lecherous sons of a rotten aristocracy."

Van Wyck won handily, and the whole town exploded in celebration on election night. New York had returned to its "free and easy life." The honest police chief, John McCullagh, was quickly replaced. Uptown and downtown, organized vice made its comeback. Nobody was particularly shocked when the New York *Times* revealed, soon after Tammany returned to power, that gambling was big business once again; that a Tammany "commission," consisting of two state senators, one city official and the czar of the city's poolroom syndicate, was collecting $3,095,000 each month in graft.

4

IF THE TROUBLE with reform was that it didn't know when to stop reforming, the trouble with Tammany was that it didn't know when to stop stealing. Inside two years the Van Wyck administration made itself so unpopular through unbridled greed that it was obvious another and more thorough housecleaning would be needed. Under amendments to the city charter, the administration's term in office had been extended from three to four years and the mayor was given prerogatives previously unknown, which Van Wyck and his puppet-masters used to the utmost for their own purposes.

Out of this increasingly malodorous situation, Judge Jerome intended to lift himself from judicial obscurity, and did so with such gusto that his one-man campaign against the underworld and its overworld protectors became a political legend. No man in political life at the turn of the century blazed up so spectacularly as William Travers Jerome. To the newspapers he was "St. George of Manhattan," singlehandedly confronting the dragons of vice and crime. To the public, as a singularly swashbuckling type of judge and later as a fiery, intrepid prosecutor, he became as glamorous a figure as one of those gunfighting marshals of the Old West.

His fame and his career were grounded, like those of a town-taming peace officer, in having a plenitude of villains to oppose him. Essentially a fighter rather than a moralist or reformer, he needed worthy opposition to prove himself. He needed something to fight. Born in another time, he would have been forced to moulder away in a humdrum law practice; like St. George he needed a perennial crop of dragons to slay, and the times provided these. Everything about the man, his personality, his convictions and, of course, his ego, thrived on the circumstances provided by Tammany Hall and its cohorts.

In brief, during the Van Wyck administration, New York's complacency over having kicked the reformers out was shaken by the following events:

(1) New Yorkers not only were permitted "beer on Sunday" but soon found the Tenderloin operating wide-open again, the lower East Side brothels and gambling houses running full blast, and 10,000 "cadets" roaming the streets of the city and recruiting their daughters for prostitution. The utterly corruptible Bill Devery was installed as police chief, and with Big Tim Sullivan, Tammany's satrap below Fourteenth Street, was collecting unprecedented amounts in tribute.

(2) Boss Croker, reveling in his unofficial title of "King of New York City," insolently announced what was apparent but better left unsaid: "I am working for my own pocket all the time."

(3) The equally insolent Asa Gardiner had to be removed by Governor Roosevelt as district attorney after he condemned the indictment of Police Chief Devery by a runaway grand jury as an "outrage." Devery was charged with having issued a seditious order to his force which in effect would have encouraged police officers to condone violations of the election laws. Gardiner's

removal was a severe blow to Tammany Hall, since he was replaced by an honest man, Eugene A. Philbin.

(4) And this was the climax to Tammany misrule: the investigation by the Mazet Committee of the State Assembly. The committee conducted hearings for a year, and summed up its five-volume findings by pointing out that "we have in this great city the most perfect instance of centralized government yet known . . . We see that government, no longer responsible to the people, but to a dictator. We see the central power, not the man who sits in the mayor's chair, but the man who stands behind it . . ." But complaisant New York was not shocked by this, nor by further evidence, along the lines investigated by the earlier Lexow Committee, that vice was organized and controlled by the police and the politicians. The shocker — and it was the most disastrous blow struck at Tammany since the Tweed Ring was smashed a generation ago — was the disclosure of how the Ice Trust operated. The American Ice Company, headed by an unscrupulous financier named Charles W. Morse, obtained a monopoly on the sale of ice throughout the city with the assistance of Croker, Van Wyck and others, who gave Morse the exclusive right to land ice at the municipal docks and thus choked off his competition. Ice, in those pre-refrigerator days, was needed to keep children's milk from spoiling, and the tenement-dwellers suffered accordingly, with an alarming rise in the number of infant deaths, when Morse did away with the custom of selling five-cent chunks and forced people to buy hundred-pound cakes, for which many were unable to spare the necessary sixty cents. In return, Mayor Van Wyck alone acquired $500,000 worth of American Ice Company stock and was unable to prove that he had paid for any of it. The ordinary New Yorker now saw the price he had to pay for his Sunday beer-drinking and other minor pleasures; the Ice Trust scandal rubbed his nose in the dirt and made him feel a share of responsibility for it.*

* A newspaper cartoon showing Croker holding in his tongs a cake of ice

But the Tammany administration still had another year in office, before the fall election of 1901, and perhaps they hoped to live down the Mazet Committee revelations, relying on the traditional short memory of the electorate. Jerome did not propose to give Tammany this breathing space. He suddenly erupted from the Court of Special Sessions and its daily grind of misdemeanors to electrify the city with his personal assaults on police-protected vice. To do this he had to cast his black robes, figuratively, to the four winds, to plunge into nonjudicial matters and to demonstrate, as it was later observed, "what a magistrate can do with the powers of investigation if he wants to stretch those powers to the snapping point."

Judge Jerome began summoning police captains in whose precincts gambling and prostitution were reported and cross-examining them on why they hadn't stopped such activities. The newspapers, which began stationing reporters in his court every day now, played up these interrogations. This brought Jerome in conflict with Bill Devery.

A policeman whom Jerome had sentenced to three months in jail for refusing to support his children came up for departmental trial before Devery. Ordinarily, such a conviction would cause automatic dismissal, but the policeman's lawyer slyly brought up the fact that his client had been "railroaded" by Judge Jerome, which caused Devery to erupt.

"Jerome, hey?" he bellowed. "Case's dismissed! There's a lot of tin soldiers running around this town with popguns on their shoulders, shootin' them off in the streets, raisin' riot and rebellion and degradin' the whole damn community! It's an outrage. Jerome ain't goin' to run this town if I have anythin' to do with it. It's about time a halt was called!"*

The policemen present raised a cheer for their doughty chief.

---

with Mayor Van Wyck congealed inside was particularly effective in epitomizing the Mazet Committee's disclosures.

* Quoted in Hodder's *A Fight for the City.*

Jerome joined an organization known as the Committee of Fifteen, reviving memories of the committee which four years earlier had driven Tammany to cover. It investigated reports of graft and corruption, turning the information over to Jerome, and prepared to campaign in the coming election for reform-minded candidates. Novelist A. L. Hodder who also joined the committee wrote that Jerome and his associates were held together by a bond as "new and accidental as that uniting a group of Western ranchmen. They were not Westerners; they were city-bred, they were college-bred, they were even super-civilized, yet they conjured up an image of the plains."

Armed with information gathered by the Committee of Fifteen and like-minded groups, who engaged detectives to verify and ferret it out, Jerome put the pressure on the precinct captains to raid the places where gamblers and madams were holding forth. Instead the police tipped off such establishments that they were under surveillance, and when the raids took place they found nothing illegal on the premises.

Jerome exploded in his wrath. Justice was not going to be circumvented by men sworn to uphold it. If the police wouldn't do their duty, he'd do it for them. With an axe in one hand and a Bible in his hip pocket, accompanied by a pick-up force of bailiffs, friends, members of the Committee of Fifteen, he would sally forth from the Criminal Courts Building to raid gambling places on the lower East Side. He always carried a stack of John Doe warrants with him to lend a shadow of legality to his impromptu activities. Then he would "rush" the selected gambling joint, hoping to smash through its "icebox" doors and other fortified features before the inmates could take alarm and conceal evidence. ("Rushing," as Hodder explained in *A Fight for the City*, "means hustling watchmen, breaking barred doors, and a free fight, ending possibly in an exchange of pistol shots with such of the occupants of the rooms within as try to make good an escape.") Reporters and photographers also accompanied Jerome to capture in words and pictures the unorthodox jurist personally chopping his way into a gambling den. Once inside the citadel, with captured gamblers, shattered gambling equipment and exploding flash powder all around him, Jerome would haul out his Bible, post himself behind a crap table and declare court in session. Witnesses were sworn in, testimony taken, and culprits arraigned on the spot. As Jerome must have foreseen, his roving, stripped down, ad-lib court sessions titillated the public imagination; he built an image of himself as a rough and ready man of action, plowing through fusillades of underworld bullets, not one of those namby-pamby reformers who'd had their chance under the Strong administration and frittered it away snatching at the simple pleasures of the poor.

Robert Dunn, then a reporter on the *Commercial Advertiser*, recalled in his autobiography (*World Alive*) that he seldom came so close to death during a long and venturesome career as when he accompanied Jerome on his raiding parties. Axe poised, Jerome looked like one of his Iroquois ancestors on a tomahawk spree as he assaulted a gaming "fort." Dunn particularly remembered a raid on a gambling joint masked by a milliner's sign and silken drapes; the fact that it was located next to Tammany's Wigwam on Fourteenth Street only added to the joy of the occasion. The lookouts took several "pot shots" at Jerome and his party, narrowly missing His Honor and young Mr. Dunn. "No reporter ever got closer to his heaven than I that afternoon," Dunn wrote. Within minutes "a truck at the curb loaded on roulette wheels and pistol smoke cleared from the rear fire escape."

A two-volume scrapbook of newspaper illustrations during 1900 and 1901 compiled by the New York Public Library indicates Jerome was the cartoonists' delight at the turn of the century. An ax-wielding jurist was something of a sensation even in those politically spectacular days, recalling inevitable comparisons to Carrie Nation and her saloon-busting hatchet. A particularly fetching cartoon in the *World* showed Jerome hold-

ing court at a faro layout while bumble-footed police are tardily
trying to tip off the proprietors that they may be raided.

One of his more sensational exploits was descending on an
exceptionally prosperous gambling house at 20 Dey Street. He
had asked the police to raid it, but they kept stalling him, claiming they were having a hard time nailing down evidence. Jerome
and his cohorts broke in, and found eight police officers in
mufti who stoutly maintained they were "working under cover,"
had been staked out there for thirty-five days and found no signs
of gambling. Jerome smashed through another door and discovered a hundred men busy at the roulette wheels, the faro
bank, the crap tables.

After the usual scuffling and shouting died down, one well-
dressed and distinguished-looking man detached himself from the
low-life herd and came up to Jerome, whispering, "Mr. Jerome,
I can't afford to be caught here; you must help me get out."

"Court's in session," Jerome snapped. "Hold up your hand
and be sworn."

When the man refused to give his name, Jerome remanded him
to the House of Detention for contempt of court. The man then
revealed his identity. He was the Honorable Maurice Holahan —
and he was the president of the Board of Public Works.

Holahan protested to the newspapers that he had come to the
gambling house in search of his "wayward son," an alibi which
"caused the town to shake with irreverent laughter." His paternal
concern, at any rate, was ill rewarded. Wayward or not, Holahan's son so resented being used as an alibi that he spilled out
the story of his father's crooked dealings with contractors doing
business with his department.

Wallace Irwin's satirical verses on the tender feeling the police
had for gambling houses, and Judge Jerome's brutal disregard
for this protective relationship, were widely circulated and included the following jibe:

"Tut, tut!" said Jerome with a grin,
"These games are disguised very thin;
  When you hear a cop snore
  By a strange-looking door
It's a cinch there is gambling within."

Tammany began to take alarm, fearing a recurrence of the '94 upheaval. A Committee of Five, mocking the reform group to which Jerome belonged, was appointed to investigate vice and graft. Its members all were Tammany men, and they predictably brought in a report that it was impossible to secure evidence of gambling operations. It was the day following this announcement that Jerome raided the Dey Street establishment.

Boss Croker suggested that it would be wise to throttle down on gambling and prostitution until the election was over. He was convinced that Tammany would have a hard time at the polls that fall of 1901. Big Tim Sullivan was ordered to line up the lower East Side for Tammany, disaffected though it was by the activities of police-protected pimps and procurers who snatched tenement girls off the streets. He had the Irish, the Germans and the Italians fairly well in hand, but found the Jews "stiff-necked," much more difficult to bamboozle.

Meanwhile, the Republican State Legislature dealt Tammany a severe blow by abolishing the office of chief of police and temporarily throwing Bill Devery out of work. Mayor Van Wyck remedied the situation by creating the office of deputy police commissioner for him. Devery, a three-hundred-pound buffoon with a wide streak of animal cunning, continued to hold his Thursday "courts," at which erring members of the force were called on the carpet, and to pass along such constabulary wisdom as, "When you're caught with the goods, don't say nothin'." As deputy police commissioner one of his chief functions was circumventing the reformers, particularly Jerome. A. L. Hodder took delight in studying Devery in action. His manner, Hodder wrote, was "for all the world that of the ducal tyrant of some

Italian state, in an Elizabethan play . . . His language was a
continuous performance in inspired mixed metaphor and Irish
bull." Occasionally he would disappear from Police Headquarters
for days at a time, embarked on a boozing spree during which
he liked to ride around town in a hack throwing handfuls of
silver to the sidewalk crowds. When reporters quizzed him on
some touchy matter, Devery's favorite reply was, "Touchin' on
and appertainin' to that, there's nothin' doin'." He loved to exercise his saw-toothed wit on delinquent policemen summoned to
his Thursday courts, Hodder observed. A patrolman was brought
up on charges of reckless shooting in the streets. Devery fined
him thirty days pay for "not hittin' nobody."

As election time approached, Devery was supremely confident
that his peculiar methods of administering the police department,
which incidentally had enriched him by an estimated quarter of
a million dollars, would be vindicated by the voters. Big Bill
was certain that New Yorkers didn't want another taste of
"panty-waist rule."

The much shrewder Mr. Croker, however, began looking
gloomier than ever late in that summer of 1901.

Tammany would offer Edward M. Shepard as its candidate
for mayor, Henry W. Unger for district attorney.

Croker was not at all displeased to learn that Fusion had
settled on Seth Low again as its mayoralty candidate, Low being
very respectable, utterly dignified — and damnably dull, particularly on the platform. He wouldn't set off any fireworks. But
Croker was thoroughly alarmed by Fusion's choice of his running
mate for district attorney. It was William Travers Jerome.

5

NEVER IN THE history of New York, and rarely in the politics of
any other American city, has there been such a campaign as
Jerome waged in 1901. Picturing himself as the "defender of the
oppressed," he made eighty-six speeches during his six-week

campaign, stirring up such excitement in his person alone that he distracted the electorate completely from Tammany's torch-lights, bands and beer, and all its traditional razzmatazz. He caused such a commotion, running for what was, after all, merely a county office — made such a gallant spectacle, such an invigorating drama, such a gripping morality play of his aspirations — that newspapers throughout the United States, in England and Germany played up the campaign as though it were taking place in their midst.

No one until La Guardia succeeded so thoroughly in convincing New Yorkers that their city could be, and should be, decently governed, in shaking them out of their lethargic, shoulder-shrugging, go-fight-City-Hall attitude toward injustice. More than three decades later the New York *Times* tried to analyze the galvanic effects of Jerome's campaign. After exploring the impact of the Jerome personality, it noted that "There was in addition something intangible, incapable of being written down, which made his service to this city unique and invaluable. He somehow expressed or symbolized in his person the deepest convictions and aspirations of the majority of our citizens . . ."

The moment he would bound onto a platform, someone in the crowd — quite possibly one of his henchmen, for he was not above showmanship — would shout, "Who's going to eat the Tiger?"

"Jerome!" the crowd would roar in response.

His campaign workers issued square-shaped black campaign buttons with "Jerome" printed diagonally across them in white letters, his campaign slogan being "Jerome on the Square."

He raced around the town in an automobile to fulfill his speaking engagements and reach into every section of the city. Even foreign-born audiences on the East Side, it was observed, caught his meaning when he raged against the men who lured or abducted thousands of girls annually into prostitution, and made them understand that the Tammany district leader was not only the man who dispensed free coal and groceries or put up bail when they were in trouble but enriched himself to their detriment and dishonor. "Bearded Jews and swart Italians, fathers of growing daughters, sobbed and wailed as they listened to Jerome; recalled what they themselves had seen, or even suffered; and went home vowing that, come what might, Fusion should have their vote."*

He would wave a leather belt strung with brass checks, which the madams of East Side brothels passed out to their customers to signify that they had paid their fee, and challenge his audience with the statement, "If these conditions existed in other communities, there would be a Vigilance Committee speedily organized, and somebody would get lynched."

The budding novelist Upton Sinclair, just out of college, watched Jerome waving those brass checks, which later gave him the title for one of his books. In his autobiography, *American Outpost*, he related how he "took fire" from Jerome's oratory and joined other youthful idealists in campaigning for his election. "I went out among everybody I knew and raised a sum of money and took it to the candidate at the dinner hour at his club. He thanked me cordially and took the money; but my feelings were a trifle hurt because he did not stay to chat with me while his dinner got cold. Having since run for office myself [he ran for governor of California thirty years later], and had admirers swarm about to shake my hand, I can appreciate the desire of a public man to have his dinner hour free."

Another such young recruit to his standards was Fred Stein, the son of a wealthy woolen manufacturer, who agreed to publish a weekly campaign paper in Yiddish, ten editions of 100,000 copies each. The paper, later called *The Jewish World*, not only was so successful that its publication continued after the election but it won for Jerome seven out of ten "Jewish" districts which ordinarily went Tammany.

* Lothrop Stoddard, *Master of Manhattan*.

If he concentrated on arousing the immigrant masses down-town to throw off the Tammany shackles, Jerome did not entirely neglect the smug and well-heeled citizens uptown who had tolerated corruption for decades. A sort of upper-class rally was held at Carnegie Hall, with the so-called better people set-tling back in their seats and waiting for a genteel appeal to their civic consciences. Instead he shocked them with words they had never heard from a political candidate, or anyone else:

"My friends, you are of my own class. I was born and bred with you. But I want to say to you that you are of no use to this city. I feel bitterly against you because of your heartlessness.

"Morally, you are as bad as the people I am fighting in the lowest dive. Morally, you are not worth the powder to blow you out of existence.

"You are too respectable to care about the teeming tenements and the hovels where crouch in darkness a million people of this city. It is you, the better people, who are responsible for the conditions in this city today. Every dollar you have laid by, every step you have climbed in the social scale has laid upon you an obligation of civic leadership, and you have failed. You are not bad people. You are heartless people and, above all, stupid people.

"And you came here tonight to get from me some words of reassurance that I shall do nothing to ruffle you. Do you think I want your votes?

"Take your votes to Tammany, that is where they belong. But remember this: by reason of your neglect of your civic duty, your lack of civic pride, you have also shown your lack of patriotism.

"You should be ashamed of yourself.

"The only civic and welfare work that is being done in this city today is being done by the Irish Catholic Charities, the Russian Jews, and the Socialists. Shame on you. When I look around in the clubs of social position I have not yet found a single man who, from the point of view of civic honor, is worthy of a decent burial."

Jerome may have lost a lot of aristocratic votes with his blunt words that evening, but reports of the speech won him many more south and west of Carnegie Hall.

The youthful Arthur Train, an assistant district attorney and a new recruit to the Jerome cause, was impressed — and occasionally appalled — by Jerome's reckless honesty. "He never minced his words, never hesitated to speak his mind whether to a political boss or to an audience of a thousand people. If there was an inopportune occasion for speaking the truth, it seemed as if Jerome always selected it. There was never a crisis, when Jerome's friends were hoping great things for his own advancement, that he did not make a savage attack on some prominent official or influential citizen in such a way as apparently to court political extermination."

A striking example was his treatment of Republican boss Tom Platt's reluctant support of Fusion, offered after twice having refused it in '94 and '97. It is a first principle of politics to welcome support of any kind in an election and settle accounts later, when you've got the office and the power. But Jerome couldn't stomach the idea of Platt marching under his banner; only pure hearts and clean consciences might enlist, and he would rather have Platt as an open enemy than a devious ally.

At first he referred sarcastically to "that winged saint, Thomas C. Platt"; then, warming to his task, he declared from the platform that Platt "has done more to debauch public life in New York than any other man," and finally he charged that Platt, in concert with William C. Whitney, head of the soon to be malodorous Metropolitan Street Railway, was secretly plotting his defeat. In another time and with another candidate, such a quixotic maneuver might have been disastrous, but the Jerome magnetism was overwhelming. "Whether he was right or wrong in his surmise," wrote Arthur Train, "the people felt that here was a man who was afraid of nothing, who was bound to have out the truth whatever the personal consequences to himself might be . . ."

Whatever the beneficial effects on the electorate of his slashing attacks, the political leaders of both parties sized him up as the most dangerous kind of maverick: honest, dedicated, incorruptible, and — worst of all — unpredictable. Jerome might achieve the district attorney's office, but his higher ambitions would suffer. The men who run politics from City Hall to the White House are never eager to espouse the career of a candidate who can't be "handled," who refuses to compromise, who believes his strength lies in the voter rather than the practical politician.

"The mob," as Train succinctly put it, "would have followed his alert, square, high-shouldered figure anywhere . . . he was the popular hero of the slums and Fifth Avenue alike . . ." but the professional politicians would never overlook his tendency to kick over the traces.

Jerome's bluntness of speech was exceeded only by that of his Number one target, Deputy Police Commissioner Devery. Smarting under Jerome's charges that he was not only the operating head of the police department but the real commander of the city's cadets, pimps, procurers and madams, Devery lost his temper and bellowed at reporters: "That man Jerome ought to be locked up on Ward's Island! He ain't sound mentally. There's somethin' the matter with him. He's like the rhinoceros up in the Park. Every time he goes down under the water he comes up with a gulp and blows it all over everybody . . . It wouldn't take me ten minutes to go and take him by the scruff of the neck and lock him up. But that wouldn't do just now . . . Will they put me out — Low and those fellers? . . . G'wan! Never! Devery stays right here!"

That arrogant assertion amused Jerome but got Devery called on the carpet before Boss Croker. Tammany's candidate for mayor promptly denied that a Democratic victory meant that

Devery was secure in his office. But the damage was done by then.*

By the end of October Jerome was so confident of victory that he began relaxing a little on the platform and lacing his speeches with humorous jibes at his opponents. One anecdote he told became known as "Jerome's lemon story," which ran as follows: "Just to show what chances there are for graft in a city like New York, let us suppose that there is a shortage of lemons in the city, and two ships loaded with lemons came into port. Whichever ship can get its cargo first to market can make a fortune. Under the law, the city fruit inspectors are required to examine every box of lemons. But suppose that one of them accepts a bribe and lets one cargo be landed ahead of the other — you can see what graft there would be for somebody."

The day after this anecdote was published in the newspapers a city fruit inspector whom he knew approached Jerome and plaintively inquired, "How the hell did you find out about those lemons?" Jerome did not bother to explain that the anecdote was the product of his imagination.

He was more amused than annoyed by a sanctimonious outburst from Big Tim Sullivan, who charged that "Jerome lives on highballs and cigarettes." Not only did he confess to a liking for them, but he went on to attack the Sunday closing laws: "As to the question of closing saloons on Sundays, I have never found that my own thirst stopped at twelve o'clock on Saturday night and began again at five o'clock on Monday morning; I have always found that I was just about as thirsty on Sunday as on any other day; and I have never understood that drinking whiskey in moderation, even on Sunday, was a moral evil. I wish to make the confession that when I have wanted a drink on Sunday I have taken it . . . The great majority of men use alcohol, and use

---

* Devery was retired a short time later and with Frank Farrell bought the franchise for the American League baseball team, then known as the Highlanders. They sold the club in 1915 to Jake Ruppert.

it in moderation . . . and they will no more consent to have their habits regulated by law for the protection of weak brothers who drink too much than for the protection of weak brothers who eat too much. The weak brothers are about the least important members of the community for whom any considerable body of decent men can be asked to make a sacrifice . . ."

His last major speech of the campaign was addressed to a "big audience of Germans" at the Grand Central Palace, where he summed up the issues and concluded with, "When you appeal to the plain people Abraham Lincoln loved for what is right and true you will get what's coming to you every time." The rally ended on a highly sentimental note, with the candidate taking his weeping wife in his arms (though her tears stemmed more from rage and humiliation at being subjected to this public demonstration than any wifely sentiment, a fact fortunately invisible to the audience), "kissing her tenderly again and again" (while she winced at the vulgarity of it all), and also hugging his eleven-year-old son William Travers Jerome, Jr. while the crowd roared its approval. "He was again the husband and father," the *Herald* noted with an unusual touch of sentiment, "no more the candidate for office."

On November 3 the *Herald* published the results of its "postcard poll," a straw vote which forecast a general Fusion victory, and that organ, published by an old friend of the Jerome family, declared editorially that day, "If the people want blackmailers and other criminals vigorously prosecuted without fear or favor they will elect Judge Jerome." Not much later Bennett's paper, as reversible as its publisher's temperament, would be denouncing him with even greater enthusiasm, but now it was predicting that Jerome would be swept in and Tammany swept out by a "cyclone of popular condemnation."

The last day of the campaign Jerome appeared at the Café Liberty, "in the heart of the ghetto," as the *Times* put it, with Mrs. Jerome, his former law partner Daniel Nason and the celebrated author and editor Richard Watson Gilder at his side. "My fight is fought," he told the throngs gathered in and around the café. "Now it's up to you."

On election night the town went wild as the first bulletins indicated a Fusion victory, and the same crowds which several years ago had snake-danced through the streets shouting "To hell with reform" now cheered the other side. Tammany conceded defeat at 10 P.M., upon which hundreds of thousands of citizens milling around Madison and Herald Squares roared their approval in "one vast diapason of sound." Low and Jerome won by a fair margin, the latter's plurality running to 15,890 out of 163,000 votes cast. Thousands of votes for his opponent, as it later developed, were thrown out on a technicality. Many had voted the straight Democratic ticket, except for Mayor Van Wyck, who was then running for the State Supreme Court. Van Wyck was so detested for his Ice Trust participation that thousands defaced their ballots by writing scurrilous comments around his name. Such ballots were legally void and could not be counted. Had they not been thrown out, Jerome's margin of victory would have been dangerously slender.

Next morning the *Times* editorial page said of Jerome that "his canvass has been one of the most inspiring things that New Yorkers can remember." *The Times* of London praised his "fearless and stirring denunciations." Berlin's *National Zeitung* commented that "Political morality has gained a brilliant and, we hope, decisive victory."

Jerome heard the news with his family at their country retreat in Lakeville, Connecticut. Evidently still carried along by the momentum of the campaign, he told reporters who interviewed him on his porch that "that winged saint Thomas C. Platt" must be eating crow for breakfast. Then he hurried back to town to begin laying plans to carry out the bold and sweeping promises he had made.

4

The Unfrocking of "His Reverence"

N OT UNTIL the blithely irresponsible and unselective twenties, when Jimmy Walker was mayor and master of the revels, did New York have a public official with the glamor and popularity of William Travers Jerome. The two men had little in common morally or intellectually — and nothing, certainly, in outlook — but both had a dashing manner, an irreverent wit, a flair for removing the pomposity from their official functions, and both flourished in pleasure-loving and relatively carefree times, the Edwardian years no less than the twenties, in which the stuffed shirt was not welcomed in public life.

Until Jerome came along, Arthur Train had written (in *From the District Attorney's Office*), the public's image of a prosecutor was "that of a bull-necked gladiator with an undershot jaw, whose only object was to convict every unfortunate charged with crime, whether guilty or not." He was the ranting inquisitor obsessed with sending men to that new contraption up the river, the electric chair. If there was a hero in the courtroom, it was the accused man or his defense lawyer.

Jerome, on the other hand, soon became known as a prosecutor who was tolerant of a certain amount of human frailty and who would tell an over-zealous assistant who had secured too stiff a sentence for some unfortunate:

"That's like hanging a man for the murder of a cigar-store Indian."

He made so attractive a figure, challenging the forces of evil and injustice, yet never losing his sense of proportion (or humor, which is practically the same thing) that he brought about a small revolution in contemporary drama and literature. Almost immediately after he entered the district attorney's office, Train has noted, "the curtain to every second act arose upon a ground glass door bearing the then mystic words 'District Attorney's Office,' from which emerged at the crucial instant an official Sir Galahad — brave, resourceful, perennially young, and clad in a nobby business suit and bowler hat. He smoked cigarettes; the senatorial villain puffed cigars; and the play ended with the powers of darkness on the run." In current fiction, too, the fighting young prosecutor, modeled after Jerome, became a standard hero.

After winning the election, Jerome had retained his place on the Special Sessions bench so that Tammany wouldn't be able to fill the vacancy with one of its own appointees. During the seven weeks between the election and the end of the year, when he would take over the district attorney's office, he spent most of his time laying plans for rooting out the gamblers, from the princely Dick Canfield on down, who until now had been immune to police interference. He also enlisted a young and vigorous staff, and conferred with Mayor-elect Low on the problems of shaking up the police force. Devery and other Tammany-tarred cops were persuaded to resign, and Colonel John N. Partridge was selected to see to it, as the new police commissioner, that the department straightened itself out. Max Schmittberger, ex-bagman in the Tenderloin, was allowed to remain and was duly promoted to inspector, so evident was his zeal to serve the cause of cleaning up the city.

Even before taking office, realizing that getting inside information was absolutely essential in dealing with the gamblers, Jerome secretly engaged a man to work undercover and quite unofficially. The spy, according to Alexander Gardiner's biography of Canfield, was:

a soft-spoken Southerner who knew his way around the town. Jerome used his own money to pay this man's salary, and although the relation of employer and employee continued uninterruptedly through the eight years he was district attorney, he never saw the man during that time, and only once was the spy inside his office. Though the man is now dead, Mr. Jerome does not care to give his name. Many times in the years that followed the gamblers suspected that someone on the inside was giving tips to the district attorney, but evidently they were never lucky enough to fasten on to the spy. The former district attorney assured me recently that he is quite certain his informant did not doublecross him, leaving that characteristic piece of work to another private detective.

On taking office the first of the year, Jerome found himself sinking in a morass of work left undone, inefficiency, incompetence and demoralization; nothing, certainly, had changed for the better since he had left the office a dozen years before. Eight hundred and sixty-one indictments had piled up in a bureaucratic logjam, awaiting a top-level decision on how to proceed. He had inherited a crumbling bureaucracy staffed for several generations mostly by dimwits and political appointees. It was like walking into a Roman house after it had been buried under volcanic ash for centuries and expecting the plumbing to work.

His first order of business was to install his fire-eating young assistants, clear out the deadwood, clean up the docket, and get the office running again on a day-by-day basis. One fiscal matter had to be corrected immediately. Until he took office, collections on forfeited bonds had averaged only $11,000 annually. Jerome got his detectives on the scent and soon raised the collection average to $100,000 annually.

At the same time, to keep his promise to the people of the lower East Side that their daughters would be protected from the pimps and procurers, he immediately opened a combination "branch office" and dormitory at 8 Rutgers Street. The place was to be kept open night and day so that complaints could be heard and investigated without delay.

Every night from ten to forty people visited the "branch office," slowly becoming convinced that Jerome meant it when he said that justice would be dispensed at every level of society.

One complainant, recalled by A. L. Hodder, was a sewing woman who earned fifty cents a day. She wanted her fifteen-year-old daughter rescued from a house of prostitution. Jerome himself happened to be on "Ghetto duty" — as his irreverent assistants soon were calling it — that night and heard her plea. She tried to give Jerome ten dollars, all she had, because experience had taught her that no politician would keep his promise without an emolument. When Jerome insisted on returning the money to her, she burst into tears and fled, convinced that his refusal meant he wouldn't do anything about restoring her daughter. Before the night was out, however, his detectives had located and returned the daughter to her mother.

Almost every night, after a full day at his desk in the Criminal Courts Building, he listened to a litany of woe and injustice, which only reinforced his determination to bring about a respect for the "rule of the law" in every level of metropolitan society.

He chose as his assistants mostly young men, many of them only a year or two out of law school, enthusiastic about the idea of public service. Many had been recommended by civic reform groups or highly reputable lawyers.

"In the old days," Jerome was fond of saying, "the district attorney's office was the mouth of hell."

He replaced its air of moldy futility with a brisk collegiate atmosphere, in which the necessarily grim work of law enforcement was accomplished in a brighter and saner climate. Once the place reeked of shady deals, grimy compromises and the exercise of pull. Now the wire-pullers and influence-peddlers who had scrounged a living around the Criminal Courts Building for years had to scatter and seek gainful employment, until the day when reform once again subsided. One depressed Irishman, a veteran camp follower of justice, was heard by Arthur Train to complain, "In the ould days a feller could use his pull; now, the divil take it, to get anythin' done you got to hold up your hand and yell 'Hay-vard, Hay-vard, Hay-vard.' " The Harvard Law School, as usual, had contributed more than its share of recruits to a progressive movement.

Among the bright young men Jerome gathered around him as assistants were: Arthur Train, whose ability as a lawyer was first-rate but whose literary ambitions were to carry him even farther; George W. Schurman, a future partner of Charles Evans Hughes; Charles C. Nott and Joseph Corrigan, future judges of the Court of General Sessions; the future Chief Justice Kernochan of Special Sessions; George W. Whiteside, Francis P. Garvan, William Rand and Charles A. Perkins, future luminaries of the New York bar.

And last, but far from least, Isidor Jacob Kresel, perhaps the most brilliant of them all. Kresel had almost everything going against him. First of all he was Jewish, in a day when men of his faith found it exceedingly difficult to gain a foothold in the legal profession. (Partly, he once told a Jewish civic group many years after leaving the district attorney's office, this was their own fault. He had just conducted an investigation which resulted in the disbarment of seventy-four Jewish lawyers in Brooklyn for ambulance-chasing. "There seems to be something in the Jewish mind," he said, "which causes them to confuse the law as a profession with a business such as selling shoes or dry goods.") Also many of his new colleagues considered that Kresel just didn't fit. Many of them were socially prominent, elegantly turned out, impeccably Anglo-Saxon (except for an odd Celt or two). Kresel was a tiny creature who weighed only ninety-five pounds, and was so short that, as the office wisecrack had it, he could "run under a table wearing a high hat." He had a long head, with a receding brow, a sooty mustache and beady little black eyes, and tiny feet which barely touched the floor when he sat at a counsel table.

His social qualifications were nil. Born in the Polish province of Galicia, he was brought to the United States at the age of eleven by his widowed mother and raised on the lower East Side. Mrs. Kresel worked in a sweatshop and sacrificed herself to educate her son. Isidor justified the sacrifice by winning Pulitzer scholarships to the Horace Mann School and later to Columbia, teaching in night schools to lessen the burden on his mother. At Columbia he came to the attention of Seth Low, then president of the college, and Low recommended him, at the age of twenty-three, to Jerome.

Jerome not only appointed him an assistant district attorney but assumed the role of guardian angel. Anyone making cracks about Kresel or his rodentlike appearance in Jerome's hearing was blistered from head to toe. Kresel was one of the two men from the district attorney's office whom Jerome took with him into private practice, and subsequently became a first-rate trial lawyer and a master of cross-examination. As an assistant district attorney, however, he took over as chief of the investigative functions of the office; his ability to speak Yiddish, Russian, German, Polish, French and Italian also came in handy in the many cases involving the immigrant population. As Jerome's "digger-in-chief," Milton MacKaye has written,* he "sat at the council table and watched other men detonate the ammunition he had mined . . . He was shy in his social contacts — in later years he would be something of a recluse — but, placed in the same room with twelve bushels of confusing documents, he would tunnel into corporate mysteries for all the world like a miner with a lamp in his hat and come out with an action ready for trial — conviction guaranteed." Kresel was the first to bring scientific method to investigations, basing them on records of every kind, bank

* *The Tin Box Parade.*

accounts, income tax returns, brokerage and expense accounts, leases, mortgages, records of telephone calls. From these records, Kresel was "able to build up his picture of a given witness or a given situation; it was a process of elimination performed before anyone was called upon to testify . . . Only relevant facts, plucked from the tangled skeins of an official history, came into open court."

Almost from the outset of his first term, Jerome served notice that he considered Fusion a fine principle for winning elections but that he would not be governed by sentiment stemming from associations in the political victory of the past November. It was hardly necessary for him to issue this warning, and certainly not in the harsh, tactless terms in which he couched it. The occasion he chose was a banquet held on January 12, 1902, just a dozen days after he assumed office, which was intended to be a feast of reconciliation between County Democrats and the regular Republicans.

"I'm not going to get too friendly with the reform administration," he bluntly told the love feast, shattering the whole mood of the occasion. "I might have to indict some of them.

"I'm not running on schedule, and I don't have to look out for red lights or green lights.

"*I'm running wildcat.*"

Then, amid a stunned silence, he abruptly sat down.

For his running mate, Mayor Seth Low, he had little esteem and treated him, it was observed, with "a lack of courtesy little short of contempt." Nor did he hesitate to discourse on the reasons for Low's unpopularity, which became apparent at the outset of his administration. This disaffection, as Jerome openly analyzed it, stemmed from "the unlovable personality of the man himself . . . Egotism, self-complacency, and constitutional timidity are not the elements to make a leader."

Aside from their temporary political affiliation, Low and Jerome had little in common. They were direct opposites in temperament. A stout, red-cheeked burgher who had inherited a prosperous silk and textile importing company, Low was stolid, earnest and well-meaning. He had attained the presidency of Columbia though "he never in his whole life taught anything more than a Sunday School class," and the mayor's office in Brooklyn with little experience in practical politics.*

Nor did he possess the sense of humor that Jerome valued in a man. One of his few recorded essays in wit was undertaken at a banquet, where he was seated on the dais between Tammany boss Dick Croker and Republican boss Thomas C. Platt. When he was called upon to speak, Low observed, "I am between the Devil and the deep T.C."

Jerome's dislike of the man, based largely on matters of personality and possibly also on the fact that Low was accused of favoring the Republicans in his administration, was a considerable factor in Low's downfall after his first term. The Fusionists renominated Low in 1903 but his hopes were dashed when a letter written by Jerome and addressed to Thomas A. Fulton, secretary of the Citizens Union, somehow was leaked to the press. Low's re-election, Jerome wrote, "would prove the wickedest thing that has been done in political life in my recollection." Jerome made apologetic noises, but the damage was done and the Tammany candidate, George B. McClellan, son of the Union general, won by a 56,000 majority.

Jerome himself was not without flaws, which became more visible when he began running the district attorney's office and getting a real taste of power after years of frustration. "He was sentimental and emotional," observed Arthur Train, "often carried away by his own enthusiasms and resentments . . . He knew his own ability and political availability, and had champed at the restraint incident to an inconspicuous minor judgeship. It made him authoritative, somewhat domineering, even slightly arrogant. He was a bit of a swashbuckler."

* Benjamin R. C. Low's *Seth Low*.

Train also disapproved of certain "boulevardier" tendencies, which Jerome undoubtedly inherited from his lighthearted father, and observed that "his rather limited social experience in youth and young manhood led him to relish fashionable attention . . ."

Just possibly Train's initial impressions of Jerome were influenced by the fact that he suspected Jerome was prejudiced against him. Train was a holdover from the Philbin regime; he also had the well-bred Bostonian's diffidence toward the more exuberant New Yorker's bonhomie. Eventually, after spending several weekends roughing it in the country with Jerome and his friends, joining in the joking and drinking and debating, he found himself regarded, he said, as a "regular feller." As a sign of acceptance, Jerome nicknamed him Mock Duck after a Chinese tong leader whom Train had prosecuted on murder charges.

Aside from Train's initial wariness, Jerome's bright young men worshiped him, from all accounts. He was not only their superior but their inspiration, idol and defender. Loyalty up and down was the keynote of his administration. The young lawyers whom he had recruited not only admired his legal brilliance, his inspiring personality, his long record for having fought corruption without backsliding or losing faith, his genial and easygoing manner outside official duties, his sophistication (always fascinating to youth), but the way he came to their rescue when they fouled up. With Jerome it was his assistants, right or wrong. One of the sights of the Criminal Courts Building was Jerome charging down a corridor, coattails flying, when he received word that one of his trial deputies was being bullied by a judge. He would stride into the courtroom, take full responsibility for the actions of his deputy and start hammering away at the judge, displaying an amazing ability at tightroping around the boundaries of contempt.

His quick-tempered assistant, Joe Corrigan, always remembered how Jerome backed him up when the former was prosecuting the keeper of a disorderly house. The opposing counsel made himself obnoxious by putting Corrigan on the stand and trying to show bias in the prosecution. On leaving the stand after parrying a particularly insulting line of questioning, Corrigan paused at the counsel table and whispered to his opponent: "You're a dirty shyster."

Boiling with indignation, the lawyer rushed over to Jerome's office the moment court was adjourned. "I demand an apology," he told the district attorney. "Mr. Corrigan called me a dirty shyster."

Jerome, who had been gazing at the tips of his shoes, which were parked on top of his desk in a characteristic posture, stood up, stared thoughtfully at the lawyer for a moment, and then quietly said, "Mr. Corrigan is a truthful man."

Augustin Derby, a Harvard Law School graduate who had served a year as secretary to Justice Oliver Wendell Holmes, found Jerome "the exact opposite in everything except character" from his first employer. Jerome, Derby later wrote, "cared nothing about the party affiliations of his staff, and chose men upon whom he felt he could depend for personal and not political reasons."

Appointed as deputy to Arthur Train, Derby considered Jerome "the perfect chief, wholly democratic and with no air of superiority, who counselled with his young men and stood behind them in all their mistakes, taking the blame himself."

I remember, [Derby recalled years later,] that I tried a case of larceny from the New York Central Railroad before a particularly bullheaded Irish-American judge, which seemed to me to be ironclad until, at the close of the People's case, the wily lawyer for the defense made a motion to dismiss the indictment on the ground that I had not proved that the New York Central . . . was a corporation. Excited and angry, I said, "Does the counsellor expect me to call the Secretary of State from Albany and prove that the State has granted the New York Central a charter, which everyone knows that it possesses?" . . .

The Court, however, sustained the motion of the defense to dismiss the indictment on the trivial ground offered.

White with anger I said, "I protest the Court's decision which will cause a grave miscarriage of justice." Then the judge's violent Irish temper boiled over, and he threatened to commit me to jail for contempt.

I sent the process server for Jerome, who appeared in court within a few minutes. He addressed the Court scathingly, I was not committed, but the decision of dismissal was allowed to stand.

Afterwards I wished that I had been sent to the Tombs. Imagine the daily papers in headlines printing that Judge X had sent a young assistant of Jerome's to jail because he protested a decision that it was necessary to prove that the New York Central Railroad was a corporation. He would have been laughed off the bench.*

Within two months of taking office, Jerome managed to introduce an unusual element of efficiency in his department, quashing some of the old indictments and pressing for immediate action on others. Meanwhile, most of the gambling houses around town were reported to have closed up, at least temporarily, convinced that Jerome meant business. A few of the places were said to open an hour or two daily to accommodate old customers who could absolutely be trusted to keep their mouths shut. "Lay low" was the order of the day; sooner or later Tammany would find a way of getting around Jerome. The gambling Bradleys, who ran a plush trap with Florida decor, cleared out completely and set up shop down south. In the Tenderloin, most of the bawdyhouses had shut down and their inmates scattered all over town, establishing themselves in apartments and rooming houses to carry on their activities on a less organized basis. In this professional crisis they turned to the notorious personals column of the New York *Herald* to advertise their wares more or less openly. Federal court action subsequently forced Bennett to clean up his want ads.

* From the late Mr. Derby's unpublished manuscript, in the author's possession.

In all, Jerome appeared to be holding himself strictly to his word and keeping the lid tightly closed on the professional purveyors of pleasure. He also succeeded in avoiding the blue-nose stigma by making it plain that he was opposed only to *organized and politically protected* vice, which infected the whole bloodstream of metropolitan government. "I like to gamble a bit myself," he explained, "but a man can get all the gambling he needs in a social game with friends." It was no secret that he liked to relax frequently over a poker table, nor that pinochle players in the back rooms of neighborhood saloons, as well as card players in his own clubs, were to be let alone.

Still, there was one problem that nagged at him, and would concern him for months — Dick Canfield's elegant establishment at 5 East Forty-fourth Street, next to Delmonico's. Rumor had it that one of the young Vanderbilts had dropped hundreds of thousands at Canfield's tables just before Jerome took office; the grapevine also reported — with equal accuracy — that Canfield had shut up shop the night before Jerome was sworn in, and was out of town. The more reform-minded newspapers, particularly the *Tribune,* still demanded that Canfield's be cracked and its doors padlocked forever, even though the existing laws were rather feeble in sustaining any actions taken against private property used for gaming purposes; gambling equipment, for instance, could not even be confiscated until Jerome pushed stricter laws through the state legislature. At the same time everyone knew that Canfield, whose patrons were the richest and most influential people in North America, was only biding his time.

If Jerome had a problem those first months as district attorney, it could be summed up in two words — Dick Canfield.

2

THE NEWSPAPERS called him the "Prince of Gamblers," and in manner, if not in appearance, he was indeed princely, if not imperial; he was also the most successful gambler, up to the rise of

Las Vegas's well-named "industry," in American history. At one time his fortune was estimated at more than $12,000,000, and despite Wall Street reverses he managed to die a millionaire.

He was soft-spoken, cultured, never talked shop but preferred to discuss art and literature with anyone whose knowledge of those subjects approached his own. Gambling was only a business with him, a coldly calculated, lucrative business which supplied him with the means to enjoy fine food and rare vintages, first editions and paintings.

Richard Canfield may have been the perfect gentleman he wanted to be, when he wasn't pressing for collection of a gambling debt, but even his admirers couldn't claim that he looked like one. Forty-seven years old when he and Jerome confronted each other in 1902, he was a pudgy fellow with brown hair parted in the middle, bartender style, and would have looked perfectly at home with a bung starter in his fist. He was five feet, eight inches and weighed two hundred and forty pounds, with a fat, florid, emotionless face. He wore corsets to contain a bulging midriff. His eyes were gambler's gray, the coldest color this side of the Greenland icecap.

Among those who liked, admired and valued him as a companion was James McNeill Whistler, the celebrated painter, who executed a portrait of Canfield looking his most episcopal with pudgy hands folded piously on his massive stomach. Whistler titled his painting, aptly enough, "His Reverence."

One of the few callers he had deigned to receive with any regularity was District Attorney Jerome's late uncle, the dashing and unconventional Leonard Jerome — a friendship which edged with irony the fact that Canfield and Travers Jerome detested each other with a rare passion.

In his last years, his fortune gone and his appetite for gaming quenched, Leonard Jerome often visited Canfield in the top-floor private apartment the latter maintained in his place of business. Here Canfield kept his books and paintings, rarely entering the gaming rooms below. He and Leonard Jerome spent hours discussing the "finer things."

"Such passion for the rare and beautiful," wrote Leonard Jerome of his nephew's future adversary, "gives one a feeling that the man is alive, much more so than most of his clients."

He was flattered that Canfield honored him with the confession that he acquired a taste for literature while serving a six-month jail term.

The eminent gentleman-gambler was born in New Bedford, Massachusetts, the son of a sailor who signed on with the whalers until he was crippled, forced to learn the printer's trade and began publishing the Fall River *Patriot*. Early in his twenties Richard Canfield came to New York and worked as a night clerk at the Union Square Hotel, which was operated by a relative.

In 1879, Canfield went back to New England, married Genevieve Martin of Pawtucket, and for two years operated a poker room in her native city. Then, ambitious to rise above the petty adventures of a milltown poker table, he opened a roulette and faro layout in Providence. It was there that the police cracked down suddenly, raided Canfield's place and sent him to jail for six months. After serving his sentence and improving his mind, he decided to buck the tiger in New York. Mrs. Canfield was established in a home in Providence, where she stayed from then on and where her husband occasionally visited her.

He climbed rapidly in the metropolis, first opening a house on Broadway near Eighteenth Street, then expanding to a four-story brownstone at 22 West Twenty-sixth Street where the rent was six hundred dollars a month and the tab for police protection was two hundred dollars monthly. A year or two later he established the Madison Square Club at 22 West Twenty-sixth Street from his earnings on Broadway. He opened houses in Saratoga (1894) and Newport (1897) to accommodate the compulsive gamblers in the summer as well as the winter. By 1898 he had accumulated enough loot to open what has been called "the most elaborate gaming palace in the western world," in which a quiet elegance would today have put to shame the mechanized sucker-traps of Las Vegas and Reno, at 5 East Forty-fourth street, next to Delmonico's, which occupied the corner at Forty-fourth Street and Fifth Avenue. He was the first American gambler to accept sizable I O U's, which were generally secure enough, considering that the Vanderbilts, Lucky Baldwin, Bet-You-a-Million Gates and the high-rolling United States Senator Edward O. Walcott of Colorado were among his steady patrons.

The house on Forty-fourth Street — "next to Del's," as it was known among the worldly — was a masterpiece of interior decoration. The gaming rooms were paneled in white mahogany inlaid with mother-of-pearl, teak and Spanish leather hand-tooled in gold. They were decorated with Whistler oils and etchings, Chinese Chippendale, rare bronzes and Chinese porcelains. Food was brought in from Delmonico's, vintages from a $75,000 wine cellar, with supper served free every night at 11 o'clock.

From his various establishments, according to his biographer, Alexander Gardiner, he took a total of almost $5,000,000. In the three years of its operation, the "million-dollar house" in Forty-fourth Street alone brought in $1,500,000. Later, turning to an even riskier form of gambling, he raked in $7,500,000 speculating on Wall Street, much of it lost in the panic of 1907.

Canfield once gave a newspaper interviewer some of the secrets of his pre-eminence, admitting that he had "no more morals than a cat." He said, "I have always told the loser that his loss was to be expected, and that if he played again with the hope of recouping it the chances were that he would lose still more. I never tried to 'jolly' the customers in that way, as the expression goes. It is not necessary. To be a successful gambler, more than in any other occupation, truth and honesty are essential. There is no use whatever in lying to your customers. They will gamble anyway, and it is much more satisfactory to be honest than not." If he could have lived his life over, he said, he would rather be a professor of literature than anything else.

Canfield did have one bad habit he didn't confess to in his odd moment of self-revelation — every night he got so drunk he could hardly make it to bed under his own power. For all his magnificent self-possession, the "Prince of Gamblers" obviously suffered from a certain splintering on the underside of his psyche.

3

THE PRESSURE on Jerome to "close up Canfield's" mounted, even though the anti-gambling laws gave him little leverage under the circumstances. He had promised the electorate to do just that, but Canfield had played a dirty trick on him by closing down on midnight, December 31, 1901, and slipping away to Europe. Whether Jerome was convinced that Canfield's was indeed shut down isn't clear, because he gave an interview indicating he believed otherwise. "It would take at least a thousand dollars to get into Dick Canfield's place and get corroborative evidence," he told reporters. "Do you think the comptroller would stand for a bill of two hundred and fifty dollars lost at roulette? He would say that the city isn't going to spend its money in that way." This statement may, of course, have been a smoke screen to conceal his bafflement at how to proceed against Canfield. Raiding an empty gambling palace, at any rate, wouldn't have been his idea of a coup.

He would probably have liked to play a waiting game with Canfield, lulling the gambler into a false sense of security and then smashing in at the head of a brigade of axmen. But the newspapers would give him no rest, playing up reports that Reginald Vanderbilt, just turned twenty-one, had dropped between $300,-000 and $500,000 in Canfield's during five nights of jousting at roulette and baccarat, although that happened months before.

The New York *Tribune*, a Republican organ which may have been acting as a mouthpiece for Boss Tom Platt, prodded Jerome with an editorial titled "Canfield's" and suggesting that the "Prince of Gamblers" was still operating and paying "a large amount of cash" for the privilege. It continued:

District Attorney Jerome says that if the comptroller would pay his bills, which would be heavy, he could close this and every other gambling house in the city; but he takes it for granted that the comptroller would refuse to pay them, and says that he is certainly not going to spend his own money for that purpose.

Perhaps Mr. Jerome is right, and yet public recollection of things done by Mr. Jerome himself in that general line is fresh. It has not always been very expensive to avoid the police, catch gamblers at play and get away with the apparatus.

If in this instance the district attorney is right, it is a disgrace that he is not wrong. But what if it would cost some hundreds or thousands of dollars to shut up the most famous and familiar hell in town? The evidence of crime often comes high. Mr. Jerome thinks, or used to think, that every liquor dealer in New York ought to be nabbed as often as he violated the law, if it cost a million and required the services of the whole police force. Isn't it pretty nearly as important a duty to stop the enormous gains of a notorious gambling house as to interfere with the illegal sale of a glass of beer?

It may be conceded that it is not so easy to secure admittance at Canfield's front door as at the family entrance of a groggery. But we won't concede either that the public authorities could not put a stop to this business if they were bound to do so without submitting the city to a heavy expense, or that a heavy expense would not be wisely incurred in ending a scandal which, whether they recognize it or not, is attaining monstrous proportions.

Jerome could only fume and keep his own counsel under such constant needling.

His press notices were generally bad, because he lashed out at so many sacred cows and stately totems and had no visible respect for the opinion of newspaper publishers. Furthermore he delighted in his own unpredictability. "He enjoyed, when there was an adequate excuse, doing startling, unconventional things — the more daring the better," as Arthur Train noted. The newspapers had no more use for a public official who ignored their advice than the politicians had for a candidate who could not be reasoned with. Even the New York *World*, a Democratic organ proud of its crusading policies, attacked him in the most underhanded way. A *World* photographer managed to grab a shot of Jerome as, groggy from overwork, he catnapped with his head resting on folded arms one night at his desk. Here, said the *World*, was evidence that Jerome slept while malefactors ranged the city. It liked the picture so much it reprinted it several times.

Finally, however, Jerome got the break he was waiting for, illusory as it turned out to be.

Late in November a man named Joseph Jacobs, who was employed as a detective by the Citizens Union, reported that he had obtained entry to Canfield's, had lost money there and was willing to swear out an affidavit to that effect.

Jerome was galvanized. Affidavit in hand, he appeared in the chambers of Judge Wyatt of Special Sessions on December 1 and obtained a warrant allowing him to enter and search the house at 5 East Forty-fourth Street.

He was in such a hurry to raid Canfield, in fact, that he failed to ask himself certain precautionary questions: How did Jacobs, on his twenty-five dollars a week salary from the Citizens' Union, manage to join the play when Canfield's clientele was so carefully screened? What about those reports that Canfield's was still shut tight as a drum? And what about the rather unstable character of Jacobs himself?

The sleuth was a fanciful type, given to elaborate disguises and tall tales about once having operated a gambling joint himself until he was horrified by a murder at his poker table. And this was his story of how he joined the high-rollers at Canfield's: "I posed as a Java prince and wore a black curly wig and a black beard. I had my face colored to complete the disguise. It was a great success. I first played roulette and lost. Then I tackled the faro game and won . . ."

All that interested Jerome, however, was that affidavit. It was the wedge he needed to pry open Canfield's citadel, and he lost no time using it.

Early that same afternoon, just after Judge Wyatt issued the warrant, the devious Mr. Jacobs telephoned David W. Bucklin, Jr., Canfield's manager, and warned him that the place would be raided that night. Bucklin called Canfield long distance in Providence, where the latter was visiting his family. Canfield hurried to catch a train for New York, instructing his attorney, John Delahunty, to meet him at the house in Forty-fourth Street and join the reception committee for Jerome. It promised to be an interesting first meeting between the Prince of Gamblers and his appointed Nemesis.

4

THAT EVENING, having laid his plans under an elaborate cover, Jerome attended the annual dinner of the St. Andrew's Society in the ballroom at Delmonico's, happily located just around the corner from Canfield's. Mayor Seth Low and other civic dignitaries were seated on the dais at the speakers' table. Jerome and Deputy Police Commissioner Piper were together at a small table in a far corner of the huge room, only half listening to the Scotch jokes of the after-dinner speakers, nervously awaiting word that everything was ready for the raid on Canfield's. A few minutes after eleven o'clock a young aide of Jerome's slipped into the ballroom, went over to Jerome's table and whispered his message to the district attorney.

Jerome and Piper quickly rose, got their hats and coats and walked out into the cold starry night. They hurried around the corner and into East Forty-fourth Street, past Number Five. The windows in all four stories of the house were blazing with light.

It looked like a good night to break in on Mr. Canfield. A ram-shackle old wagon was waiting at the curb.

"All right," Jerome snapped. "Let's go."

Suddenly from the rear of the wagon a Keystone Kop eruption occurred — a score of detectives, investigators and assistant district attorneys tumbling out with enough equipment to break into the Federal Reserve Bank.

Even this human battering ram couldn't have dented the huge bronze doors which formed the portals to Canfield's, so two detectives ran up with a ladder and placed it against a window nearest the door. A detective scampered up the ladder, ax in hand, and smashed the window. Then Police Inspector Nicholas Brooks hurled himself inside, with his revolver drawn. He opened the bronze doors from the inside, and in poured Jerome, Piper and the whole mob. They were followed by a second wave of newspaper reporters who, of course, had been alerted, along with a full complement of photographers, to record the historic assault on the place their editors had maintained would never be breached.

The whole mob rushed up the baronial staircase, to be greeted on the second floor by a remarkably calm but indignant trio. Canfield, Bucklin and Delahunty awaited them in full evening dress, with the Negro servants who staffed the place drawn up behind them.

Jerome and Canfield ignored each other while Joseph Jacobs, double-dealing detective, was pushing to the fore. Under Jerome's formal questioning, Jacobs identified Bucklin as the man who had dealt the faro game when he played there six nights before, but he said Canfield had not been on the premises then.

The district attorney and his raiding party quickly searched every room of the mansion but found no players, no gambling equipment, no evidence that the place had been in operation.

Jerome was naturally taken aback. He ordered a closer search of every room in the house. Bucklin, meanwhile, was placed under arrest on Jacobs's say-so.

Perhaps half an hour later the sharp-eyed Inspector Brooks was tapping the walls of a storeroom on the fourth floor, having noted that the chamber wasn't as deep as it apparently should be. One of the walls sounded hollow. He sent for an ax and summoned the district attorney. A few minutes later, the ax crashing through a plaster-and-lath wall, Canfield's hiding place was uncovered.

"By God!" Jerome exclaimed. "At last we've got the stuff."

"The stuff" included: Five long roulette tables. Three roulette wheels. A faro layout. Thousands of ivory chips — the white for one dollar, red for five dollars, blue for ten dollars, yellow for one hundred dollars, brown for one thousand dollars. Several packs of playing cards.

Detectives carried all this paraphernalia down to the wagon at the curb and loaded it aboard while a throng of 5,000 watched.

Canfield told reporters that "not a card has turned in my house for months," that the raiders had found "nothing," adding: "They sounded the walls and floors, looking for mysterious hiding places, and finally on the top floor they found a place I have reserved for storing gambling equipment which does not belong here. It is used in my Newport establishment, which is closed, and it was simply sent here for storage."

He allowed that Jerome had been "very courteous and friendly . . . very nice to me . . ." but that was the last kind word he had for the district attorney.

Jerome himself was exuberant in discussing the raid with reporters. "It cost less than fifty dollars to get Canfield, and a wild and woolly Westerner [Jacobs] with no social connections did the job. Therefore I conclude that Canfield is like all the other gamblers, willing to take every cent a man has got, no matter what his station."

The newspapers, of course, gave the story a tremendous play, including minute descriptions of the house where Edwardian magnificoes gambled away hundreds of thousands in a night. They even found room for Mr. Canfield's complaint that some-one had walked off with one of his small peachblow vases worth $8,000. (The culprit was a souvenir-hunting reporter, who gave it back.) Much was also made of the fact that $300,000 worth of Reggie Vanderbilt's I O U's were found in Canfield's safe. (They were later settled for $130,000, an arrangement which indicated that a gambler's sense of honor was somewhat superior to that of a nabob's.)

Jerome was naturally triumphant, convinced that he could sew up a case against Canfield by summoning as witnesses men who were known to have gambled in his place. A *Times* editorial congratulated him on his coup, and added, regarding the police, "Whatever assurance of immunity they may give to powerful gamblers they cannot keep the pact so long as this terrible district attorney is in office." When a friend of Canfield's was quoted as saying that Jacobs had never set foot in the house in Forty-fourth Street until the night of the raid, Jerome denounced him as a liar, a crook and a hophead. It just so happened that Canfield's friend was telling the truth about Jerome's star wit-ness.

5

As THE LONG and hard-fought legal contest between Jerome and Canfield began, the two men, to the delight of the newspapers, sparred verbally and quoted poetry at each other. Jerome an-nounced that secret hearings, "star chamber" proceedings, would be held before Judge Wyatt of Special Sessions, at which Jesse Lewisohn, Jr., Arthur A. Housman, Harry Payne Whitney and Mortimer L. Schiff — all big names on Wall Street and the society pages — would be invited to tell about their alleged sessions at Canfield's. The worst thing that can happen to a gambler with a Gold Coast clientele is to have them publicly identified; Canfield, properly stung, retaliated by filing complaints against Jerome, Police Inspector Brooks and Deputy Police Commissioner Piper charging them with illegal entry.

"A felon like Canfield," Jerome snorted to the press, "has got an intolerable cheek to go blowing around about his constitutional rights. But the animus and purpose of his proceedings are quite plain and they don't disturb me a particle." He quoted Tennyson's line on "men of long enduring hopes" caring little for the actions of "little would-be popes."

Canfield's riposte was suave and equally literate: "It is absolutely impossible for an unlettered felon to cope with the intellect, the culture and refinement of a person like the district attorney, therefore I would make a most pitiable spectacle of myself in attempting to reply . . . Then, too, I have always supposed that the proper place to try legal actions, criminal or civil, was in a court of law. The district attorney evidently thinks the place to try his cases is in the newspapers . . . If I am found guilty of any crime I must take the consequences of it like any other criminal. In the meantime I hope to establish the fact that a citizen of New York has certain rights in any house where he may be abiding which the police and even the district attorney must respect." His punch line was a quotation from John Greenleaf Whittier to the effect that he would shun no "pang beneath the sun" where "human rights are staked and won."

Lewisohn and the others appeared in Judge Wyatt's chambers under subpoena, beginning a long fight over whether they were required to answer the question, "Do you know Richard A. Canfield?" — and any others that might occur to Jerome. Lewisohn refused to answer, was cited for contempt, and appealed; the others similarly refused to answer until the Lewisohn case was decided. Eventually the Court of Appeals ruled Lewisohn was not legally bound to answer.

Mr. Canfield celebrated by going to England to have his famous portrait done by Whistler, drawing from Jerome the comment, "It is too bad Mr. Canfield has gone so far and at so great expense to have his portrait painted. If he had remained here a while longer he might have had his picture taken at the expense of the public."

While trying to figure out a way of prying information out of reluctant witnesses and finally nailing Canfield's hide to those massive bronze doors, Jerome kept the lid on the town, and the New York *Sun* quoted a "prominent gambler" as saying, "Today there is not a gambling house of any account doing business from the Battery north. New York was never so free from gambling houses, as going concerns, as it is now." He also pressed the state legislature to pass the Prince and Canfield anti-gambling laws, which plugged up so many loopholes that even Honest John Kelly, whose place at 156 West Forty-fourth had been shuttered temporarily in the hope that Jerome would weaken, and who was one of the kingpins of the gambling world, finally gave up hopes of reopening.

Kelly appeared in Jerome's office one day, doffed his bowler, and announced, "Judge, you've got us in a bind. I want to get on the bandwagon. Shall I send my stuff down?"

"Sure," said Jerome, "send it along."

Later that day Kelly sent two truckloads of gambling equipment down to the district attorney's office. It was some years before Kelly was able to open another "store."

On Canfield's return from England, Jerome had him arrested on a charge of being a common gambler — uncommon gambler though he was — but he couldn't make the charge stick. Reggie Vanderbilt, in the meantime, had successfully dodged subpoena-servers until the Court of Appeals finally ruled that Lewisohn and other Canfield patrons could not be forced to testify.

To anyone less tenacious than Jerome, it would have appeared that the law was stymied in its efforts to punish Canfield. But Jerome merely continued the battle on another front: back to

Albany for another law to plug that particular loophole, and loosen the tongues of reluctant witnesses. State Senator Victor J. Dowling was persuaded to introduce a bill which would amend the criminal code to refuse a witness in a gambling case the right to stay mum on the grounds that testifying against a gambling house keeper might tend to degrade him. That was the argument successfully used by Jesse Lewisohn. Such witnesses would be granted immunity to prosecution. They could be questioned before a judge in chambers.

There was strong opposition to the Dowling Bill, effectively led by Senator Edgar T. Brackett, once Canfield's attorney, who was especially vigorous in his attacks on District Attorney Jerome as the "real sponsor of the Dowling Bill." He charged that Jerome, by leading raids with judicial robes flying, while a judge of Special Sessions, had demeaned himself and his position; that as district attorney he had not hesitated to "commit crimes to obtain evidence." Jerome, he roared on the floor of the State Senate, was "half child and all wild [Jerome was then forty-five but still invincibly youthful in manner and appearance]." Why, he demanded, did Jerome want stricter gambling laws while relaxing enforcement of the laws governing drinking on Sunday? Brackett suggested that the paradox was traceable to "a mental lapse, the possible explanation of which is to be found in the habits of the young man."

Dowling defended Jerome and his motives with equal vigor: "No one thought of attacking him as long as he proceeded against cheap gamblers. But when he declined to consider 5 East Forty-fourth Street as an art museum and, passing by the bric-a-brac, broke open the hidden receptacle of gambling implements, he became obnoxious to the high society connections now opposing this bill. It is worthy of remark that Jesse Lewisohn refused to answer whether he had ever been in those premises on the ground that it would incriminate him, which is proof absolute that the reputation of the place as a gambling resort must have been well established . . . The proposition simply is whether the green columns and bronze doors of 5 East Forty-fourth Street shall continue to flaunt their open defiance of decency, law and order in New York."

After weeks of recrimination and debate, the bill was passed and Jerome had his absolute weapon for the final campaign against Canfield and anyone else who proposed to defy him. He withheld action against Canfield until that fall, waiting with unaccustomed patience as the Appellate Division of the Supreme Court ruled the Dowling amendment constitutional and the Court of Appeals, on November 15, 1904, concurred.

Now (he was certain) he had his man. Canfield, on conviction, would be sent to Sing Sing for two years as a two-time loser. It had taken him three years to corner the Prince of Gamblers — three years of near-misses, journalistic taunts, endless sniping from Canfield's influential friends, battling in the halls of the legislature, badgering of witnesses afraid to admit they'd frequented a gambling house — but the triumph would be all the sweeter for the obstacles surmounted.

All this time, ticking away like a time bomb, an ex-detective with a self-proclaimed flair for disguises had been stifling his impulse to bare his breast and tell all. The retired gumshoe was, of course, Joseph Jacobs.

Just as Canfield and his lawyers were conceding that Jerome had outmaneuvered them and that it looked as though Canfield would have to do a little time, Jacobs popped up, all tear-stained and contrite. He appeared in the offices of Benjamin F. Tracy, of Tracy and Britt, Canfield's new counsel of record, and told him that he had sworn falsely when he claimed to have gambled in Canfield's place. He would affirm this in return for enough money to get out of the country, away from Jerome's wrath.

Tracy obtained Jacobs's affidavit but, instead of keeping his part of the bargain, turned him over to Jerome. The district attorney now contemplated three years' work lying in ruins, and was in no mood for forgiveness. Jacobs was rushed to trial for swearing out a false affidavit and sent to Sing Sing for a year.

Obviously the trap on Canfield was broken. His place had been raided on perjured evidence. Yet he could still be mightily embarrassed, along with his rich friends, if Jerome proceeded with the prosecution and forced the Wall Streeters to testify.

Under the circumstances, a deal was in order, much as Jerome detested the necessity of compromise. Canfield was to plead guilty to being a common gambler, and Jerome was to recommend a $1,000 fine. Canfield's trial, therefore, was anti-climactic; two former servants at 5 East Forty-fourth testified they had seen gambling on the premises; Jerome made his recommendation that Canfield be fined, and the court accepted it.

Canfield had escaped with a slap on the wrist, but in the long view Jerome had achieved his purpose, even though the headlined fruits of victory had escaped him, for Canfield never again operated a gambling house in New York City. "His Reverence" had been effectively unfrocked.

Jerome was, of course, bitterly disappointed, and the New York *Herald* rubbed salt in his wounds by publishing a cartoon showing him tipping the scales of justice so that Canfield escaped with a fine while Jacobs went to prison. "What a farce!" a *Herald* editorial sneered, labeling Jerome's efforts as a "fuss-and-feathers campaign." It ignored the fact that a few days after the Canfield trial every prominent gambler in town trooped into Jerome's office, one by one, and promised that they would conduct no more games of chance while he was district attorney, and that anyone bearing his card would be admitted to their properties day or night to see that they were keeping their promises. About all that inveterate gamblers had to console them, in New York City, was the occasional floating crap game or poker session in a hotel room.

All in all, Jerome had every reason to reflect that between his Uncle Leonard's crony Dick Canfield and his father's favorite drinking companion, James Gordon Bennett of the *Herald*, he could hardly afford any more old friends of the family in his life.

6

UNSUSPECTED by anyone outside his family, concealed by the heartiness of his public manner, a private and domestic tragedy curdled and embittered success for Jerome. He and his wife had discovered they were not only incompatible but wretchedly mismated. There was virtually nothing they could agree on; nothing but a mutual respect, an impersonal regard for each other's dignity, and a mutual concern for the welfare of their son to keep them together. Jerome found that he had escaped from the unhappy home of his youth to an equally uninviting home at least partly of his own making. It only rubbed salt into the wound that he had to pretend to be a happy, home-loving husband and father.

Lavinia may well have made an admirable wife for someone else, but she was unable to adapt herself to the unexpected demands created when her husband entered public life. She had thought she was marrying a lawyer but instead, in spite of her retiring and self-enclosed nature, found she was expected to step boldly into the limelight and play the often fatuous role of a politician's wife. After he was elected to his first term as district attorney, she simply refused to continue playing her part. She never again appeared on the public platform with him, after being hugged and kissed, and smiling tautly all the while, as thousands cheered at the climax of his first campaign. Furthermore, detesting politics in their every aspect and abhorring politicians even more, she firmly discouraged Jerome from inviting to their home the people who might have advanced his career. Nor did she approve of his nonpolitical friends, his boisterous bull sessions with male companions or his inclination to turn their home into a debating society.

They disagreed in almost every particular, including the relatively trivial. She insisted on furnishing their homes in up-town Manhattan and in Lakeville in the drabbest browns and grays, while his nature demanded a setting of bright colors. She was an extremely untidy housekeeper, who left everything in disarray; as her daughter-in-law, who otherwise was exceedingly fond of her, frankly recalls, the condition of her household was always "disreputable." This grated on her husband, who highly prized order and neatness around him.

A much more serious difference concerned the upbringing of their only son. He objected strenuously, and futilely, to her "coddling" and "smothering" him, recalling his own mother's suffocating devotion. His greatest fear was that William Travers Jerome, Jr. would grow up a weakling, unable to face life on his own, an apprehension only sharpened by the fact that she insisted that their son attend Hotchkiss and then Yale, despite Jerome's urgent pleas that he be allowed to prepare for and attend Harvard, because those schools were closer to home. . Another point of contention was her pet name for her son, "Chinky Dinky," which caused Jerome — and later the young man himself, who was known throughout his collegiate career as "Chink" and took years to live it down, and then only with the determined assistance of his wife — to shudder every time he heard it.

It didn't help that he was called upon, early in their married life, to take in her two brothers as permanent guests. Gus and Nick Howe had lived with their mother until she died, and the burden of supporting them fell upon Jerome. They were "gentle-men of the old school," as Jerome's daughter-in-law characterized them, gentle, charming and utterly ineffectual, who "never lifted a finger to support themselves." Nick had been educated for an architect's career, but his only known effort along professional lines was to design the Jeromes's summer home at Lakeville. Jerome considered this oddly-shaped house, all but impossible to heat, an architectural disaster, and disliked it so much that he lived in cramped quarters in the metal-working shop he built as a refuge on the grounds. His brother-in-law Gus "could not even make a pot of tea for himself," as Jerome's daughter-in-law once discovered when she came across him pottering helplessly around the kitchen. Everything had to be done for them. Jerome never objected openly to being handed custody of two grown men, whom he supported from then on, but it could hardly have been a cause for rejoicing.

In contrast to his gregarious nature, Mrs. Jerome's only extramural interest was her membership in the Colonial Dames of America (one of her ancestors was Lord Pell, who was enabled to establish Pelham Manor through his marriage with the daughter of an Eastchester Indian Chief).

Another cause of resentment may have been the serious automobile accident they had. Jerome was a dashing pioneer in the dawning automotive age, and one of his prized possessions was a sporty, speedy Stutz roadster. One day, with Mrs. Jerome as his sole passenger, he hurtled around a curve and into a tree. Lavinia suffered a badly fractured leg which refused to heal properly and left her semi-crippled for the rest of her life. Jerome himself escaped injury.

By the time he was elected district attorney Jerome found home life all but intolerable and spent much of his time, outside the Criminal Courts Building, at his various clubs and the "night office" in Rutgers Street, which Mrs. Jerome considered a ridiculous operation and refused to visit.

It was almost inevitable, given the warm-blooded and impulsive Jerome temperament, that he would fall in love with another woman; also that, given the strait-laced Hall sense of ethics, he would never be able to bring himself to cut his emotional losses and divorce Lavinia.

Somewhere, and at some time during his service as district attorney, he met and fell in love with a beautiful, cultivated and sympathetic blonde lady. Her name was Ethel Stewart Elliot, and she was about twenty years younger than Jerome, then in his middle forties. She had been divorced and was the mother of one daughter. Mrs. Elliot had been trained since childhood for a musical career, had appeared with some success as a concert singer, and was a close friend of the operatic star Geraldine Farrar. Inevitably, she possessed many qualities that Mrs. Jerome did not: she ran an impeccable household, was witty, understanding and quick-minded, and shared Jerome's love of conversation and sociability.

From all accounts Mrs. Elliot really deserved something better than the semi-clandestine fate that awaited her as the love of William Travers Jerome's life. She was unselfish enough to insist herself that nothing in their relationship should be allowed to damage his political career. She was as ambitious for Jerome as he was for himself — and that was saying a lot, during the early years of their affair. Everyone who knew her, and none more wholeheartedly than Jerome's kinfolk, approved of her, admired her and loved her.

From then until his death, Mrs. Elliot was the most meaningful and comforting element in Jerome's life.

And by way of punishment for this happiness, as a public man and more ironically as a standard-bearer of civic morality, he had to keep it a secret. One of the greatest successes of his career was the fact that he managed to avoid an uproarious scandal during the years when his enemies, plentiful in number, would have given anything to expose the flaws in his private life. One misstep, one moment of indiscretion could have ruined him. No miscreant or evildoer in New York walked a tauter tightrope than the man whose sworn duty it was to bring them to justice.

5

A Duel of Wits with Little Abe

ALL THROUGH HIS strenuous eight-year career as district attorney, William Travers Jerome was bewitched by the
prospects of higher office. His personal popularity, his national
fame as the archfoe of the underworld, his magnetism on the
platform — so he and his friends thought — should have added up
to a dazzling political career. Furthermore there was solid evidence that his fortunes were not tied to the ebb and flow of reform movements. By the time he campaigned for re-election in
the fall of 1905 Seth Low had been turned out of the mayor's
office in favor of George B. McClellan, a Tammany favorite, but
Jerome was still the hero of the metropolis.

His opponents for re-election were James W. Osborne, the
Tammany candidate, and Clarence J. Shearn, counsel for William Randolph Hearst, who with his patron was running on the
Municipal Ownership ticket. Hearst was running for mayor
against McClellan and William M. Ivins, a Republican.

In a rousing windup to his campaign at Carnegie Hall, Jerome
demanded of his supporters, "Do you think that for four long
years it has been a bed of roses?" and then went on to catalogue
the burdens of his office — "racked with the misery and sorrow
that is brought to you" — until many of his auditors must have
wondered how he could bring himself to seek re-election. "One
of the greatest evils of the present time," he said, "is that small

groups of men, and not infrequently a single man has obtained control of the executive machinery of party organizations and nominating conventions and stands between the public servant and the voters. The result is that one in public office usually has to choose between a termination of his public career and subservience to such a man or group of men." Here was a clear indication that he was thinking ahead to the possibility of seeking higher office than that of district attorney, a venture for which he would need organized support.

He made it clear during the 1905 campaign, however, that he would never make a deal with Tammany for the support of the "executive machinery of party organizations." The current Tammany bosses, he said, were only "faint imprints" of the departed Dick Croker. "Though I fought him [Croker] for twenty years, he was a real man — a man with a jaw — a man that stood up and never lied to a friend."

Nor had he any kind words for the financial and commercial powers which often exerted decisive influence on political decisions. "The corruption of our public life in a large measure simply reflects the corruption of our business life."*

The distinguished lawyer Joseph H. Choate, himself a Republican, hailed Jerome as "a courageous, chivalric man fighting alone against all the powers of darkness in the city . . . one of the bravest lawyers who ever opened his lips in court," and compared him with St. Jerome, who plucked a thorn from a lion's paw. "And now not only the Republican lion but all the whelps follow him."**

When the voters registered their decision on November 7, Mayor McClellan was returned to office by a margin of 3,000 votes over Hearst, who claimed he had been robbed of the vic-

* From the New York *Times* and New York *Herald* coverage of his campaign speeches, Oct. 24–Nov. 6, 1905.
** From a collection of speeches in the possession of William Travers Jerome, III. The speech was made on November 1, 1905 at Carnegie Hall.

tory. Jerome, running as an Independent and against the Tammany tide, was re-elected by a comfortable 119,638 votes to Osborne's 108,188 and Shearn's 72,492. He was, as the New York *Herald* conceded, "the great figure of the campaign."

Some historians have remarked on the perversity of fate in denying him greater rewards, quite possibly the governor's mansion in Albany, not improbably the White House. Others have suggested that untoward events of his last year or two in office killed off his chances — and undoubtedly they would have been a great handicap. But there were more immediate and equally insuperable obstacles in the upward path for Jerome: Tammany's vengeful and unceasing opposition, which would have made it difficult if not impossible for him to obtain the gubernatorial nomination of the Democratic party; the natural suspicion of all politicians for a man of his maverick independence; a certain public coldness, combined though it may be with admiration, for the prosecutor as a type (Thomas E. Dewey was only one of many who could not shake off its traditional chill).

The greatest handicap at this stage of his career, however, was his make-up as an individual, his go-to-hell attitude, his willingness to offend and make enemies even when unwarranted by the circumstances. His defiance took such forms as getting up at a dinner given by the Mayflower Descendants and gratuitously denouncing the Puritans and the Pilgrims as hypocritical bores, labeling Thomas Jefferson a "faker" at a banquet gathered to celebrate the virtues of the Founding Fathers, flaying the whole New York City judiciary as a "body of incompetents." He even offended the decorum of his profession, as a *Tribune* reporter observed, when a "thin trickle of smoke could have been seen from Mr. Jerome's cupped fingers while he was trying a case."

Arthur Train considered him a "synthetic personality . . . a combination of Savonarola, St. George and D'Artagnan," with a touch of the prima donna in his character which made it impossible for him to kneel in the dust and chickenbones of the political alleyways and join in the eternal crap games of the heelers, leaders and bosses. His unabashed ego, too, worked against him, Train picturing him as "a picturesque, voluble, unrestrained and often injudicious talker . . . One couldn't imagine Jerome as a mere listener." Yet, Train conceded, he gave promise of "a spectacular career in which we hoped to share." Later Train saw that these hopes were impossible of achievement, if for no other reason than that Jerome "knew little of national politics . . . knew little of international affairs and was unfitted by temperament and equipment for the Presidency." It should be said that other contemporaries, quite as close to him as Train, were equally certain that Jerome *was* fitted for the Presidency — and never ceased speculating on how much better it might have been if, say, Jerome made the governorship, obtained the Democratic nomination for President in 1912 instead of Wilson, and with his more pragmatic approach had presided over America's participation in the war and the shaping of the post-war world. It would not, certainly, have been a Wilsonian concept . . .

His first stab at promoting himself to Albany was undertaken in the summer of 1906.

The generally sympathetic New York *Sun* noted in an editorial on August 11: "We understand that Mr. William Travers Jerome is considering the propriety of offering himself as a candidate for the governorship of this state.

"If Mr. Jerome runs Mr. Jerome will be elected."

Eight days later Jerome announced that he would seek the Democratic nomination.

The only other prominent candidate was William Randolph Hearst, publisher of the New York *Journal* and *American*, whose eye was also transfixed by visions of the White House. He had already served in Congress. In those days his newspapers proclaimed themselves the tribunes of the "common man" and danced on the verge of socialism. Not yet the remote lord of San Simeon, Hearst had acquired a considerable following, and his aspirations were not quite so ridiculous as they appeared to some of his biographers.

The Jerome–Hearst rivalry placed Tammany's leaders in a quandary. Both were cordially hated under the Wigwam. Twice Jerome had damaged Tammany severely in elections, and before that in the Lexow investigation; and besides he had dried up many sources of its financial nourishment. Hearst, on the other hand, had published cartoons showing Charles F. Murphy, the current boss of Tammany, rigged out in convict's stripes.

In the end Tammany's chieftains, presented with this distasteful choice, decided that Hearst's insults could be swallowed easier than Jerome's long record of intransigeance. The publisher accordingly was nominated, running against the glacially dignified Charles Evans Hughes. There were no manly tears around the Wigwam when Hughes defeated Hearst.

The Jerome ebullience, at any rate, was undiminished. He was still only forty-seven years old, and there would be many other elections. Yet he must have been a trifle envious when he contemplated the swift rise in public affairs of his British cousin, Winston Churchill.* Fifteen years younger than Jerome, Churchill had served as any army officer, watched Kitchener take Khartoum, covered the Boer War as a correspondent, had twice been elected to Parliament and made a name for himself as the razor-tongued critic of the Conservatives, and had just been advanced to junior ministerial rank as Under Secretary for the Colonies in the Liberal government. Jerome must often have envied his cousin the relative urbanity and gentlemanliness of British politics, in which family connections still counted for something; how far would Winston have advanced in the squalor and indignity of New York City's political life?

---

* Technically, genealogists say, they were double first cousins once removed.

On his part Sir Winston has professed great admiration for his American cousin. The two men met in the twenties when Churchill himself was in eclipse and Jerome had long abandoned his political aspirations. Perhaps they compared notes, though no record of their conversations survives. Many years later, however, Sir Winston told one of Jerome's grandsons that he had followed Jerome's career from abroad with great interest, and that he believed he "might have gone on to the Presidency had he wished to pay the price."*

Jerome, unabashed, continued to flaunt his official honesty like an all-conquering banner. At times he was almost boorish in his display of rectitude, and more than once he stigmatized financial and political figures as crooks and grafters on very slight evidence. There were times when his friends suspected that he viewed himself as the only honest man in public life. He had a habit of going off half-cocked, without divining the true depth of other men's motives. Once an elderly and distinguished gentleman presented himself in Jerome's office, evidently believing that Jerome knew who he was. He asked if Jerome would have any objection to a governor's pardon for an inmate of Sing Sing who had received a particularly heavy sentence on questionable evidence. The Jerome temper flared up immediately in resentment at what he took to be pressure from Albany.

"You go back to Albany," he snarled, "and tell the governor we don't think any more of him down here than we do of monkeys!" Badly shaken, his venerable caller was shown the door and would not have been greatly surprised if he had been kicked downstairs. The last thing he heard was Jerome shouting to an aide, "Who the hell was that old geezer?"

"That," a quieter voice informed the district attorney, "was the former presiding justice of the Appellate Division of the Second Department."

---

* From a record kept of his conversation with Sir Winston, at Chartwell on July 12, 1952, by William Travers Jerome, III, when he and his family visited with members of the English branch of their clan.

Usually, if no pressure was applied on behalf of leniency, Jerome ranged himself, with a determination uncommon in prosecuting attorneys, on the side of compassion and understanding for the convicted person. He never favored harsh sentences unless the crime was truly barbarous. Often, his assistants have recalled, he intervened with the court on behalf of men his office had worked hard to convict.

One such case involved a longshoreman who had killed a man with his fists during a dockside brawl. The man may have been a brute, a simple-minded brawler of the West Side saloons, but he was a killer only by accident. He had been convicted of manslaughter, however, and it appeared that he would be sent up for a number of years. Jerome called in Train, who had handled the prosecution, and asked him what he thought about the prospective sentencing, nodding in agreement when Train advocated penalties just severe enough to "teach him and his associates to be more careful with their fists."

"What's the judge likely to give him?"

"Anywhere from five to fifteen years, I'm afraid," Train replied.

"That won't do," Jerome snapped.

He marched over to the judge's chambers and, in effect, delivered a plea for the defendant, citing his lack of education, his brutish upbringing in the waterfront streets where boys began swinging their fists before they learned to walk. Instead of a long term in Sing Sing, the longshoreman was given a few months in jail, Train said, to "cool his heels and ponder upon the inadvisability of amateur pugilism."

Such merciful interventions occurred only in cases of the poor and defenseless who were overmatched in their struggle with the law, cases which aroused Jerome's considerable sense of chivalry. Men who were equal or superior in wit, influence and resources, whose crimes sprang from calculation rather than

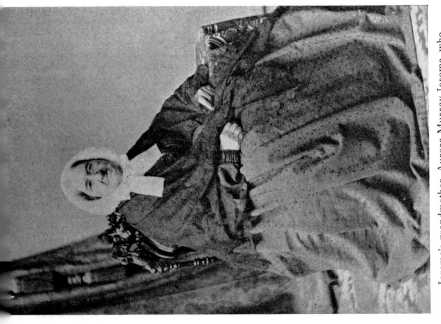

Jerome's grandmother, Aurora Murray Jerome, who was also Winston Churchill's great-grandmother.

Jerome's grandfather, Isaac.

Lawrence Jerome and his four sons — (l to r) William Travers, Lawrence Roscoe, Roswell Hart and Lovell Hall

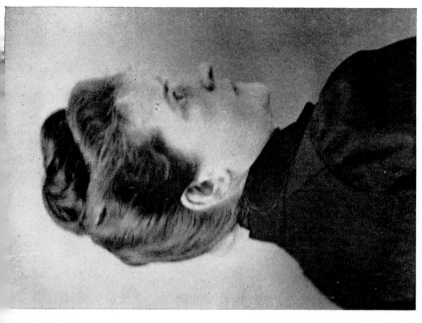

Lavinia Taylor Howe at the time of her marriage to Jerome.

The stern but unsuccessful matriarch — Catherine Hall Jerome, his mother. Her abhorrence of liquor was passed along to none of her four sons.

Boss Croker, who gave Jerome his first steady
job and lived long enough to regret the gesture.

SOME VIEWS OF CANFIELD LISTENING TO DELAHUNTY.

Studies of Richard Canfield

Dick Canfield, sketched by a New York *Herald* artist, as he
listened to his attorney address the court.

Jerome at his desk in the district attorney's office. In less formal moments he usually
had his feet on it.

The lordly William F. Howe and his shrewd little partner, Abe Hummel, as conceived by a New York *Recorder* artist.

Nan Patterson, "the girl in the hansom cab" and the first of the Floradora girls to get herself in trouble.

Jerome at the door of his workshop on the grounds of his Lakeville, Connecticut, home. This was his refuge from politics, his wife and her two brothers, his permanent guests.

Two forensic opponents of Jerome's photographed in later years. Martin Littleton (right) successfully defended Colonel William D. Mann and, at his second trial, Harry K. Thaw. John B. Stanchfield (left) was a member of the Thaw defense battery at the first trial.

impulse, who were accustomed to thinking that cold cash weighed heavily in the scales of justice, were confronted by the Savonarola as well as the D'Artagnan in the Jerome temperament. In such cases, Jerome's quest for justice became a passion, an obsession, which gave him no rest until it had been satisfied.

His fame as a prosecutor whose tenacity had been amply demonstrated in the contest with Dick Canfield rests even more securely on two of the most famous and strenuously fought cases in American jurisprudence. The first of these, the Dodge–Morse–Hummel case, was an all but incredible duel of wits with the wiliest criminal lawyer then practicing in New York, a violently picaresque affair involving chases on land and sea, attempted kidnapings, a threatened war between the Texas Rangers and the Wharton County Woodpeckers, an historic debauchery, a tattooed lady, and a highly important set of false teeth, to name but a few of the more volatile ingredients — not the least of which was the deadly chess game Jerome and Little Abe Hummel played behind the scenes.

2

"I'M A CROOK and I'm a blackmailer," Abe Hummel once confessed in a conversation with the late Samuel Hopkins Adams, when Jerome was hot after his scalp. "But there's one thing about me — I'm a neat son-of-a-bitch."

He was indeed neat, from his derby-crowned bald head to the tips of his sharply pointed patent leather shoes. His suits were always black, tailored for his gnomish figure; his linen was so white and crisp it gleamed. Counsellor Hummel always looked as though he had stepped out of a truncated bandbox, his manner as unruffled, even under dire circumstances, as his linen. He was also neat about covering his tracks: when Jerome tried to subpoena the records of his law firm during their long grapple he found they simply didn't exist. Hummel had neatly filed all the sordid facts of his practice under his bare bulging skull, where they were quite safe from prying minds.

Since the death of his outsize partner, William F. Howe, several months after Jerome began his first term in office, no pricklier mercenary in the war against law enforcement existed. Eliminating Hummel came next in the order of business for Jerome after Dick Canfield. The district attorney had first tangled with the firm of Howe and Hummel during the various investigations into the Tenderloin, most of its madams being represented by the partners. He realized that the burdens of his office would be immeasurably reduced if Hummel, as the underworld's trickiest mouthpiece, could be forcibly retired. Seeking clues to Hummel's remarkable survival through decades of suborning perjury, bribing judges and concocting extortion plots, Jerome checked back on his career soon after he took office.

One incident in Hummel's past which excited his interest was the attempted bribery of a judge in Westchester County, who had been trying a Howe and Hummel client, some years before. They had Abe dead to rights in his bribery attempt, and he was disbarred. A few months later Hummel was mysteriously reinstated. The methods by which Hummel wangled reinstatement were, Jerome said, "too sordid even to discuss"; presumably the sordidness stemmed from the ways Hummel found to persuade his peers to forget their concern for professional ethics. In another notable instance of Howe–Hummel rascality, it was discovered that the partners were representing both the plaintiff and the defendant in a civil suit — and once again they escaped punishment.

Hummel's specialty was extracting money from indiscreet husbands. Contemporaries said that between 1885 and 1905 the number of men shaken down by Little Abe numbered in the hundreds, "most of them well known and respected people — big merchants, politicians, members of old families . . . and a few bishops, too." But there was one thing to be said of a Hummel shakedown — it was never repeated. The evidence, packets of love letters, or whatever, was burned before the eyes of the victims in an iron brazier which was the centerpiece of Hummel's office and charred black with the smoke of so many dead and disillusioned passions.

By the time Jerome came to grips with him, Hummel had moved his offices from Centre Street to the basement of the New York Life Insurance Building at 346 Broadway, bringing with him the serviceable iron brazier and his magic telephone. The latter instrument was unconnected. Hummel used it to hold supposed conversations with judges and other public officials and impress clients who wanted him to use his influence with various bigwigs. When a client would ask Abe if he knew the judge trying his case, he would be told with an expansive gesture, "Sure I know him — have lunch with him practically every day." Abe would pick up his dead phone, giving an imaginary number to a phantom operator. "Hello? Judge Nemo? Hello, Jack! Yes, this is Abe. Say, I want to talk over a little matter with you before we go into court. How about lunch? One o'clock? I'll be there. So long, Jack."

Such a one-way conversation had a marvelously tranquilizing effect on a nervous client; whispered recollections of it to the client's friends, when they too needed a lawyer, helped to broadcast the rumor that a Hummel case was always "in the bag."

In both the underworld and street-level society, the word spread that Howe and Hummel, with its tenacles reaching everywhere in the metropolis, was both omniscient and omnipotent. Even "more respectable members of the bar," according to Arthur Train, found the firm invaluable. "Apprehension of what they might disclose operated as a powerful lever on politicians, 'big shots,' millionaire playboys and certain members of the judiciary . . . A family skeleton is the criminal lawyer's strongest ally and Howe and Hummel possessed what was probably the largest collection on record."

One exception to the general "apprehension" over what captured skeletons might be exhibited by Hummel at the appropriate moment was District Attorney Jerome. His record was clean, his amiable vices were known to all, and he had nothing to fear personally from the cunning mannikin of 346 Broadway (the affair with Mrs. Elliot not having started at this point). If there had been any leverage to exercise against Jerome, Hummel would have known how to use it.

Jerome had served as district attorney for two years before an opportunity arose to put Hummel out of action. Better still, it would also serve to even the public's accounts with Charles W. Morse, the brains and moneybags of the ice trust, whose activities Jerome had investigated immediately after taking office but who had covered his tracks so well that no actionable evidence against him could be found. The cast of characters in this lengthy legal chase,* as melodramatic as any horse opera, included, in addition to its square-jawed peace officer (Jerome) and its crafty villain (Hummel), the following principals:

CHARLES W. MORSE himself, a man in his middle forties, born in Bath, Maine, who had worked his way along the darker alleys of finance and small-time banking to Boston and finally New York, where he set up an ice monopoly with the help of Mayor Van Wyck and other officials.

CHARLES F. DODGE, a Vermont farm boy who drifted around the country as a hotel clerk, usually in inferior establishments, with occasional stints as a restaurant manager or railroad conductor. A frail, nondescript little man, his only distinction was

---

* An exhaustive account of this affair was given by Arthur Train in *From the District Attorney's Office*. It may be traced in even greater detail through the files of the impartial New York *Times*, in lesser but more biased detail in the New York *Herald*, whose proprietor had always been friendly with Hummel. A brisk modern account may be found in Richard Rovere's biography of Howe and Hummel.

an heroic, almost a monumental capacity for dissipation, particularly in the form of sex, drink and drugs. Thanks to his strategic place in Morse's designs, he may well have enjoyed the longest and most expensive freeload in history; it took hundreds of thousands of Morse's dollars to keep him "entertained" and out of Jerome's hands.

CLEMENCE CHRYSTIE COWLES DODGE MORSE, wife to both the ice magnate and the itinerant hotel clerk. Like her first husband, she was a complete neuter in personality and appearance, a dumpy colorless woman, meager in looks and charm.

JESSE BLOCHER, private detective extraordinary, employed by the district attorney's office. Train called him "one of the most capable, resourceful, adroit and quick-witted knights of adventure who ever set forth upon a seemingly impossible errand." Nobody looked less like the standard fictional representation of the private eye. Blocher was a quiet little man with a round face and twinkling blue eyes. He was soft-spoken and avoided violence whenever possible.

EDWARD BRACKEN, also a private detective, formerly a policeman, who often performed shadowing jobs for Howe and Hummel. He was appointed Dodge's unofficial guardian, and seldom did a man spend more money for another man's pleasure. His deliberate debauchery of Dodge could only be compared to the force-feeding of a Strasbourg goose.

An unlikely assortment of humanity, with even odder characters playing smaller roles, they found themselves involved in a complex drama no playwright this side of the Elizabethan era would have dared to imagine.

It started with Dodge's marriage in San Francisco, where he was clerking in a hotel in 1877. His bride was Clemence Chrystie Cowles. They stayed together for three or four years while Dodge drifted from one job to another, one city to another. Then they separated as casually as they had married, neither seeking a divorce.

Twenty years after their marriage, Mrs. Dodge was operating a rooming house in the Park Slope section of Brooklyn, Dodge was clerk at the Everett House in Manhattan, at Fourth Avenue and Seventeenth Street. For some reason, Mrs. Dodge decided to sue for divorce, and engaged an attorney named William A. Sweetzer. Dodge was served with the papers at the Everett House and retained an attorney named Benjamin A. Ruger to represent him. The case was heard by a referee, who granted Mrs. Dodge her divorce in the spring of 1897. Although she was a pivotal character in the whole affair, from then on, through litigation in many courts and a four-year harvest of headlines, she never again made an appearance but remained drably in the background. None of the newspaper accounts give the slightest clue to her appearance or personality; in the dramaturgical sense, it was like casting a scrubwoman to play Helen of Troy.

Four years later Mrs. Dodge met Mr. Morse, who had been applying the methods of frenzied finance to the ice business with considerable success. The Mazet Committee's revelations had broken his monopoly and a number of political careers, after causing untold misery in the tenement districts, but Morse escaped unscathed and was using the proceeds to buy control of a number of coastal shipping lines and Montana copper mines. With all that loot, Morse could have found a more glamorous wife than Mrs. Dodge, certainly, but he was a widower with four children and what he really wanted was a competent house-keeper. Mrs. Dodge, with her rooming-house experience, filled the bill nicely from the standpoint of Yankee practicality. So they were married.

Sometime during the following two years, as the Morse interests recovered from the shock and degradation of the ice trust scandal, Morse met another woman who in other particulars than keeping house would have suited him better as a wife. He wanted to marry her, but she was a Roman Catholic and couldn't do so unless he received an annulment, rather than a divorce, from the current Mrs. Morse.

For a man in Morse's predicament, standing in need of legal miracle, there was only one recourse: Abe Hummel.

The financier's uncle, Captain Jim Morse, a retired sailing master of Bath and presently treasurer of the Morse enterprises, acted as his emissary.

Uncle Jim, as he became known in journalistic prose, which adorned him with all the saltiness and horny-handedness expected of a Down East mariner, asked Hummel if an annulment could be obtained. He mentioned a $60,000 fee, with a $15,000 retainer. For that kind of money Abe would separate a man from a whole harem. The problem, Abe said, was to nullify Morse's marriage by canceling out Mrs. Morse's divorce from Dodge. One way to do this was to prove that Dodge had never been served with the notice that his wife was suing for divorce. But all this was mere detail work. Uncle Jim could leave it to Little Abe and his versatile helpers; Mrs. Morse would soon be Mrs. Dodge again, and the ice magnate could take a third wife without raising priestly objections.

Hummel and his assistants set to work immediately. First Dodge had to be located, and private detective Edward Bracken was assigned to this chore.

Bracken quickly traced Dodge to Atlanta, Georgia, where the little lecher was busy as a bee, dividing his time between opening a restaurant and pursuing a colored woman named Marie Laws. Bracken offered him $500 if he would drop his various pursuits and come to New York for an interview with Abe Hummel. Sure, said Dodge, reaching for the five hundred.

In New York, Dodge listened amiably to a proposition from Hummel that he commit perjury for $5,000. All he had to do was swear out an affidavit that Ruger had never been retained as his attorney and that Sweetzer (Mrs. Morse's lawyer) had never served him with a summons. Ruger, it was pointed out, had since died and could cause them no trouble. Dodge agreed, and was flattered when the great Hummel reached over, patted his knee and called him "my mascot." Dodge then returned to Atlanta with his $5,000, dropped plans for opening a restaurant, set up light housekeeping with Mrs. Laws and proceeded to spend the rest of the money in the city's brothels and opium pads. Along with his beanbag of a wife, so soon to be tossed back at him, he had acquired in San Francisco a taste for smoking an occasional pipe, the poppy being a popular turn-of-the-century tranquilizer.

Meanwhile, Hummel was solemnly writing Morse and informing the financier that his marriage to Mrs. Morse — that is, Mrs. Dodge — was invalid. The news, of course, was something less than a shock to Morse. And Mrs. Morse was flaccidly inclined to accept the situation. It looked as though an annulment would have clear sailing, except that Sweetzer, the attorney who obtained the Dodge divorce, began offering objections. He was highly offended at the suggestion that he had engineered a divorce by fraudulent means, remembered very well that he had served Dodge with the papers, and announced his intentions of contesting the annulment.

On October 20, 1903, Hummel obtained a Supreme Court order requiring Mrs. Dodge–Morse to show cause why her divorce from Dodge should not be declared invalid. A referee was appointed to hear the evidence.

Just before the hearing took place, Hummel laid an ingenious trap for Sweetzer. The latter had seen Dodge just once, six years before, when he served the summons. Hummel or one of his assistants found a man named Herpich sitting on a park bench; he was about the same age, size and weight as Dodge. Herpich agreed to appear at the hearing for twenty-five dollars.

A little late and out of breath, Sweetzer rushed into the referee's office. He apologized to the referee, then noticed Herpich, Hummel and Benjamin Steinhardt, a junior partner of Hummel's, sitting with their backs to the window, their faces in shadow. He knew Hummel and Steinhardt and accordingly greeted them. Taking it for granted that the man with them was the one he had served with a summons six years before, he then turned to Herpich and said, "How do you do, Mr. Dodge?" The hearing was over before it began. Hummel had little difficulty in persuading the referee that, since Sweetzer had mistaken Herpich for Dodge, he was probably mistaken in claiming that he had served Dodge with the divorce papers.

Accordingly the Dodge divorce was declared null and void; Mrs. Morse was Mrs. Dodge again, and Mr. Morse was legally a bachelor.

And William A. Sweetzer was mightily embarrassed, not to say chagrined. His professional honor was at stake. Furthermore he knew that he had been tricked. Somehow he had to turn the tables on Hummel and whoever was behind him.

Hummel wasn't worried; he'd arranged a thousand deals as tricky as this one. Just to make sure that the woman in the case wasn't too embittered at being declared Mrs. Dodge again, she was packed off to Paris with a more than adequate allowance. She was heard of no more. Little Abe turned his attention to other matters requiring the Hummel touch, which was known to be infallible.

3

SEVERAL MONTHS LATER the outraged Attorney Sweetzer took himself and certain documents to the district attorney's office. Jerome's customary brusqueness turned to joviality when he learned what Sweetzer was bringing him. A few days before, doggedly trying to obtain proof that he had been diddled by Hummel, Sweetzer had visited the offices of the late Benjamin A. Ruger, who had represented Dodge in the divorce case. Among Ruger's effects he found several letters from Dodge to Ruger in which it was made plain that the former had engaged counsel, furthermore that he had been served with the divorce papers.

Obviously the two men who headed Jerome's private list of public enemies were now brought within range of his artillery — Hummel for subornation of perjury, financier Morse on the same charge, plus conspiracy — if certain testimony could be obtained to back up the evidence already in hand. It was just possible both men could be nailed. More likely, one could be induced to testify against the other in return for a lighter sentence. Probably what he planned was to use Hummel to get Morse, who certainly out-ranked the shyster as a menace to society; even if Hummel thus escaped a prison sentence, he would be disbarred. Hummel's foreseeable argument that he was simply acting in good faith as Dodge's attorney could be knocked to pieces once the much-traveled hotel clerk was put on the griddle and himself confronted with the possibility of a perjury conviction. That Hummel was acting on behalf of Morse could similarly be proven. Almost at once a hint was thrown out that Hummel could save his own skin at Morse's expense, a member of Jerome's staff being quoted by the *Times* as saying, "The net, when it is dragged in, is ex-pected to contain leaders in the world of finance." It was also reported that Jerome privately made offers of such a deal to Hummel.*

Little Abe, however, in his own words was too "neat a son-of-a-bitch" to smear his reputation for keeping his mouth shut and violate his own peculiar code of ethics.

He chose to fight Jerome every step of the way.

The district attorney's first step was to send detectives to Atlanta, arrest Dodge and bring him back to New York. The

* Richard Rovere, in his *Howe & Hummel*, has pointed to a subsequent parallel: "The situation was in a way comparable to the one which Thomas E. Dewey faced some years later when he got the goods on Dixie Davis, attorney to the underworld leader Dutch Schultz and Schultz's errand boy to Jimmie Hines, at that time the center of corruption in Tammany Hall. Dewey did not prosecute Davis, the mouthpiece. Instead he exchanged a promise not to prosecute Davis for Davis's promise to testify against Hines, whose conviction, in 1939, put Dewey in line for all the blessings he has since enjoyed."

moment Dodge was arraigned on a perjury charge, Hummel sent word to Morse that he'd better supply bail instanter, before Dodge could be induced to talk. Uncle Jim came on the run with $10,000, Dodge was bailed out and was promptly placed in custody of Hummel's operative, Edward Bracken, who whisked him off to hiding in New Orleans.

No Dodge, no airtight case, was Jerome's dilemma. For more than a year he was to fight tooth and nail, using every resource of his office and whatever he could commandeer from state and federal governments, often outbid and outmaneuvered through the hundreds of thousands Morse spent to frustrate him, to extradite the elusive hotel clerk. It became a classic among extradition cases, subject to endless citation, *a cause célèbre* of the law libraries.

For several months Jerome, through local police everywhere in the nation, searched fruitlessly for Dodge, who was luxuriating all that time in a first-rate hotel, the St. Charles of New Orleans, and enjoying all the women and whiskey he could handle. A tip came into the district attorney's office that Dodge was hiding out there, despite reports to the contrary from both the New York and New Orleans police departments. These denials made the tip seem all the more promising to Jerome, who knew how bribable were the police of both cities. He decided to follow it up, but without the knowledge of any of his supposed helpers in either of the police departments.

On January 23, 1904 he summoned to his office Jesse Blocher, a private detective known to be uniquely incorruptible, and commissioned him to find Dodge, keep him under strict surveillance but not to let him know he was being watched. Checking out the New Orleans tip was to be his first assignment. That same afternoon Blocher left for the Louisiana city, a pudgy, mild-mannered little man who looked more like a ladies'-wear drummer than a manhunter.

It took Mr. Blocher less than an hour to accomplish more than the combined police departments of the nation.

He checked into the St. Charles, upon arrival the next day, then went out to hunt up a stationery store, where he bought a bright red envelope for two cents. He addressed it to Charles F. Dodge. Waiting until the mail clerk at the St. Charles had his back turned, Blocher slipped the envelope on the desk and then retreated a few paces. Unaware that he was being watched, the busy clerk glanced at the name on the envelope and automatically slipped it into the box for room 420. Blocher had already ascertained, of course, that Dodge wasn't registered at the hotel under his own name.

A few minutes later the detective asked the room clerk if he could be switched to room 423 (across the hall from Dodge's suite), which held sentimental memories from a previous visit. The clerk, who understood such matters, was glad to oblige.

Blocher kept watch on room 420 through a crack in his door. Soon Dodge and his guardian, Bracken, left their suite and went down to breakfast. Blocher, with the help of a generous tip, persuaded a chambermaid to let him in room 420. He found several letters addressed to Dodge lying on a table. The suite, he also learned, was rented to a Mr. Bradley.

The detective immediately wired Jerome: BIRD LOCATED AT ST. CHARLES. At 3 P.M. that afternoon he received a telegram in reply: NEW ORLEANS POLICE DEPARTMENT CLAIMS PARTY NOT THERE. LEFT FOR MEXICO THREE WEEKS AGO. ASCERTAIN CORRECT DESTINATION AND WIRE AT ONCE. To which Blocher replied: NO QUESTION AS TO IDENTITY AND PRESENCE HERE AT THIS TIME.

Blocher's continuing stakeout of room 420 was rewarded that evening by glimpses of several callers at the Dodge hideyhole. One or two obviously merchandised sex and drugs. Another was a plainclothes detective from the New Orleans Police Headquarters. Apparently he brought information that Jerome was hot on the trail, for the next morning Dodge and Bracken, their shadow not far behind, checked out of the St. Charles and boarded the Sunset Limited. Somehow Blocher managed to catch a glimpse of the fugitive's ticket, which was about a yard long and indicated extensive travel: Dodge and his companion were bound for Mexico City via Houston, San Antonio, and Eagle Pass. At the Limited's first stop that afternoon (January 26, just three days after Blocher left New York) the district attorney's man wired Jerome that their quarry was fleeing the country.

Naturally Blocher expected that the train would be met at one of the next stops and Dodge removed by local police armed with telegraphed warrants. At Beaumont and at Houston, he waited anxiously for the law to appear, but apparently his telegram had been delayed. He almost missed the Houston–San Antonio train. Just as he was running to catch it, a squad of police appeared on the run from Houston headquarters. The train was just beginning to chuff up steam for departure when Blocher and the Houston police boarded it, ordered the conductor to pull the emergency cord and hauled Dodge out of his berth. At headquarters Dodge admitted his identity but said, "I know what I'm wanted for, but I will never return to New York." Dodge still had faith in the long arm of Little Abe, and rightly so.

Back in New York, Hummel and Jerome were beginning their long battle of writs, wits, plots and counterplots. For months their agents in the field struggled over possession of the small, dissipated person of Charles Dodge, ranging over most of the state of Texas, but every move was planned in New York. Often, according to Arthur Train, the opposing forces held their skull sessions not more than ten yards from each other, the scene being Pontin's, the bar and restaurant favored by the legal profession.

The judges of General Sessions had a table there, so did the Special Sessions bench, the district attorney's office, and the firm of Howe and Hummel. Hummel and his assistants would be plotting some cloak and dagger maneuver at their table, while halfway across the room Jerome and his underlings would be discussing their countermoves and promising each other that Little Abe would soon be spending up to twenty years in an atmosphere less congenial than Pontin's.

Before the struggle of almost a year was over, close to a hundred writs had been fired like shellbursts between the two tables, although they were actually issued in such obscure Texas towns and counties as Alice, Bee County; Point Isabella, Corpus Christi, Laredo, Nueces County, and other frontier localities which turned a sophisticated crime thriller into a crude horse opera. Before he was through, the city-bred operative Blocher was riding stagecoaches drawn by broncos and galloping across deserts with the sorest rump north of the Rio Grande. Hummel's agents likewise acquired their saddle sores. Their masterminds suffered nothing harder than Pontin's bar stools.

The day after Dodge was taken into custody in Houston, a local law firm engaged by Hummel obtained his release on a writ of habeas corpus; he was rearrested before he could leave the courtroom; a second writ was obtained, and he was released on $20,000 bail. Jerome engaged the services of a Houston law firm to represent his office in the involved skirmish of writs and injunctions. Meanwhile, Hummel was speeding reinforcements to Houston, among them his nephew, Abraham Kaffenburgh, who was also a partner in Howe and Hummel.

Then also began the long series of misadventures which befell Sergeant Herlihy of the New York Police Department. Governor Odell of New York had signed extradition papers, with which the detective was dispatched to the Texas capital at Austin. Governor Lanham of Texas issued a warrant commanding that Dodge be handed over to Sergeant Herlihy for return to New York, but the opposition obtained an injunction preventing this, also a new writ of habeas corpus returnable in the United States District Court. Dodge in the meantime was being kept at the Rice Hotel, where Sergeant Herlihy was detailed to keep him under observation, Jesse Blocher being detained in Austin.

The tedium of Sergeant Herlihy's stakeout was being relieved by new-found friends overflowing with Texas hospitality. Herlihy, a convivial type, did not inquire as to their motives, but allowed them to ply him with champagne and brandy in such quantities as an honest cop hadn't seen since the good old days before the Tenderloin was turned into a rump roast.

Next thing Herlihy knew he was waking painfully in a strange hotel room with a nasty taste in his mouth but without the warrant for Dodge's extradition. A call downstairs informed the suffering sergeant that he had come to in the Menger Hotel. "In Houston?" the sergeant inquired hopefully. "In San Antonio," he was told.

While Herlihy was nursing his hangover on the train back to Houston, Jesse Blocher had discovered that the "bird" — code name for Dodge — once again had flown. This time he was accompanied by Bracken and Kaffenburgh, who were instructed to get him out of the country if they had to hire the Mexican Navy. While Blocher was nosing around to get on the scent again, other expeditions bearing extradition papers were being launched from New York. One party got as far as Austin, all right, but they'd hardly stepped off the train before hospitable strangers were insisting on showing them the sights, including half the joints in town. They, too, woke up in strange surroundings minus their documents. Jerome patiently dispatched a third squad, which managed to evade Hummel's minions and, thirsty but proud, deposit their papers on Governor Lanham's desk. By this time, of course, Hummel's snafu-makers had tangled up service of the warrant in another snare of writs, and besides Dodge was in flight again.

The fugitive, in fact, was hiding aboard a British ship lying in the harbor of Galveston while Hummel agents were chartering a seagoing tug from the Southern Pacific Railroad which, it was agreed, would transport him to Tampico for $3,000. Blocher got wind of the scheme, however, and prevailed upon officials of the railroad to participate in an elaborate hoax which would save their chartering fee but keep Dodge in the United States. The tug put out to sea, according to plan, and when it was well under way the captain announced to his passengers that he had been ordered not to take them to Tampico but to put in at Browns-ville. They offered him another $5,000 to disobey orders but he refused. Later he said it was a pleasure to turn Kaffenburgh down because of his arrogant and self-important manner. He also took malicious delight in informing the landlubbers that the barometer was falling fast and they'd have to ride out a Gulf of Mexico storm.

Now Blocher had to devise plans for intercepting the seasick voyagers. He traveled by railroad as far as the town of Alice, the southern terminus, then caught the stage for Brownsville, one hundred and seventy miles across the desert. For two days and nights Blocher went sleepless as the stagecoach bucketed along the wagon road, pausing every fifteen miles to pick up a fresh relay of broncos. While he was jouncing across the desert, Captain John R. Hughes, commanding Company D of the Texas Rangers, who had agreed to cooperate during Blocher's brief stopover at Alice, was detailing his border detachment to keep Dodge and his companions under surveillance from the moment the tug put them ashore at Point Isabella, on the mouth of the Rio Grande. The fugitive was trailed from Point Isabella to Brownsville, where he and his protectors checked into the Miller House under assumed names, rested up, then headed for Alice.

Now the travel-worn Blocher had to double back on his tracks, having missed his quarry in Brownsville. Dodge, Bracken and Kaffenburgh were aboard the stage on its return trip to Alice, and Blocher had to shuttle back as best he could. Buying a horse and saddle, he headed back to Alice without even pausing to catch a wink of sleep. It was seventy-four miles to the Santa La Cruz Ranch. Blocher rode all day and made it by nightfall. Fortunately there was a telephone at the ranchhouse because it enabled him to alert Ranger Captain Hughes to the fact that Dodge was on his way to Alice and should be watched. Then, indescribably saddle sore, he hired a buggy and a team of horses to complete the journey to Alice.

By the time Dodge and Company checked into the City Hotel in Alice, Captain Hughes, following the telephoned strategy suggested by Blocher, had substituted a Ranger named Harrod for the regular night clerk at the hotel with instructions to wheedle his way into the Dodge party's confidence. Blocher arrived three hours later and was so weary he could barely make it to his room. While he fell into a twelve-hour sleep, the Rangers took admirable care of his interests.

Ranger Harrod made himself so agreeable to Dodge and his companions that they confided their travel plans to the supposed night clerk. Mr. Dougherty, as Dodge was now calling himself, was journeying to Mexico for urgent reasons of health and wanted to leave early the next morning. His friends would appreciate it if the obliging Harrod would go over to the railroad station and buy three tickets for Monterey, Mexico. Harrod obliged. And now the trap was sprung. By the time Blocher was awakened early the next morning, he had proof that Dodge was trying to skip the country and could have him taken into custody again.

Dodge, Bracken and Kaffenburgh, whose names when linked sounded like a man falling downstairs, appeared at the International Railway Station well in time for the trans-border train, settled themselves in the smoker and congratulated each other on having finally outrun the adhesive Mr. Blocher. A heavy hand descended on Dodge's shoulder. It belonged to Captain Hughes, who removed Dodge from the train under arrest. For good measure he also arrested Bracken, but couldn't make that charge stick.

Again there was a flurry of habeas corpuses obtained in surrounding counties. Peace officers arrived from Nueces and Bee Counties to assume charge of the prisoner. Captain Hughes announced to all comers that he would retain custody, and tempers were beginning to run high in Alice. Thoroughly alarmed, a federal judge in Houston ordered that Dodge be turned over to the United States Marshal. Again Captain Hughes said no, which meant that county, state and federal authorities all were now contending for possession of the prisoner. Finally a compromise was reached: Dodge was returned to Houston in the joint custody of Hughes and the United States Marshal and was released in bail of $50,000 pending the outcome of appeals to the United States Circuit Court of Appeals at Fort Worth and the United States Supreme Court in Washington. The uppity Mr. Kaffenburgh had incurred the wrath of the federal judge by spiriting Dodge to Galveston and had to flee Houston one step ahead of a summons for contempt of court. His replacement was another Howe and Hummel partner, David May, "as urbane as Kaffenburgh had been insolent," who "fluttered into Houston like a white dove of peace," as Arthur Train put it, promising one and all that no further attempts would be made to cause Dodge's disappearance. Despite Mr. May's soothing announcements, Hummel's field forces did not give up trying to eliminate Dodge as a witness against Morse and Little Abe. While both sides awaited the rulings from the higher courts and watched each other's every move, various original schemes were tried out for getting rid of the star witness. They included:

Plan A: Bribe Blocher to look the other way. First he was offered $3,500 to "get lost" for a day or two while Dodge was being slipped over into Mexico. Blocher refused.

Plan B: Offer Blocher a bigger bribe. This time the offer was $25,000, coupled with a statement from Bracken that his side would spend a million dollars if necessary to keep Dodge from being returned to New York. The offer only encouraged Blocher to redouble the precautions he had taken to see that Dodge obeyed the conditions of his release on bail, which included the proviso that he was not to leave Harris County, in which Houston was located.

Plan C: Smuggle Dodge out the country in a traveling circus. The circus was appearing at San Antonio during the State Fair. It was scheduled to leave for Mexico on completion of that engagement. Dodge was to impersonate the tattooed lady or the lion tamer. Presumably, in his debilitated state, it would have been the tattooed lady; he hardly looked capable of taming anything livelier than the giant sloth. Blocher learned of this scheme when he went through the pockets of Bracken's coat in a poolroom and found detailed plans for transportation, passing luggage through customs, obtaining hotel accommodations in Mexico City and Tampico, even steamship tickets from Tampico to Europe. Blocher thwarted this operation by letting Bracken know he was wise to the plan.

Plan D: A systematic program of boozing, gambling, wenching and opium-smoking, by which Dodge might kill himself with pleasure. Dodge was subjected to such a course of debauchery, during the spring, summer and fall of 1904, while a decision was awaited on the appeals, that it was a miracle he was still ambulatory at Thanksgiving. Such an abundance of distractions could hardly have existed in the hotel clerk's wildest fantasies. "His feet never touch ground," as Blocher reported to Jerome, who began to wonder whether he would ever retrieve a live and breathing Mr. Dodge.

Dodge, with Bracken as his dark angel, was established in a suite at the Rice Hotel. Wherever they went, Bracken carried sheaves of currency in a black satchel, so Dodge's every whim could be satisfied.

As Blocher reported to Jerome, Dodge's schedule began with a breakfast of solid whiskey at 9 or 10 A.M., followed at noon by a luncheon consisting mostly of alcohol. In the afternoons they would visit the poolrooms and lay bets on the horses, with an occasional matinee at a brothel or an opium joint. After dinner he played faro till about midnight, when he adjourned to a certain brothel on Louisiana Street where he spent the night. He never slept more than two or three hours. Nothing was denied him, provided it was likely to help ruin his health. Frequently Bracken "spent as much as fifty dollars a night for wine," with Dodge "invariably ending in a beastly state of intoxication."

As the first blue northers darkened the Texas sky, Dodge grew weaker, thinner and paler but no less determined to enjoy himself on the millions his patron had extracted from the ice business. Occasionally, the worried Blocher observed, a physician had to be called to treat him. Usually a day or two on the wagon, alcoholically and otherwise, would restore his vitality.

By Thanksgiving, every tooth had fallen out of Dodge's head due to the inroads of malnutrition, beriberi and similar disorders. He was reduced to indistinct mumbling, the Hummel budget was evidently unable to cover a pair of false teeth — and besides his sponsors had no interest in restoring his natural garrulity.

If a ruling didn't come soon from Washington, obviously, it would be a race between the undertaker and the district attorney of New York County.

On December 3, 1904, after more than ten months of hide-and-seek, the Hummel faction heard the bad news. The Supreme Court ruled against them, and Dodge, or what was left of him, was ordered to be surrendered to the United States Marshal.

Dodge's private saturnalia thus came to an abrupt end, just this side of apoplexy and cirrhosis. His new custodians, fearing the onset of delirium tremens, supplied him with enough liquor to keep him well lit until he could be returned to New York, but playtime was over. The question for Hummel was whether Dodge would be grateful enough for his paid vacation to keep his mouth shut, or spill everything to the district attorney, definitely incriminating him and possibly Morse.

Little Abe decided he couldn't depend on Dodge's sense of

gratitude, particularly if Jerome supplied him with false teeth
and restored the power of speech to him. He had one more shot
in the locker: kidnaping.

A Hummel partner named Nathan Cohen arrived in Houston
just as the Supreme Court was handing down its ruling, and
immediately began laying plans for a jail delivery on the grand
scale. Armed with the usual suitcase crammed with currency, he
repaired to Wharton County, as Blocher later reported to Jerome,
and prevailed upon the sheriff to enlist a posse of a hundred men.
The possemen were members of a gang of ruffians known as the
Wharton County Woodpeckers. Each Woodpecker was armed
with a rifle and given one hundred and fifty dollars. At Cohen's
signal they were to descend upon Houston and storm the Harris
County Jail. It was Blocher's opinion that the Hummelites hoped
that during the gun battle Dodge himself would catch a bullet.
By now Blocher had organized an intelligence service rivaled in
the past only during General Phil Sheridan's occupation of Texas
in the Reconstruction years; the federal authorities were alerted,
and Dodge was sent on his way back to New York before
the Wharton County Woodpeckers could hurrah the Houston
lockup.

Thanks to Jesse Blocher's sleepless vigils, midnight rides and
dogged blocking of every Hummel maneuver, and to the Texas
Rangers' unswerving devotion, District Attorney Jerome finally
got his indispensable witness, and Abe Hummel his lesson that not
every man has his price. It must have been hard for Little Abe
to believe after thirty-five years as a New York criminal lawyer.

4

ON CHRISTMAS EVE of 1904 it looked as though the rodeo had
come to the Criminal Courts Building in New York.

Surrounded by the tall hats, holstered revolvers and bulky
shoulders of a score of deputy United States marshals from Texas,
Charles F. Dodge, wobbly from a year's violent dissipation, was

carried along by the elbows to the district attorney's office. The armed delegation had come along with Blocher and his prisoner to make sure that Dodge's former custodians did not try to get him back by wrecking a train or some other last desperate measure. Once they had dumped the fugitive in Jerome's office, the Texans, whooping with joy, scattered over Manhattan like coursing hounds, and reports of their depredations were coming in to Jerome, as their nominal host, for days afterward until they were finally packed back to Texas.

Hummel heard of Dodge's arrival in the midst of a party he was giving for his theatrical friends. He lost no time in slipping away to the Criminal Courts Building. After all, he was Dodge's lawyer, and the travel-weary hotel clerk was entitled to legal consolation. Furthermore he just might be persuaded not to turn state's evidence; the possibility was slight, but it had to be explored.

Dressed in evening clothes and jauntily swinging an ebony cane, Little Abe approached the reception desk at the head of the shadowy corridor leading to Jerome's office.

"I'm Mr. Hummel," he told the cop on duty, "and I've come to see my client, Charles F. Dodge."

"He isn't your client any longer," the cop said. "He's got another lawyer."

Dodge had started talking the moment his rump hit the chair in front of Jerome's desk. Rarely had anyone seen so cooperative a witness. The only trouble was, nobody could quite understand the mumble that issued incessantly from his toothless mouth. Jerome ordered that in the next few days Dodge was to be sobered up completely and measured for a set of store teeth. Meanwhile, over the holidays, Jerome kept throwing out hints in the press that Hummel need not go down the drain if, like Dodge, he was prepared to come clean. One such inference could be read in the *Daily Mail* which said it might be wrong to assume that "the Dodge–Morse case will affect high legal circles" and that "no lawyers at all may be involved." If Jerome expected Hummel to snap at the bait, he was disappointed; and he may well have been bitterly disappointed, since Hummel's testimony could sew up a case against Morse, whom the district attorney really wanted on Blackwell's Island.

Hummel, Bracken and Benjamin Steinhardt were indicted for conspiracy to obstruct justice. Only Hummell went to trial, Bracken skipping the country and the indictment against Steinhardt being eventually dismissed.

Little Abe faced trial stoically, with DeLancey Nicoll, a former district attorney, defending him. The state called as its first witnesses Cohen and Kaffenburgh of Hummel's firm, and both declined to testify on the grounds they might incriminate or degrade themselves, which had the effect of further incriminating their senior partner. Dodge, flashing his new teeth, testified volubly, told in detail how he had been suborned to perjure himself in the divorce case, then had been virtually kidnaped all over the Southwest. Hummel refused to testify in his own defense. It took the jury just eighteen minutes to find him guilty.

Appeals were taken, but the conviction was sustained. Rarely vindictive in triumph, Jerome reportedly recommended to the judge that Hummel be treated with leniency, since his career was ended and he could no longer thwart justice in his highly original way. Jerome had, in fact, whittled the indictment down to one count of conspiracy in the course of the trial. So Hummel was sentenced to only a year on Blackwell's Island, and began serving his sentence March 8, 1907. On release from prison, he left the country and spent most of his remaining eighteen years comfortably expatriated in Paris and London.

The number one villain of the whole affair, Charles W. Morse, escaped punishment, except for the estimated million dollars it cost him in the futile effort to smuggle Dodge out of the country. A few years later, however, he was indicted on federal charges of tampering with the books of the Bank of North America and was sentenced to fifteen years in prison. He was released in 1912 on the findings of a medical board that he had only a few months to live. His dire condition, it was later believed, was induced by swallowing a concoction of soapsuds and other chemicals. If nothing else, he was a bold and persistent scoundrel. During World War I, he conned the government into turning over millions of dollars to build ships in nonexistent shipyards. At the time of his death in the 1930's congressional investigating committees were still trying to unravel the methods by which he obtained so much government money with so few visible means of support.

Aside from Morse's escape from punishment, there was another vexation connected with the windup of the long and bedeviling Dodge–Morse–Hummel case — the matter of Dodge's new false teeth. Without the choppers, Dodge would have been an incomprehensible and therefore valueless witness; yet an officious gentleman, the Honorable Edward M. Grout, the City Comptroller, objected.

Jerome's auditor had confidently put through a voucher reading "Two sets of false teeth, upper and lower — $40." It seemed a modest expenditure, considering the invaluable role their wearer played on the witness stand.

Comptroller Grout, however, notified Jerome that he declined to "certify this or any other bill of similar character." Soon he and Jerome were involved in a bureaucratic feud joyfully seized upon by the newspapers.

"Whoever heard of buying false teeth for a witness?" Grout complained to reporters. "Clothes to cover his nakedness and make him presentable in court, yes. Board and lodging, yes. But false teeth! Ye Gods! What a nerve!"

While Grout fumed, Jerome discovered a loophole. Several months before the Hummel trial the Board of Estimate had voted the district attorney's office a special appropriation of $35,000 to defray the expenses of tracking Dodge down and bringing him back from Texas. Grout himself was a member of the board, and had voted for the appropriation.

Jerome applied for permission to transfer forty dollars from his "general office equipment account" to his "contingencies account" for the specific purpose of paying for Dodge's teeth. Grout protested to the Board of Estimate, and a full-scale hearing into the matter was scheduled.

The New York *Star*, in particular, had a field day with the story:

HE NEVER SLEEPS
Grout Unearths Conspiracy to Defraud City
DECLARES DODGE SHALL NOT CHEW
AT PUBLIC EXPENSE!

The Star has learned on reliable authority that Comptroller Grout discerns, behind an innocent-looking application for transfer of $40 from one account in the District Attorney's appropriation to another, the first step in a conspiracy to have all public officials and city employes masticate at the public expense . . . In order to save the board, and especially our energetic comptroller, from further embarrassment *The Star* herewith starts a popular fund to pay for the molars in question, limited to a maximum of one cent from each contributor.

The Board of Estimate hastily approved the transfer of funds, Jerome tasted a victory almost as sweet as Hummel's comeuppance, and Dodge disappeared into history with title to his teeth free and clear.

6

A Floradora Girl, a Naughty Old Man
and a Vicious Valet

So MANY OF District Attorney Jerome's celebrated cases, in addition to a lesser swarm attracting only a few paragraphs in the newspapers, tended to overlap and proliferate in retrials and appeals that for most of his eight years in office, particularly his last term, he was hard pressed to keep up with all the details of the cases being prosecuted. His life was a merry-go-round of courtroom appearances, conferences with his trial deputies and long bouts of paperwork. Week in and week out he worked twelve- to sixteen-hour days, the tedium of which were relieved only by nipping over to Pontin's for a round of drinks and occasional weekends in the country.

On the Hummel case he could not rest easy until the cell door clanked shut on Little Abe in March, 1907, but meanwhile the Stanford White murder case had erupted, and just before it, still actively contending with Abe Hummel, he had to deal with the famous murder in the hansom cab, the prosecutions attending the campaign against *Town Topics*, the society scandal sheet, in which so many large but vulnerable reputations were involved, and the unique and long-fought case of William M. Rice.

2

"TELL ME, pretty maiden," the six young men in silk hats and cutaways sang to the six young ladies wearing black picture hats and twirling pink parasols, "are there any more at home like you?" The young ladies, who were members of the Floradora Sextette, trilled in reply that there were a few, "simple girls, and proper too." It was just as well they stayed home. The pretty maidens, by themselves, created quite enough havoc, domestic, legal and financial, without the help of any offstage sisters. Before the first decade of the new century was out, two of them were involved in sensational murder cases, several had married millionaires, and others — including replacements of the original sextette and members of the numerous road companies — wrecked a few homes and broke more than a few hearts.

The source of all the emotional disturbance was a musical comedy titled *Floradora,* imported from England and starring Edna Wallace Hopper and Eddie Foy, Sr., which opened at the Casino Theater on November 11, 1900. It was the biggest hit on Broadway — the theaters were still on Broadway then — in many seasons. The grace and beauty of the Floradora girls were largely responsible for its long run. Some of the town's leading connoisseurs of feminine beauty held reserved seats for the show's entire life.

Two of its leading girl graduates were Evelyn Nesbit, in whose magnificent eyes men fancied they glimpsed volcanic depths, and Nan Patterson, fleshier and less exotic but almost equally attractive to men. The difference between the two girls was that Miss Patterson had no mother to guide her — in the direction of the sportive millionaires who clustered around every stage door — as Miss Nesbit most certainly had.

Nan fell in love with a prosperous bookmaker named Francis Thomas "Caesar" Young, fourteen years older than she. In his younger days he had attained a measure of fame as a long-distance and cross-country runner. When his legs gave out, he turned to gambling, worked for the Poolroom Syndicate, and in 1899 went into business for himself, taking bets at the various racetracks around the country. His athletic career over, Caesar broke training in a big way, ate like Diamond Jim Brady and drank like Dick Canfield. He also chased the girls with a like enthusiasm, uninhibited by the fact that he was married, his wife intended that they should stay married, and, most importantly, his half-million-dollar fortune was tied up in Mrs. Young's name.

Nan, the daughter of John B. Patterson, supervising architect for the United States Treasury for many years, left home when she was sixteen to marry a young man named Martin. That was in 1898. A year later she left Martin to join the chorus of a musical comedy playing on Broadway. Still later she joined the Floradora Sextette and toured with a road company of the show. After that she danced in the chorus of *A Chinese Honeymoon*. The New York *Herald* described her as a young woman of "more than ordinary attraction," with a mass of dark brown hair. "Her eyes are blue and her features are regular . . . her fingers are covered with rings, most of them of great value. She had a heavy gold chain around her neck and a diamond pin in her bosom." A more precise *Evening Telegram* reporter recorded that she was five feet seven inches tall and weighed one hundred and thirty-five pounds, and that "although she might not be termed beautiful she is a woman who would quickly attract attention and would be termed good looking."

Nan and Caesar met on a train bound for California early in 1903, and by the time they reached Los Angeles they had decided they were made for each other. She became his mistress and followed him up and down California attending race meetings. That spring she divorced her husband, with Caesar footing all the bills. Later that year the idyll was forcibly interrupted. Mrs. Young and his bookmaking partner, a former prizefighter named John D. Millin, intercepted them just as they were about to board a train in Los Angeles for New York. There was a flurry of fists, ending with Caesar laid low on the station platform. He was persuaded to come along quietly with his wife and partner, all of them returning to San Francisco. In February, 1904, however,

Caesar escaped from custody and met Nan in Los Angeles. When the diligent Millin caught up with them, they were sleeping off a terrific binge in what must have been an exceedingly broad-minded Turkish bath. Millin knotted his fist; Young quickly agreed to return to his wife, and Nan was packed off to New York with a train ticket and $2,800 in cash.

That spring the Youngs themselves returned to New York, and the bookmaker secretly resumed his affair with Nan Patterson. According to later testimony, she began pleading with him to divorce his wife and keep his promise to marry her. Nan, then twenty-two years old, was determined to legalize the arrangement. Caesar Young, an amiable boozer who hated domestic discord, much as he courted it, hoped that the present arrangement of wife and mistress could be maintained. He was registered with Mrs. Young at the Hotel Walcott; at the Hotel Imperial with Nan as "Mr. and Mrs. J. B. Patterson," which happened to be her father's name. There was immense pressure against the status quo. His wife and his rock-fisted partner, who considered Nan a gold digger, if not a diamond digger, insisted that he give the girl up immediately. Nan and her sister, Julia, who was married to a no-good named J. Morgan Smith, were equally insistent that he give up his wife. As Julia wrote Caesar, "You know that I love Nan better than anything on earth and she loves you above and beyond everything. To see her absolutely wild as she is breaks my heart." Sister Julia demanded an interview to "get the whole thing straightened out." This note was intercepted by Mrs. Young, leading to yet another shattering domestic scene. Caesar, shuttling between the Imperial and the Walcott, was a sorely beset man.

Seeking a way out of his dilemma, he first tried to persuade Nan to sail on the *Teutonic* a few days hence for a European vacation. Nan not only balked at leaving the field to his wife but announced, untruthfully, that she was four months pregnant. Caesar had to give up that idea.

Then Mrs. Young decided that a European vacation was just the thing to save her marriage. Without consulting Caesar, she booked passage for them on the *Germanic*, sailing June 4, 1904. It would be a second honeymoon, she announced to her husband. Caesar agreed to go along. On June 3, the day before sailing, Caesar met Nan, her sister Julia and her brother-in-law Morgan Smith at the Sheepshead Bay racetrack; between races he slipped her the news that he was going abroad with his wife. And at six o'clock that evening a man and a woman — whom the state later contended were Mr. and Mrs. Smith — purchased a .32 caliber revolver in Hyman Stern's pawnshop at 516 Sixth Avenue.

On the following morning, by prearrangement, Caesar met Nan on Columbus Circle at eight o'clock. The *Germanic* sailed at 9:30 A.M. Nan would drive down to West Fulton Street to see him off on his second honeymoon. His wife would already be aboard the liner, and Caesar, whose profession accustomed him to taking chances, could only hope that she was not out on deck to catch a glimpse of him being seen off by her rival.

Nan and Caesar got into a hansom cab, driven by Frederick Michaels, which was waiting at the curb at Fifty-eighth Street and Eighth Avenue. On the way downtown, Caesar instructed the cabbie, he wanted to stop at two places, (1) a hat store, and (2) a saloon. Caesar needed a replacement for his rather shabby derby, and even more, for his daily alcoholic intake was a joy to the distilling industry, a bracer or two to tide him over until he reached the haven of the *Germanic's* bar.

The cab clopped on its way downtown, halting first at a hat store in the Fifth Avenue Hotel, then at a saloon on the corner of West Broadway and Bleecker Street. Caesar and Nan went in through the family entrance, and Caesar had two quick drinks before they resumed their journey. At West Broadway and Fulton Street Michaels heard a pistol shot. A moment later Nan lifted the trap on the roof of the cab and told the cabbie to drive quickly to a drugstore. Michaels saw Caesar lying across

Nan's lap. At a nearby drugstore they were directed to the Hudson Street Hospital. A police officer, William J. Junior, who had been on traffic duty, jumped up on the footboard for the dash to the hospital. Later he testified hearing Nan crying over and over again, "Caesar, Caesar, why did you do this?" At the hospital Caesar Young was pronounced "dead on arrival." A bullet had entered his body just below the left shoulder.

Nan's story was that Caesar had committed suicide, awkward though it would have been for the most desperate man to have shot himself in the back, and in the narrow confines of a hansom cab at that. The police consigned her to the Tombs without bail, while Park Row trotted out its tallest type to announce that a "rich bookmaker" had been killed in a "hansom cab mystery" involving his "Floradora sweetheart," and Mrs. Young, having been notified just as the gangplank was removed, sorrowfully unpacked.

Mostly, perhaps, because of the immense publicity being given the case, Jerome took a leading role at the outset. All the facts pointed to Nan Patterson as having pulled the trigger, yet convicting a woman of first-degree murder, particularly one as young and attractive as the ex-Floradora Girl, would be difficult. The case presented a challenge which was only increased by the accused girl's choice of defense counsel, the firm of Unger and Levy. Henry W. Unger had opposed Jerome in his first campaign for the district attorney's office. His partner, Abraham Levy, was considered by Arthur Train to be the most brilliant criminal lawyer in the country, a short, bald, Pickwickian man who, as Alexander Woollcott wrote, "managed to suggest that he was just a shabby neighbor of the jurors, trying to rescue a fluttering butterfly from the juggernaut of the State." Obviously Jerome felt that his office could not afford to take a trouncing from a firm which included his late rival for office and a man renowned as "The Last Hope" for his successful advocacy of all-but-hopeless defendants.

The district attorney's chances of obtaining a conviction were greatly diminished months before the case came to trial when Nan's sister and brother-in-law, whose parts in the death of Caesar Young appeared to be more than interested bystanders, suddenly disappeared. Jerome naturally suspected that the defense may have encouraged their disappearance. Well, if Unger and Levy wanted to play dirty pool, Jerome knew a trick or two himself. One counterploy was "trying the case in the newspapers" (as its victims generally label it), thereby influencing prospective jurors.

Thus Jerome allowed the news to leak out to reporters that the reason the Smiths had disappeared, probably, was because they could be identified by a pawnbroker as having bought the gun with which Young was shot and which inexplicably was found in one of the victim's pockets after the shooting.

Regarding Jerome's impromptu mating of the law and journalism, Newman Levy, son of his opponent, himself a noted lawyer and author of the objective and perceptive *The Nan Patterson Case*, has written: "If, as has been said, Waterloo was won on the playing fields of Eton, it can be said with equal truth that many murder trials at the beginning of the century were won in the pages of the *World* and the *Journal* as much as in the courtroom."

Levy and Unger, in fact, were equally resourceful at enlisting public opinion through the journalistic medium. With their encouragement, reporters pictured Nan as wasting away in the Tombs, provided touching descriptions of her white-haired and grieving father and polled a "jury" of twelve Broadway show-girls who returned a unanimous "verdict" that Nan Patterson was innocent. "It is too much to hope," as Newman Levy commented in his book on the case, "that the jurors who were subsequently to determine Nan's fate did not read this, for everybody was reading everything about the case."

Journalistic and public interest was positively feverish by the time People *v.* Nan Patterson was called for trial in Supreme

Court, on November 15, 1904. At the prosecution's table sat Jerome and two of his ablest assistants, William Rand and Francis Garvan. Jerome was to be present at almost every session but the actual conduct of the prosecution was entrusted to Rand, a brilliant young graduate of Harvard Law School. In addition to legal aptitude, unfortunately, Rand possessed a rather toplofty manner which did not always sit well with commoners on the jury. "He was a brilliant advocate," Alexander Woollcott observed, but suggested "an English squire addressing the tenantry."

The dramatic highlight of the trial was contained in this exchange between the accused girl and her counsel:

LEVY: Nan, look at me. Did you shoot Caesar Young?

NAN (in a quiet, steady voice): I did not. I swear I did not. God knows that if I could bring him back to life I would.

Rand's cross-examination was pitilessly searching but the girl could not be shaken in her assertion that Young had taken his own life in despair over being "trapped" into taking his wife on a trip abroad. The prosecution even brought a skeleton, borrowed from a medical school, into court to demonstrate how difficult it would have been for Young to have shot himself in the manner described by the defense.

In their closing arguments, the defense rested upon an emotional appeal to let Nan "go and sin no more," while the prosecution incisively marshaled the tremendous weight of evidence against the possibility that, a few minutes after buying himself a new hat, Caesar Young had suddenly decided to shoot himself just below the left shoulder.

The jury deliberated for a total of fourteen hours before reporting itself hopelessly deadlocked. Six stood for acquittal, six for conviction. The court had no alternative but to discharge them.

Jerome could, of course, have decided to drop the case, but

under the circumstances, particularly the nature of the evidence, and not inconsiderably the psychological grip a closely fought action exercises on a prosecutor, involving his professional pride, skill and ego, he would not let go.

He was convinced that Nan shot Young — how could it have been otherwise? The fair possibility that the bullet was fired during a struggle over the gun hardly entered into his calculations. To a large share of the public Nan Patterson may have seemed the proverbial moth fluttering helplessly in the Mazda glare of Longacre Square, a girl caught up in and despoiled by the whirligig life of the cabarets and lobster palaces. Lenient as he could be with lesser offenders, Jerome considered her an amoral creature and believed her case should be prosecuted to the hilt.

The case, he decided, would have to be tried again. A few months after the first trial ended, in March, 1905, his office was heartened by news that its detectives finally had managed to locate Julia and Morgan Smith, Nan's sister and brother-in-law, in Toronto. If pawnbroker Stern could identify them as the persons who bought the .32 caliber revolver which killed Young, no jury would be inclined to hesitate over conviction.

The second trial, set for April 18, 1905, was to be held in General Sessions before Jerome's former associate, Recorder John W. Goff, with whom Jerome had served as counsel for the Lexow Committee.* Since Goff was notoriously conviction-minded, the newspapers generally expressed the opinion that Nan didn't stand much of a chance in his court, particularly in view of the old alliance between bench and prosecution. Actually, for some personal reason never divulged, the two men had fallen out. Newman Levy said there was, in fact, "a bitter feud" going on between them. In recent years, Goff had grown more irascible than ever, probably the result of a stomach ailment. He could

* The title of Recorder, bestowed on the senior member of the General Sessions bench, was abolished when Goff moved up to a higher court.

eat nothing but milk and crackers, a diet reinforced, so Levy's father told him, by frequent swigs from a bottle of Irish whiskey which he kept under the bench. To the late Lloyd Paul Stryker (*The Art of Advocacy*) he was the epitome of the razor-tongued "hanging judge" so firmly embedded in English fiction and undoubtedly derived from plentiful living models. He had "the cold visage of a python," Stryker wrote, and "a cold heart and a sadistic joy in suffering." In his study of the Patterson case, Newman Levy noted that if Jerome expected any of the breaks Goff usually gave the prosecution (as members of the New York bar always maintained), "he did not quite live up to the prosecutor's expectations. Not that Goff was unfair; he was temperamentally incapable of that. But many of his rulings, particularly on certain critical questions of evidence, were definitely favorable to the defense." Levy thought that Goff might also have been prejudiced by the "haughty" manner of Assistant District Attorney Rand, who again conducted the state's case. During the second trial, Jerome attended every session, determined to offset in whatever way he could the animosity radiating from the Recorder's bench.

This time the crucial testimony was given by Hyman Stern, the Sixth Avenue pawnbroker who sold the death weapon to a couple who, the state hoped, he would be able to identify as Nan's sister and brother-in-law. The prosecution's confidence in Stern as its key witness should have been diminished, however, by three factors: he was extremely nearsighted, he had sold the gun almost a year ago to a couple he had no reason to suspect of any criminal motives, and he was an almost painfully conscientious man.

Stern peered intently at both Smith and his wife, hesitated so long that he was impatiently prodded by Recorder Goff, and then said he could not be certain they were the persons who appeared in his shop the night before Caesar Young's death. Crash

went the prosecution's case in that instant; for Stern could not
be persuaded out of his uncertainty.

Yet the evidence weighed heavily against the defense's claim
that Young killed himself, as Rand caustically emphasized in his
summation. If one went along with that theory, Rand told the
jury, certain questions would have to be asked. "Where would
he naturally, being a right-handed man, shoot himself? Well,
here is the brain, that is the quickest death, the roof of the mouth,
the temple, the heart . . . You don't think, do you, that he would
have held the revolver upside down and pulled the trigger with
his thumb? You don't suppose that having suddenly decided to
die and knowing how fatal a shot in the heart would be, you
don't suppose that he would be going to shoot himself through
the apex of his left lung to the fourth dorsal vertebra?"

Logic, however, is seldom an imperative in determining the
decision of a jury. Once again the jury disagreed; this time the
vote was eight to four for acquittal.

Nan Patterson crossed the Bridge of Sighs leading from the
Tombs for the last time May 12, when she was brought into
Recorder Goff's court to learn whether she would be held for a
third trial.

Until now Jerome had been a silent, if hardly inactive partner
in the long battle to convict her.

Now he rose to take full responsibility for his office's course
of action. Whatever his assistant Rand did, he told the court,
"he did right — he did bravely, efficiently and well." He could
not conceal his bitterness at certain aspects of the press coverage,
particularly published claims that the two trials had cost the
state between $200,000 and $300,000. The total cost, he said, was
$8,000. And he added:

"This case has been misrepresented to the public, and the trial
has resulted in a miscarriage of justice. I have looked at the
trial in all its aspects. I have no criticism to make of the judge
or jury. They performed their duty."

Then, gritting his teeth, he made the statement that sentimental-
ists all over the world were waiting to hear:

"I ask that the defendant be discharged on her own recog-
nizance. Another trial would be unavailing."

"The motion," Recorder Goff said, with no visible reluctance,
"is granted."

All over the nation, which was much more engrossed by Nan's
fate than by the Russo–Japanese War or President Roosevelt's
jousting with the trusts, a great, slack-minded sigh of relief went
up. A crowd of two thousand cheered their heroine when she
left the Criminal Courts Building. A few weeks later she was
touring the vaudeville circuits and cashing in on her notoriety.

Even the most sentimental, who believed that Nan had been
the victim of a vile seducer who plugged himself in the back when
the burden of his guilt became overwhelming, were somewhat
taken aback by succeeding events. Nan remarried her first husband. And Mrs. Young, who had fought so bitterly to hang onto
her wayward husband, married John Millin, the ex-partner of the
late Caesar, who had also labored mightily to straighten him out.
Happy endings all around.

Who, then, killed Caesar Young? There is no definitive answer.
It was, perhaps, of extra-legal significance that at a banquet cele-
brating Nan Patterson's acquittal one of her lawyers reportedly
toasted her as "the guilty girl who beat the case."*

3

A FASCINATING VARIETY of villains cropped up in Jerome's professional life. Charles W. Morse, the conscienceless financier;
Abe Hummel, the craftiest of criminal lawyers; Dick Canfield, the
intellectual gambler; Bill Devery, the roaring bully-boy of the
constabulary, and Mock Duck, the intrepid hatchetman of the
Chinatown tong wars, all were characters so colorful, so devilish
in their different ways, that even such masters of literary extrava-

* According to Arthur Train, *From the District Attorney's Office.*

gance as Mark Twain or O. Henry would have thought twice
about inventing them. In picaresque and roguish qualities, however, these gentlemen were pallid conformists compared to yet
another of Jerome's gallery of rascals.

His name was Colonel William D'Alton Mann, whose name
stands high on the roll call of Edwardian scoundrelly, yet is seldom
mentioned by the more respectful historians of American society;
for the Colonel discovered and ruthlessly exploited a sensitive
area among the people who had arrived not too long ago on
Fifth Avenue, an exposed nerve common to the genus parvenu.
The Colonel's discovery was simply that the social newcomers
could not bear to have their occasional misconduct, their gau-
cheries and miscalculations retailed in a public print. He appointed himself their Father Grundy.

Even the briefest rundown on the colonel's career — his military title, which many thought self-bestowed, was a brevet commission but nonetheless genuine — indicates a man of astounding
versatility, an abounding resourcefulness. Humbly born in Ohio,
his rich Alabama accent led people to believe he was an offshoot
of the plantation aristocracy. He commanded the hard-fighting
Seventh Michigan Cavalry through most of the Civil War, but
afterward, as a newspaper publisher and cottonseed oil manufacturer in Mobile, Alabama, he also joined the Ku Klux Klan.
Later turning his interest toward invention, he obtained patents
for the Mann Boudoir car, which he sold for a pittance to
George Pullman, thus losing both the money and the credit for
developing the first railroad sleeping car. He also patented the
Mann Refrigerator car, and invented the vestibule which allowed
train passengers to pass from one car to another. A military treatise
published in England presented the colonel's plans for what
amounted to a pre-Wehrmacht blitzkrieg by mounted riflemen.

Early in the nineties the fertile brain of Colonel Mann was
attracted to the possibilities of combining a fringe form of
journalism with a fringe form of blackmail. He did the real

spadework in the field which produced, in all its weedlike syndicated glory, the gossip column. His brother, E. D. Mann, had been publishing a society-gossip sheet called *Town Topics*, but wearied of the venture after being convicted of sending obscene matter through the mails. The Colonel took over *Town Topics*, but was careful to avoid charges of libel, scurrility and obscenity by a leering, winking and nudging style of retailing gossip which was quite as offensive but less actionable.

Mann also quickly grasped the fact that the real money wasn't in circulation but in advertising and in "loans" from people who didn't want their social careers blighted. If his agents, who were planted in every strata of society, came across a damaging item about some bigwig, the latter was summoned to the Colonel's office and invited to lend him money or to contract for advertising. The unuttered agreement was that, in return, the Colonel would spike the story. He circulated the boast that his safe was crammed with enough unpublished scandal to rock the island of Manhattan. Whenever the spirit moved him, he also produced special "Wall Street Editions," through which shady financial dealings were threatened with exposure. Some of the mightiest names on the Street contributed to Mann's private welfare fund rather than risk having their operations described in malicious detail by *Town Topics*.

By the turn of the century, Mann and his weekly scandal sheet had created a reign of terror among socially aspiring people. Nowhere was the paper more widely read than in the metropolitan dailies' offices, which condemned Mann as a vicious scandalmonger but did not hesitate to lift the exclusive news he published, such as the supposedly sealed details of Colonel John Jacob Astor's divorce.

The Colonel, a patriarchal-looking old devil with lilac whiskers, flaring white mustachios, lively blue eyes and extraordinarily dilated nostrils which seemed to be constantly sniffing for the slightest whiff of useful gossip, was Foxy Grandpa to the last saintly white hair. He was assisted in avoiding any breach of the libel or extortion laws by a city magistrate named Joseph M. Deuel, who was vice president and general counsel of the *Town Topics* publishing company and read every line that reached print.

Until District Attorney Jerome began taking an intrusive interest in his affairs, the Colonel was a happy old blatherskite. He lunched and dined daily at Delmonico's on platters of mutton chops served with lashings of vintage champagne. A dollar cigar always jutted from his face like a small cannon. He entertained the ladies on a lavish scale, an employee later recalling that "women trooped through his office all day long." And he was allowed to indulge, sometimes quite profitably, in speculating in New York real estate. That was his favorite pastime, aside from chasing female visitors around the desk in his office. It was recalled that he "could ask for a third mortgage without blushing." He bought up a number of lots on Thirty-eighth Street between Eighth and Ninth Avenues, and pulled wires endlessly but unavailingly to have the new post office erected on them. The New York *Herald Tribune* occupies property once owned by the Colonel in his wheeling and dealing days.

One of his most lucrative inspirations was publishing a volume titled *Fads and Fancies of Representative Americans,* for which subscribers paid $1,500 a copy. "The timorous paid to avoid exposure," it was observed, "and the vain paid to secure a flattering biography." With such names as Duke, Vanderbilt, Astor, Huntington, Flagler, Whitney, Lorillard, Ryan, Hyde, Belmont and Fleischmann on the list of subscribers, the Colonel cleared a neat $90,000 on the publication. He included on this list the name of Theodore Roosevelt, and was outraged when the President publicly denied having joined the roll call of *Town Topics'* sponsors. His pique over being snubbed by the White House, and his bitter distaste for everything Rooseveltian, eventually and indirectly brought him into collision with the law.

The Colonel regarded himself, at least publicly, as a great force for social betterment and the sanctity of the upper-class home, as the self-appointed guardian of society's manners and morals. No one could scold a debutante for using a touch too much mascara more righteously that the Colonel; none could be so shocked by goings-on at Newport, Bar Harbor or Palm Beach as he and his writers professed to be in the *Town Topics*. "Scandal!" he would bluster at anyone accusing him of running a gossip sheet. "Harumph! Harumph! Nothing of the sort! We're only pointing a moral. *Town Topics* stands for moral purity. Written by gentle folk, for gentle folk, on topics of interest to gentle folk."*

As matters stood in the summer of 1905, the Colonel had made a fortune out of shearing black sheep, no one had protested his methods (thanks to the eternal vigilance of Judge Deuel), and neither the law nor society seemed capable of curbing the professional blabbermouth.

Since early in his first term, Jerome had been meditating ways of deodorizing this particular form of skunk journalism, but no one could be found to admit that the Colonel had extorted money from him in return for silence in *Town Topics*. No one, in fact, would admit being interviewed by him. Nor could any basis for criminal libel action be found in the weekly's columns, so skillfully did the Colonel's hacks skirt around their subjects, though Jerome read *Town Topics* as religiously as any city editor on Park Row.

Jerome and certain of his clubmen friends — including Robert Collier, son of the *Collier's Weekly* founder; Norman Hapgood, *Collier's* editor; Harry Payne Whitney, Charles Dana Gibson, Finley Peter Dunne and Mark Sullivan — had long discussed ways of exterminating *Town Topics*. The overthrow of Colonel Mann

---

* Quoted by Robert R. Rowe, a former *Town Topics* reporter who covered Newport parties disguised as a tambourine player, in the *American Mercury*, July, 1926.

was planned in Manhattan's clubs, just as Tammany's was in 1901. Several of the anti-Mann forces had personal reasons for joining in the undercover crusade: Whitney's father had been clipped by the Colonel and *Collier's* was a favorite target of the *Town Topics'* more venomous paragraphs. Old Peter Collier, so the Colonel alleged, among other things, once sold Catholic Bibles to innocent Protestants in the Catskills.

Jerome was a particularly close friend of the brilliant young Hapgood and, as was disclosed subsequently in legal proceedings, mapped the strategy which lured the Colonel out of his protective shell and into the hazardous territory of open court.

But it was the Colonel and his hatred for the Roosevelt family who opened up possibilities of exposing the way *Town Topics* operated. In the summer of 1905, his spies tipped him off that Miss Alice Roosevelt, the President's daughter, who was strenuously opposed to stuffiness of any kind, was having a very gay summer as a guest of the Ogden Mills family in Newport. Rumors also reached the Colonel that "Princess Alice" was joining in the tippling for which certain Newport circles were notorious. As Miss Roosevelt herself frankly said later, she "danced the hootchy-kootchy on Grace Vanderbilt's roof."

If Princess Alice was unable to see any reason why a girl shouldn't have a good time merely because her father happened to be President of the United States, Colonel William D'Alton Mann was only too ready to offer a correction. With heavy heart, yet with enough discretion to avoid prosecution for libel, he ran a "blind" item in his columns of chitchat; Alice Roosevelt was not mentioned by name but any knowledgeable reader knew who *Town Topics* was tattling on. "From wearing costly lingerie to indulging in fancy dances for the edification of men was only a step," the journal observed. "And then came a second step — indulging freely in stimulants . . . Flying all around Newport without a chaperone was another thing that greatly concerned Mother Grundy. There may have been no reason for the old lady making such a fuss about it, but if the young woman knew some of the tales that are told at the clubs in Newport she would be more careful in the future about what she does and how she does it."

Collier's Weekly not only leaped to Alice Roosevelt's defense but scaldingly denounced *Town Topics* ("a degraded, sewer-like sheet") and its fabricators of gossip, from Colonel Mann on down. Judge Deuel was chacterized in Norman Hapgood's editorial as "part owner of a paper of which the occupation is printing scandal about people who are not cowardly enough to pay for silence." As for Colonel Mann, his "standing among people is somewhat worse than that of an ordinary forger, horse thief, or second-story man."

When they read that scorcher, Judge Deuel and Colonel Mann differed on what must be done about it. Mindful of his judicial position, Deuel felt that they must demand that Hapgood be indicted for criminal libel. The Colonel was inclined to shrug it off; *his* reputation mattered little to him, so long as it struck terror in the hearts of his financial supporters. Perhaps his flaring nostrils scented a trap. But, unwisely, he allowed the judge to have his way.

Hapgood was charged with criminal libel and was so eager to be arrested that he hurried back to New York from his summer home at York Harbor, though Finley Peter Dunne warned him, "It is all right now, when people know what it is about, but ten years from now they will think you were arrested for writing an article in *Town Topics* libeling Alice Roosevelt, and many of them will remember your name without being sure whether you were the editor of *Town Topics* or the man who jumped off the Brooklyn Bridge." Mr. Dooley's creator was right about that, Hapgood later admitted. "Dunne's humor had in it so much of actuality," Hapgood said, "that a man on a Pullman once told me he remembered me as the editor of *Town Topics.*"

District Attorney Jerome was now placed in the position of

prosecuting his friend, Norman Hapgood, on behalf of men whom he detested, Judge Deuel and Colonel Mann.

His problem: to turn that criminal libel prosecution into some sort of attack on *Town Topics*, Deuel and Mann.

This would take some fancy footwork, and Jerome decided that he must take full charge of the case, in and out of court.

Hapgood's trial was set for January, 1906. During the months before the trial, *Collier's Weekly* lured away a number of *Town Topics* staff members who thoughtfully brought with them a number of memorandums signed by Deuel and Mann and any other documentary evidence that might damage their former employer. The Colonel, meanwhile, was hoping desperately that the case would never come to trial. His hopes rested on two possibilities, that *Collier's* would try to settle the case to get their editor off the hook, and that Jerome, whom he suspected of pressing the prosecution with something less than sympathy for the complainants, would be defeated in the fall election. But *Collier's* refused to settle and Jerome was re-elected; furthermore, the latter insisted that Colonel Mann would have to appear as a witness, the last thing he wanted, knowing all too well how the trial might be turned into a gigantic embarrassment for him.

Hapgood meanwhile was being assured by Jerome, as the editor recalled in his autobiography (*The Changing Years*), that the allegedly libelous editorial "was written in such Harvard College English that it was hard to tell exactly in what words lay the charge of blackmail. Instead of using that word, I had said that the paper abused people who were not cowardly enough to pay for protection. It was about that time that the editor of a New York daily asked his editorial writers to read *Collier's* to see how libels ought to be written. The trick was a simple one. It was to avoid epithets and instead to describe exactly what the person had done."

To justify his lack of enthusiasm for prosecuting Hapgood, his actual advocacy of the young editor, in fact, Jerome had only to cite his statutory duty to free the innocent and punish the guilty no matter what legal barriers temporarily presented themselves.

An indication of how he performed this high-wire act was shown during Jerome's cross-examination of Hapgood, a rather tongue-in-cheek affair with the district attorney affecting a mock sternness. Jerome was seeking to show that all Hapgood knew of *Town Topics* and some of the scrapes its employes got into was what he had read in the daily newspapers.

JEROME: "Was *all* you knew about *Town Topics* acquired from the newspapers?"

HAPGOOD: "No. I was influenced also by the opinion existing in the district attorney's office."

JEROME: "What was that?"

HAPGOOD: "It was to the effect that it was easy to catch the little fellows, and that the person who would deserve credit would be he who would get the big spider [that is, Colonel Mann]."

JEROME: "Who told you that was the opinion in our office?"

HAPGOOD: (struggling to keep his face straight): "You did."

On January 19, Mann himself was summoned to the witness stand, seating himself, as a New York *Herald* reporter observed, "with the air of one who is about to accomplish great things." He insisted under direct examination that any loans he received were freely given and claimed, with a twitch of his white mustachios, "I am a poor man." Confident as his manner was, the Colonel soon stumbled into error. Jerome introduced a memorandum signed with the initials W. D. M. suggesting that pressure be exerted on certain persons reluctant to have their affairs broadcast by *Town Topics*. Mann could hardly own up to authorship of the memo without admitting that his practices as a publisher were more than somewhat irregular. He denied having inscribed the initials. Jerome immediately summoned handwriting experts who assured him the Colonel was lying. Meanwhile, in court, Jerome laid the groundwork for future prosecution.

JEROME: "Now was there anything like blackmail or extortion or shaking down weak, foolish people for money to keep unpleasant things about them out of *Town Topics*, or to have printed pleasant notices about them?"

MANN (shouting): "Absolutely no, and no one can say to the contrary!"

Oliver H. P. Belmont of the banking family, however, testified effectively on just how Colonel Mann operated in the privacy of his Fifth Avenue offices. Belmont said that Mann summoned him to suggest that he buy $5,000 worth of *Town Topics* stock. When Belmont refused, Mann asked him to "loan" $5,000. Again Belmont shook his head. Mann suggested a $2,000 loan, and when that also was turned down, he warned Belmont, "It would be well for you to think the matter over." Soon "unpleasant stories" about him began appearing in *Town Topics*, Belmont said. He further testified that his brother Perry had lent Mann money and was "kindly treated."

On January 26, the jury retired, deliberated exactly seven minutes and returned a verdict acquitting Hapgood.

Jerome then proceeded to prosecute Colonel Mann on perjury charges, specifically with having lied when he denied having signed the memorandum attributed to him.

At his trial Jerome forced Mann to admit that he had "borrowed" a total of almost $200,000 from various Fifth Avenue and Wall Street figures, including James R. Keene, $90,000; William K. Vanderbilt, $25,000; John W. "Bet-You-a-Million" Gates, $20,000; William C. Whitney, $10,000; Thomas Fortune Ryan, $10,000; Collis P. Huntington, $5,000, among the larger contributors. Mann was maneuvered into admitting that he obtained almost as much in a loan from a life insurance company, not otherwise celebrated for its tendency to lend money without security.

Such society figures as Harry Lehr, the feather-footed cotillion leader much in demand among Fifth Avenue's more regal hostesses; Edwin P. Post and Oliver Belmont testified to the colonel's peculiar methods of gathering news, if it could be called news, and processing it with equal regard for his gossip-hungry readers and his own bank account.

It was generally agreed that the Colonel was cornered, branded not only a perjurer but a blackmailer. But those ephemeral "courtroom observers" had not reckoned with the eloquence of Martin Littleton, whom Mann had paid a $75,000 fee to defend him. Even the highly skilled Littleton could find little to offer in the way of legal defense. He pinned his hopes on the final argument. His voice throbbing in the quiet courtroom, Littleton launched one of the most moving pleas ever heard on behalf of a defendant. He catalogued the Colonel's services to the Union Army battle by battle, almost saber stroke by saber stroke, and did not hesitate to assign to his client the major share of credit for the victory at Gettysburg. The bearded cheeks of the jurors were matted with honest tears, all evidence was forgotten as Littleton appealed to them to "send this gallant old hero from this courtroom a free man." They did just that.

Jerome's prosecution, however, had achieved its purpose. Colonel Mann's power to terrify was dissipated by the revelations the district attorney had induced in open court, and those who had paid him off were made to feel supremely ridiculous. After that, it was noted, "advertisers shrank away and many a distinguished New Yorker began to wonder why the old rascal's bluff hadn't been called years ago."*

As with Canfield and Hummel, Jerome managed to pull the fangs of still another rascal whom his fellow citizens had regarded as being above the law, even though his full purpose was not achieved. *Town Topics* kept publishing, but without the enormously inflated profits accruing from fear of the colonel. Much later it was revealed that his safe, which he claimed was packed

* Dixon Wecter in *The Saga of American Society.*

with enough dynamite to blow high society apart, actually contained his office supply of brandy and cigars, undoubtedly the source of much of his inspiration.

4

THE RICE MURDER CASE, a classic in the annals of criminology, started before Jerome took office and finished some years after he left, but most of the burden of prosecuting it fell on his administration.

Early in the evening of September 23, 1900, a multimillionaire named William M. Rice, who was eighty-four years old and who had founded the Rice Institute of Texas, lay dying in his apartment at 500 Madison Avenue. Two elderly ladies, friends of the childless widower, called shortly after 7 P.M. with a hamper of cakes and wine for the old gentleman. No one answered their ring, though Rice's valet and sole companion in what had become a reclusive life, Charles F. Jones, was always at his side. Jones was unable to come to the door, as he later stated, because he was occupied with a more important matter. While the old ladies were ringing the doorbell, in fact, he was holding a cone saturated with chloroform over Rice's face and waiting for him to die.

The suspicions of Rice's relatives and of the authorities were aroused by several events which occurred immediately after his death. All of them involved a lawyer named Albert T. Patrick. Although Rice and Patrick had never met, the latter was named principal heir to Rice's $7,000,000 estate in a will dated June 30, 1900; furthermore, Patrick had drawn four checks on Rice's accounts for a total of $250,000, had an order giving him control of the contents of his safe deposit vaults containing more than $250,000 in securities, and also displayed a general assignment by which he received control of Rice's entire estate. What made these documents all the more suspicious was the fact that several years before Patrick had been retained in litigation against Rice which aroused the old man's hatred for the lawyer, though they never met. The documents, in any case, were subsequently adjudged forgeries. Attention of the police was also attracted by the fact that valet Jones, with lawyer Patrick's connivance, had attempted to have Rice's body cremated immediately after his death, a move that was thwarted by the dead man's relatives.

A month after Rice's death Jones and Patrick were arrested on charges of forgery. Jones, obviously the weaker of the two men, began faltering in his claim that his employer died a natural death. He tried to cut his throat with a knife which police learned had been supplied him by Patrick. On recovering Jones made a full confession: he had chloroformed Rice at Patrick's instigation, had helped him forge the documents by which Patrick intended to lay hands on the estate, and was to share in the proceeds.

Patrick denied all, confident that he could not be convicted on the uncorroborated testimony of Rice's confessed slayer.

Although Jerome's predecessor had a year to bring Patrick to trial before leaving office, the case was one of many allowed to hang fire and await action by the new district attorney. Jerome proceeded to try Patrick immediately after taking office, and despite the defense's contention that Rice's death, attributed to "a congestion of the lungs," could have been caused by embalming fluid, and that there was no corroborative evidence directly connecting him to the murder, he was convicted of first-degree murder in April, 1902 and sentenced to be electrocuted. The faithless valet Jones, in consideration of his testimony for the state, went free.

That, however, wasn't the last to be heard from Mr. Patrick. He appealed the conviction, which was sustained by the higher courts. Jerome was determined that he pay the penalty, considering it a particularly heinous and cold-blooded crime.

Early in January, 1906, while he was preparing the case involving *Town Topics*, he had to take time out to oppose a campaign to obtain a commutation for Patrick. He was accused by Patrick's counsel of "trying to influence signers of a petition for clemency," which did not deter him from journeying to Albany and arguing vociferously against any further delay in electrocuting Patrick.* Governor Higgins, however, granted Patrick a sixty-day reprieve, and later that year commuted his sentence to life imprisonment.

Jerome was a hard loser, in some cases, and he was particularly aroused by the way the wily and determined Patrick wriggled out of his clutches. In 1912, Patrick was granted a pardon by Governor Dix, who did not even consult with the district attorney's office before turning him loose. Patrick subsequently practiced law for many years in a western state.

Difficult, vexing and not altogether successful as these prosecutions turned out to be, they were mere warm-ups for the summit performance of Jerome's career, when he was provided with the opportunity to demonstrate the full extent of his abilities as a prosecutor. This came when the "crime of the century," as the newspapers somewhat overconfidently termed it, was committed in his bailiwick. Naturally what followed, again according to the brash estimate of the headline writers, was the "trial of the century." This served as Jerome's cue to step stage center in the full glare of journalistic floodlights as prosecutor in one of the most fascinating of American murder trials.

* New York *Herald*, January 16, 1906.

7

A Crime of Many Passions (I)

> When it comes to focusing the attention
> of the whole nation searchingly upon a
> single subject, and giving it a single set of
> facts on which to test its moral values, it is
> doubtful whether anything really unifies the
> country like its murders.
> — Charles Merz.

IT WASN'T MUCH of a day for news, June 25, 1906. Fretful city
editors of the metropolitan dailies had to make the best of a
story emanating from the Customs House — John D. Rockefeller's
powdered wig, imported from France for a society ball, was held
up at customs for nonpayment of duties. The city's leading news-
maker, William Travers Jerome, had departed on an early vacation, leaving a sizable vacuum dreaded by circulation-minded
editors. For table conversation that evening the city would have
to fall back upon such topics as Frenzied Finance, the latest
activities of the Black Hand, the simmering feuds among the
Chinatown tongs, Fletcherism, bloodless surgery, and the most
reliable of all, the rising cost of living (ice cream sodas had gone
up to ten cents, the theater was hoping that the new two-dollar
top wouldn't keep too many patrons away, and housewives were
upbraiding their butchers for having boosted steak to twenty
cents a pound).

As night fell, unseasonably hot and humid, three of the city's most faithful theater-goers were preparing to go out in style. Stanford White, the most famous of American architects, climbed into evening dress at his town apartment; his wife was staying at their summer home on Long Island, and he had a pre-theater engagement to meet his son and a classmate, just down from Harvard, for dinner. Uptown at the Lorraine, Fifth Avenue at Forty-fifth Street, Mr. and Mrs. Harry K. Thaw were also dressing for dinner and the theater. For the young and supremely beautiful Mrs. Thaw it was an exhaustive ritual. Thaw waited with mounting impatience while she took her time about enhancing her flawless features. Mrs. Thaw, formerly Evelyn Nesbit of the Floradora Sextette and other such comely groupings, was struggling with a new white satin gown in the Directoire style which, as one newspaper commented, "applied such searching sculptural indiscretion to the female figure," squeezing out breasts and emphasizing the curving line of hips and buttocks, that it was "little short of revolutionary."

Finally Thaw wearied of waiting and told her to join him in Sherry's bar a block away. Before he left the sumptuous apartment, he slipped a revolver into the inside pocket of his coat.

An hour later Mrs. Thaw had joined her husband and they had gone on to Martin's with its huge white and gold dining room and its glamorous terrace reserved for properly dressed celebrities. Here they met two young friends of Thaw's, Truxton Beale and Thomas McCaleb, and took a table in the dining room, since their guests were still dressed in business suits. They ordered several rounds of drinks, then dinner and two quarts of champagne. Conversation at the Thaw table was lighthearted, inconsequential. Later, it was recalled, they told each other limericks, gossiped on various subjects and remarked on how many of the young women at the tables around them were dressed and made up in hopeful emulation of the reigning young star on Broadway, Miss Ethel Barrymore.

Something of a stir was created in the dining room just as

the Thaws and their guests reached the coffee-and-brandy stage. Stanford White was making his entrance, bowed in with some ceremony by Humbert, the headwaiter. Energy and magnetism radiated from the stocky, red-haired architect. Even a country cousin being shown the town could recognize him as one of the elect by the way he charged into the room, followed by his son and the latter's friend from Harvard; by the assurance with which he made his way through the chamber, waving at friends, smiling and nodding. It was a royal procession. White and his companions, suitably dressed, were escorted to the terrace by Humbert himself.

Thaw's back was turned to the aisle down which White strode, but he was made aware of the mild sensation the architect's entrance had caused. His wife was obviously upset, casting her eyes down, biting her full red underlip. He stared at her questioningly.

She took a small gold pencil from her purse and scribbled a note, which she passed over the table to Thaw.

"That B is here," it read.

The big event in Manhattan night life that evening was the opening of a new musical comedy, *Mamzelle Champagne*, in the roof-garden theater at Madison Square Garden.

The new Garden, located at the northeast end of Madison Square and occupying the whole block bounded by Fourth and Madison Avenues, was not only the showplace of the metropolis but one of the brighter jewels in Stanford White's architectural diadem. It was built in 1890 at the cost of $4,500,000 and was the largest building in the Western Hemisphere given over to entertainment. Most of it was occupied by a huge arena three hundred feet long and two hundred feet wide in which circuses, horse shows and other spectacles were staged; surrounding it were tiers of boxes, mezzanine floors and balconies which could seat 7,000 spectators. Double that number could be accommodated for prizefights and political conventions, when seats could be placed in the arena itself. Aside from the main arena, the Garden found room for a large restaurant, a theater and concert hall, lodge and club headquarters, and most recently the theater on the roof in which *Mamzelle Champagne* was opening.

From the outside, the most striking feature of the Garden was the square, 341-foot tower which thrust itself above the rest of the structure. It was modeled after the Giralda Tower in Seville and was topped by the fourteen-foot copper statue of Diana, bare to the waist, which had been executed by Augustus St. Gaudens, the noted sculptor and friend of Stanford White. Mother Grundy seethed over that statue with its breasts bared to the four winds; clergymen denounced it from the pulpit as an affront to every decent woman in New York, and the newspapers reported that nasty old men spent hours sitting in Madison Square Park and studying the semi-nude figure through telescopes. Despite the protests, the copper-sheathed Diana was still poised high over midtown Manhattan, revolving always to point windward on its mounting of forty steel balls. People still talked about her almost as much as the elegantly debauched parties White was rumored to hold in his apartment in the tower, which was said to have mirrored ceilings in the bedrooms, divans covered with leopard skins, erotic paintings and tapestries, secret doors and sliding panels and all manner of enticements to join hands with the devil.

Among those present when the curtain rang up on *Mamzelle Champagne* in the theater below the revolving Diana were Mr. and Mrs. Thaw. As their seat neighbors afterward recalled, Thaw appeared to be in a highly emotional state hardly in key with the lighthearted proceedings on stage. *Mamzelle* wasn't much of a show even for the Garden roof, which specialized in the lightest sort of entertainment. It was all bubbles and no wine, and the professionals in the audience, between the acts, agreed that it wouldn't be running long (actually the events of the next hour guaranteed it a run far beyond its merits).

Viola de Costa, in the title role, fetchingly popped out of a giant papier-mâché bottle of Pommery Sec; Harry Short drew some snickering and nudging when he boasted in song "I Could Love a Thousand Girls," and Maude Fulton succeeded in rousing the audience from its torpor when she sang "Can I Fascinate You?"

Then came the show's big production number, with the chorus trotting out in pink tights and swishing their fencing foils.

As the ladies of the chorus paired off and playfully clashed with their foils, Stanford White strolled down the aisle and took a seat at the table reserved for him in the section just below the stage, where favored patrons could have supper if they wished. White was alone, having dropped off his dinner companions. Usually he had a young and beautiful girl on his arm for such occasions; he kept himself surrounded by feminine beauty, night and day, but this evening — possibly because of the dinner appointment with his son and his son's classmate — he was unaccompanied.

Among those who noted his entrance was a young newspaperman named Albert Payson Terhune, then a member of the New York *World* staff, some years later celebrated as the author of dog stories. Terhune had been assigned to review the opening of *Mamzelle Champagne* in place of the regular dramatic critic, who was honeymooning in Europe. Of the nine hundred persons who witnessed the offstage finale to the show's opening, he was one of the more reliable, because he was both a trained observer and was sitting only a few yards away.

Terhune's attention was distracted from the stage when Thaw suddenly rose from his seat, strode to the tables near the stage and began pacing back and forth in front of White's table. "Every time he passed the table," Terhune wrote,* Thaw "would pause to glower furiously down at the ostentatiously oblivious oldster [White]. I knew both men by sight. I knew, as did many another observer, the reason for that dramatic glower."

* In his autobiography, *To the Best of My Memory.*

On the stage, the girls were swishing their foils and their fannies, and singing:

> I challenge you,
> I challenge you
> To a duel, to a d-u-e-l.

The lyrics would have been curiously and ironically appropriate had Stanford White been armed as the glowering young man was.

The number was coming to an end, and the chorus was marching down to the footlights with their foils extended, coyly menacing the audience.

Just then Harry Thaw halted in his furious pacing in front of Stanford White, and drew his revolver. White's jaw dropped, his eyes popped in alarm, he started to get up from his chair. The gun in Thaw's hand was only two feet from his face, aimed on a level with his eyes.

". . . Three times in slow and rhythmic succession he fired . . ." as Terhune observed.

White's face was torn apart by the bullets. A dying reflex stiffened him, brought him to his feet, and then sent him crashing lifelessly to the floor. The architect died instantly in a puddle of blood.

Everyone was too stunned to panic. The curtain came down with a rush, and there were shrieks backstage. Many in the audience thought the shooting was part of the fencing number, and waited for White to get up and join the cast backstage. Then those seated nearest to White began shouting and screaming.

Terhune's reportorial instincts kept him cool, collected and observant. He watched Thaw raise the revolver over his head, break it open and shuck out the shells, as though to demonstrate that the shooting was over and no one else need fear him.

A uniformed member of the Garden's security force rushed over to Thaw, who handed him the revolver and said:

"He deserved it, he ruined my wife."

By now panic and confusion swept the audience; some stampeded for the exits, others pushed their way toward the stage in morbid excitement to stare down at White's blood-masked face and sprawling figure.

A young woman as pale as the elegant white satin she wore struggled through the near-hysterical mob to reach Thaw's side. It was his wife Evelyn. She threw her arms around Thaw, and Terhune heard her cry out:

"Oh, Harry, I never thought you'd do it that way!"

Other witnesses said they heard Thaw say to her, "It's all right, dear. I have probably saved your life."

Terhune, with a first-edition deadline looming, scrambled through the crowd and plunged down the wide red-carpeted stairs leading from the roof garden to a corridor on the next floor where a telephone booth was located. With the biggest story in years waiting to be told over the wires to Park Row, Terhune encountered a classic frustration. "A man was using the telephone for a smirking conversation with one Tessie." Terhune tried to reason with Tessie's admirer but he wouldn't give up the phone. The husky reporter yanked him away and sent him sprawling. A few minutes later, while Terhune was begging an indifferent central to connect him in a hurry and the hello-girl was taking her time about it, Tessie's friend returned with a pal who had armed himself with a chair. With one arm and one leg, Terhune managed to fend off his attackers and hang onto the line until he reached the city desk of the *Morning World* and the biggest murder story in New York since Edward Stokes shot Jim Fisk was on its way to the presses. It was the beginning of a journalistic circus — and of an orgy of misdirected sentimentality — that was to exert a tremendous and inimical influence on the workings of justice.

By the time Terhune ran back upstairs to the roof garden, the nine hundred persons in the audience who had come to while

away a few hours with *Mamzelle Champagne* but witnessed, at
no extra charge, a murder that perceptibly shook the structure
of society were milling around the corpse under the dimmed
footlights. Someone had thrown a coat over the shattered face.
The police had arrived and were leading Thaw to the elevators.
He seemed to be enjoying all the attention and was trying volubly to explain the necessity of firing three bullets squarely into
Stanford White's face.

A few minutes later he was being booked on a murder charge.
Everyone knew who he was, and Thaw knew they knew it, but
he insisted on being booked as "John Smith, 18 Lafayette Street,
Philadelphia." He gave his occupation as "student." As he was
being led into the back room of the station house for questioning, he turned to an officer and said, "Here's a bill, officer. Get
Carnegie on the telephone and tell him I'm in trouble." The first
policemen who talked to him reported that the prisoner seemed
to have no idea of the enormity of his crime but was exhilarated
by the commotion he had caused. Someone at the station house
recalled that Thaw was known to the newspapers as "Mad
Harry," and the sobriquet seemed to fit.

2

MURDER IS a whimsical casting director. In a crime of passion
particularly, the cast is often wildly diverse in character, summoned together by the accidents and perversities of human behavior. How else but under the hot, white cone of light which
society focuses upon a sensational murder case could the principals in the Stanford White affair have found themselves grouped
eternally in a notorious tableau — White himself, the artist and
promotional genius; Thaw, the psychopathic playboy from Pittsburgh; Evelyn Nesbit, the Broadway beauty also born in Pittsburgh but in a much grimier section than the wild young man
she married, and finally, much as he shied away from that searing
spotlight, John Barrymore, who was to become one of America's

greatest actors, the wayward young Jack of Park Row and the Bowery still rebelling at the theater's disciplines. In the ordinary course of events, if he had been an ordinary man with quieter tastes and pursuits, White would have known none of them; Thaw, likewise, would have been confined to his own idle but less dangerous circle; only Evelyn Nesbit and Jack Barrymore had any logical reason for acquaintance.

But it was just that strange juxtaposition of character that gave the case its lasting fascination, that provided such an eye-opening glimpse of the realities of Edwardian society, that echoed the now-discernible cracking of the pillars on which the social structure rested. Obviously society, and particularly the upper classes upon which an almost mystical regard was conferred, was disordered, in a state of demoralization, when a man like Stanford White could be associated even momentarily with characters bearing more than a whiff of the Tenderloin.

There was no mystery to lend suspense to the Stanford White murder case — no mystery but the eternal psychological one. It all turned on Harry Thaw's alleged motive for killing White, that the latter had "ruined" his wife. And if there is one unsolved mystery concerning the case, it is whether this was true. The trial records conceal more than they reveal in this respect. Thaw's partisans, incredibly numerous, maintained that he had every right to shoot White as the seducer of his young wife. White's friends, so incredibly lacking in eloquence on this one occasion, murmured that this could not be true; "Stanny" was a gentleman from his bristling red hair to the polished tips of his English boots, and gentlemen didn't go around tampering with the morals of very young females. In all the millions of words written and spoken about the case, you are given a choice of two views of Stanford White: greathearted gentleman or ruthless voluptuary. Could he, in the more modern view, have been something of both?

The truth about his character may be sensed, but only in glimmerings, in the bare facts of his background and career. Per-

haps the most significant facet of his personality was the fact that
he literally worshiped beauty, whether it was in the hard clear
lines of architecture or the softer graces of the human female
just a step or two short of womanhood. He was an apostle of
beauty in a country which was maddeningly slow to awaken to
it. Guilty or innocent of being carried away by this passion for
beauty, it was that which destroyed him: his fate encouraged
the belief, in paraphrase, that each man is killed by the thing he
loves best.

At the time of his death White was fifty-two, a vital, energetic,
gregarious man with hair that was still mostly red, a barrel chest
and a stocky build that recently had started running to fat. He
was married — happily, it seemed — to the former Bessie Springs
Smith, a descendant of Burgomaster Van Cortlandt, who governed
the city when it was still New Amsterdam. Two sons were born
to the Whites, but only one, Lawrence Grant White, survived
infancy.

White himself came of a distinguished line which he could
trace back three hundred years, his ancestor John White having
landed in Boston in 1632. His grandfather was a New York
shipping merchant; his father, Richard Grant White, a lawyer,
scholar and writer whom the London *Spectator* called "the most
accomplished and best bred man that America has sent to England within the present generation." Stanford himself was born
in New York City, but was apprenticed in his youth to the celebrated Boston architect, Henry Hobson Richardson. Eventually,
with Charles Follen McKim, another Richardson apprentice, and
with William Rutherford Mead, he formed the firm of McKim,
Mead and White. The firm not only prospered amazingly, but
its headquarters at 57 Broadway became a sort of White House of
the fine arts, the gathering place of such artistic celebrities as
Sargent, St. Gaudens, LaFarge, Millet, Carrère, Weir, Abbey,
Chase, Dewing, Wells, Hastings.

Stanford White's place in American architecture is open to

critical dispute; he was preoccupied with the beauties of the Renaissance to the detriment of originality, and he was more the enthusiast than the artist. Even his contemporaries, much as he was admired, were conscious of this flaw. Commenting on his works, in an editorial published two days after his murder, the New York *Times* said that "One may continue to insist that this is by no means architecture in the highest sense of the word, and may still insist upon the exceptional qualities that were required to do it so well." John Jay Chapman, a perceptive critic, wrote that:

Ornament was his passion. The weak side of his architecture is due in part to his too great reliance on festive ornament. Indeed, some of his work is apt to remind one of those dreaded atlases of photographs which architects keep in their sanctums and which give the motive and the detail of every famous architectural design in the world. The fact is, of course, that the age demanded an impresario who could reel out masterworks and put up seven palaces in a week. In the rush of his success White could not always take time to be correct. Besides he could not have held his post and led the procession if he had been a more serious artist. What the people demanded was glamour.

To Chapman he was "an interpreter of the age," with all its vulgarity and appetite for the overdone and overstuffed; "the protagonist of popular art, the prevailing influence not only in architecture but in everything connected with decoration and design." To the abounding newly-rich, he was a galvanizing guidon-bearer of the kind of culture they could own, feel and encompass — even understand; "he buffaloed them, he met them on all sides at once, in sport, pleasure, antiquities, furniture, decoration, bibelots, office buildings, country houses and exhibitions." In brief, he was the Edwardians' number one salesman of popularized culture. And the judgment of those who succeeded him professionally and artistically has been severe; to them he was a copyist, a creator of structural wedding cakes, and an unabashed pharisee.

But his works speak best for him, and some of them, to the untutored eye at least, possessed a genuine grace and beauty. Besides the new Madison Square Garden they included the Century and Metropolitan Clubs, the Washington Arch, the Hotel Imperial, the Players Club, Cullum Memorial Hall at West Point, the New York Herald Building, the Lambs Club, the Madison Square Presbyterian Church, Grand Central Station, the Colony Club — many of them still standing — and the residences of Henry Villard, Joseph H. Choate, Pierre Lorillard, Ogden Mills, Thomas Nelson Page, Levi P. Morton, Stuyvesant Fish, Henry W. Poor, Clarence Mackay, Charles Dana Gibson, Joseph Pulitzer, Mrs. William K. Vanderbilt, Jr. and Payne Whitney. If they offended the eye of the critical beholder, their owners largely were proud and satisfied. One of his few disgruntled clients was the cantankerous James Gordon Bennett, Jr., who complained that his new Herald Building looked like "an Italian fish market."

By birth and achievement, White was a certified member of top-drawer society, the peer and companion of such men as John Jacob Astor, Herman Oelrichs, William K. Vanderbilt, the Whitneys and Morgans and Harrimans; the longtime friend of Richard Harding Davis, Frank Millet, Richard Watson Gilder, and all the artists who made the offices of McKim, Mead and White their downtown headquarters. His talent for friendship was undeniable. Edward Simmons, the painter, recalled in his memoir (*From Seven to Seventy*) that White was the most generous of men, openhanded with his time, money and encouragement. ". . . I think he more nearly fitted Emerson's definition of a gentleman than anyone else I've ever known . . . If the word can be divided into *gentle* and *man*, Stanny was certainly both. He may have had troubles of his own, but we never knew about them, for he was always too busy doing something for someone else to talk about himself. He pulled me out of many a financial hole, sometimes with much work to himself . . . I don't think he gave ten minutes a week to thinking about himself."

Nothing gave "Stanny" more pleasure than planning elaborate entertainments for his friends. An April Fool's dinner complete with the sort of gentle joking he loved was typical of White as a host — unless one believed the whispers around Broadway that less sedate affairs were held in his hideaway apartments with less wholesome companions. On this occasion, related by Simmons, he invited his friends to dinner at his tower apartment in Madison Square Garden. The table was elaborately set, but there was no food and no host. After a long wait, Louis Sherry, the restaurateur and caterer, finally appeared and guided the party to his establishment. There they found an empty table and a sign exclaiming *April Fool.* While they were still cussing out Stanny's sense of humor, Sherry suggested that they repair to his basement kitchen. There they found a grinning host and tables laid out with Sherry's choicest dishes.

And then there was the famous "Girl in the Pie" dinner at which White was merely one of the guests, an affair of which the newspapers made much and claimed that it "wrecked the life of an innocent sixteen-year-old girl." It was held in the studio of society photographer James L. Breese — and studio then was a word that suggested all sorts of license and depravity. Among those who attended, in addition to White, were his business partners, Cooper Hewitt, William Astor Chandler, George E. Perkins, Augustus St. Gaudens and other eminently respectable men. As Simmons said, "we wanted a *blowout,* and we did not propose to be limited by New Englandism . . . Two girls — models — in exquisite costumes, one blonde and one brunette, poured the drinks, each serving the colored wine that corresponded to her complexion." The *pièce de résistance* was a huge pie — shades of Jim Fisk and the revelers of the Gilded Age! — and out of it popped the sixteen-year-old Susie Johnson. Simmons said she was "draped from head to foot in black, with a stuffed blackbird on her head."

There was so much newspaper hullabaloo about the episode, Simmons said, that "we were forced to break up our club." Hearst's pseudo-moralistic *American* claimed that Susie's life was ruined by the affair. "She later married but her husband threw her off because he heard of the 'Pie Dinner.' She is buried in Potter's Field." The *American* charged that there were many men about town who kept studios "not for the pursuit of art but for the pursuit of sin and the ruin of human souls."

From such relatively innocent affairs — no matter with what pious horror they were viewed by Hearst's editorial writers — Stanford White turned to the madder wine, wilder music and later hours of Broadway and Longacre (later Times) Square. This happened about ten years before his death, when he was in his early forties. He loved the theater and its people, was as fascinated by the feverish glow of the lights of Broadway as any gaping peasant from the corn belt. In particular, he was fascinated by the young girls of the theater, the adolescent charmers who filled out the chorus lines and played the French maids and other walk-ons. His manner toward these painted children was indulgent, semi-paternal, and perhaps a little too adoring. He sent them flowers and candy, paid their hospital bills, gave them money when they were between jobs, dined and wined them. He may or may not have been looking for his Lolita, he may or may not have been conscious of certain urges which he apparently sublimated as a worship of beauty in any form. The years he spent as the Number one sugar daddy of the Great White Way were so obscured by the smoke from Harry Thaw's pistol and all the gossip and rumor that spiraled up to the skyline after it that it is difficult to learn just how much overt or covert sexuality played its part in his activities as a patron of the theater. Still, it is straining credulity to believe that a wealthy, intelligent, middle-aged man spent so much of his time pursuing and patronizing young actresses, dancers and singers merely to afford himself the opportunity of listening to their endless prattle about backstage feuds.

In any case, White's theatrical interests were largely confined to the musical comedies. He knew all the show tunes and delighted in whistling them. Royal Cortissoz, once his office boy and later a prominent art critic, provided a rather touching picture of him as an inveterate whistler who could convey "the very genius of the music." Sometimes, Cortissoz recalled, "whistling would fail him, and, as though in despair of expressing all he felt, he would burst into a kind of song. It was as though beauty possessed him. Beauty did possess him."

The theatrical world must have been a fascinating place then with such shining names as Maude Adams, David Warfield, William Gillette, Eddie Foy, James O'Neill, Nat Goodwin, DeWolf Hopper, Fritzi Scheff, Sarah Bernhardt, Mrs. Fiske, Anna Held, Blanche Ring, the Drews and the Barrymores on the marquees and three-sheets. Undoubtedly the restless and ebullient White felt a stronger attraction from it than the stuffier social world east of Fifth Avenue inhabited by his family and his older friends. He honored the values of that more secure world, but the febrile excitement of Broadway called to him irresistibly after dark. "He constituted himself a bridge over the gap between the social world of Fifth Avenue and the social world of Broadway," wrote Frederick L. Collins (*Glamorous Sinners*); "and, although, like the famous Bridge of San Luis Rey, he ultimately fell, he managed during his lifetime to achieve something very like a community of interest between the drawing room and the green room."

Some time in the fall of 1901, when George Lederer opened his production of the musical comedy *The Wild Rose*, White was struck by the charms of a seventeen-year-old girl dancing in its chorus. It was simple for him to arrange a meeting with the lovely creature; and close up, with the stage makeup off, she was even more stunning than she appeared behind the footlights; she was appealing, demure, and in her face there was an odd, alluring combination of the virginal and the wanton. She inspired strong emotions in White, and in every man who laid eyes on her, and it was not long before he had assumed the role of her guide, patron, philosopher and protector.

Her name was Evelyn Nesbit.

Two years earlier her mother had brought her and her brother Howard to New York, where, like any good, determined stage mother, she hoped that her beautiful child would win fame and a wealthy husband, Mrs. Nesbit later became the wife of Charles J. Holman, a Pittsburgh real estate man, but at the moment the fifteen-year-old Evelyn was the sole support of her widowed mother and her brother. The stage mother has achieved a notoriety in theatrical annals second only to the fly-by-night producer who stranded his company out of town, and it must be said of Mrs. Nesbit–Holman that she played the role to the hilt. Evelyn was her mother's gold mine and she was worked right down to the tailings. Without the aggressive Mother Nesbit, there would have been no Stanford White murder case.

At first the Nesbits found it hard going in New York. Artists and producers were willing to concede that Mrs. Nesbit had a fine piece of merchandise in her daughter, but the child was simply too young to be exploited in full view of the public. The Gerry Society's agents were diligent about ferreting out underage girls employed in the theater, even though nontheatrical children were freely employed in sweatshops throughout the city. Mrs. Nesbit was advised to wait a year or two until Evelyn had blossomed out a little more.

Unwilling to face the alternative that she herself go to work and support her children, the Widow Nesbit grimly trotted Evelyn around the casting offices.

A producer named Fisher looked the girl over and snorted: "Madam, I'm not running a baby farm."

Some months passed before the lovely child was given work posing for calendar artists and magazine illustrators. Soon she was earning, as she later recalled, seventeen dollars and eighteen dollars a week, not bad in a day when candy-dippers earned only a third of that for long hours of labor. And soon her perfectly regular features and her delicately voluptuous form were appearing on "art" calendars and billboards. Charles Dana Gibson, Archie Gunn and James Montgomery Flagg captured her likeness for magazine illustrations. The producers of *Floradora* took one look at her and engaged her as a member of the Sextette which became so quickly famous. (For all the money they attracted at the box office, the members of that ensemble were paid only fifteen dollars a week.) In the studios along Fifty-seventh Street she was known as "the most beautiful artist's model in America," and one illustrator contended that she had "the most perfectly modeled foot since Venus." He must have been the only man in New York whose infatuation stopped at the instep.

A brunette with large hazel eyes, she represented the more delicate type of beauty which succeeded the fleshy blondes of the Lillian Russell period.

To Irvin S. Cobb she was "the most exquisitely lovely human being I ever looked at — the slim, quick grace of a fawn, a head that sat on her flawless throat as a lily on its stem, eyes that were the color of blue-brown pansies and the size of half dollars; a mouth made of rumpled rose petals."

Surviving sketches and photographs of her confirm every smitten word of Mr. Cobb's forget-me-not prose.

By the time Evelyn was recruited for the chorus of *The Wild Rose*, whose producer George Lederer was still another victim of her charms (according to his wife's divorce suit), her career on and offstage was the talk of Broadway and the Tenderloin. One glance from those huge pansy-like eyes and men were willing to forget wife, home and mother. She was, as a newspaper paragrapher said, "the gorgeous butterfly of Stageland, the toast and admiration of the gallants and gilded youth of the city."

And furthermore she had the sharp-eyed Mother Nesbit to weed out the men who lacked the substance to do right by My Little Girl, such as fellow actors, Wall Street runners posing as wealthy brokers, and the like. Under this sort of tutelage, she perceptibly hardened; Mother had finally impressed upon her the necessity of keeping her eye on the main chance, and she had come to understand the realistic philosophy of the chorus girls' dressing room that it was just as easy to fall in love with a man who owned a steam yacht as one who boasted about his tandem bicycle. Robert Dunn, a reporter for the *Commercial Advertiser*, who met Evelyn at a party at Shanley's lobster palace, thought her beauty "surprising but lifeless" as calculation began to replace girlish innocence.

Of the three men who came into her life while she was still in her teens — the three who figured most importantly in her emotional life — young Jack Barrymore was the first to make her acquaintance, followed shortly by White and then Thaw. On Mrs. Nesbit's scale of values Barrymore had nothing to offer but the celebrity of his family's name. White ranked high because he was sending Evelyn a twenty-five-dollar check every week she wasn't working in the theater, but he was married. Thaw was wealthy and single; he behaved like a bashi-bazouk half the time, was reputed to be a drug addict and a sexual weirdo, but he was eminently eligible.

Most people would have agreed with Mrs. Nesbit about Jack Barrymore's prospects at the time he met Evelyn. He was then nineteen, two years older than she. In the considered opinion of his family and elders, the youth showed every promise of being a bum. Beautifully gaunt, weedily handsome, Barrymore had decided that acting, the family curse, as he viewed it, would not get him, although his brother Lionel and his sister Ethel had already succumbed to their fate.

He attended classes at the Art Students League and developed a respectable talent for drawing, but it was the newspaper business — or rather, its practitioners and their reckless way of life in the saloons of Park Row and the Bowery — which attracted him. His best friend and drinking companion was the legendary Frank Butler, a huge and hard living reporter for the *Daily News,* whose senatorial manner and rumpled tailoring reminded one colleague of "a dropsical eagle that had spent the night in a coal bin." Young Barrymore managed to combine art with journalism by obtaining a job with the *Morning Telegraph* as a sketch artist. Thanks to Editor Arthur Brisbane's admiration for his sister, Jack then moved downtown to Hearst's *Journal* and a better job. Brisbane, despite his discovery that Barrymore couldn't draw the human foot and generally depicted his subjects standing ankle-deep in grass, assigned him to illustrating editorials, drawing the borders for Ella Wheeler Wilcox's weekly poems and sketching courtroom scenes. Afterwards, Barrymore looked back on his brief career on Park Row as the happiest and most carefree days of his life. He and Butler spent every dime of their meager salaries on liquor, ate off free-lunch counters and slept on their friend's floors.

It was just before Brisbane fired him from the *Journal,* and just after *The Wild Rose* opened with Evelyn Nesbit in its chorus, that Jack met the sloe-eyed charmer. They fell madly in love — madly, that is, because Barrymore couldn't have supported an alley cat, let alone a girl who was beginning to believe that she deserved the best of everything. Mrs. Nesbit was outraged. No boozing, penniless newspaperman, she announced, was going to marry her Evelyn. Jack Barrymore, she added, would never amount to anything. Evelyn would soon recover her senses and send him packing.

For once Evelyn defied her mother. Jack wanted to marry her, and she wanted to marry him.

Jack continued to live the Bohemian life of those who "slept under the sun and lived beneath the moon," largely on his family's impeccable credit rating. He moved into the Algonquin, whose proprietor, Frank Case, was a friend of the family and extended him the right to sign for his room, drinks and meals. It was understood that young Mr. Barrymore would take up an acting career as soon as a suitable vehicle could be found for his embryonic talents.

Already a master of the lordly gesture, he entertained Evelyn frequently on the Algonquin's highly elastic credit, despite proprietor Case's growing nervousness over the tab Barrymore was running up. Once he and Evelyn were feeding expensively in the Algonquin's dining room when Case made his hourly patrol, gloomily noting that most of the diners, like Barrymore, were on the cuff. Case sidled over to Barrymore's table and whispered into Jack's ear, "Couldn't you have ordered something less costly than hearts of artichoke?"

Barrymore threw down his napkin and jumped to his feet, sputtering, "By God, we'll go to a restaurant that doesn't insult its guests." He hastened to his room, packed his belongings and moved out, with Evelyn on his arm but without pausing to pay his sizable bill. Then he summoned a cab. The pair drove around midtown Manhattan for hours trying to find a hotel which would accommodate him. Jack had forgotten there was a political convention which absorbed all the room space north of the Bowery. Close to midnight they returned to the Algonquin, only slightly crestfallen, and Barrymore moved back in. He signed Case's name to a requisition for enough cash to pay off the cabbie.

Despite such misadventures, Evelyn was determined to marry him. They were seen together so much, and in such intimate circumstances, that their friends on Park Row and Broadway assumed they were secretly married — or ought to be.

The Nesbit–Barrymore idyll was described in one newspaper's theatrical section (the *Herald*) as "joy and sunshine for three months of devoted camaraderie." The account continued:

Gay and joyous with the freshness of youth, Evelyn Nesbit danced and sang her way into the hearts of all, but she showed preference to none until Jack Barrymore paid sudden and tempestuous court.

Like two happy children, the after-theater Broadway began to see them with eyes for none others in the fashionable restaurants. Nightly he waited for her at the stage door, whence she would emerge with a huge bouquet of violets as her corsage, the tribute of her admirer. In the afternoons they would drive or walk through the Park. They found each other congenial and all else dross . . .

Largely through the stage-managing of Mrs. Nesbit, however, Evelyn began to see less of Barrymore and more of White — even after, as Evelyn was to testify, the architect plied her with drugged champagne and had his way with her. During the following year, 1902, a new suitor entered the lists, not at all handicapped by his well-deserved nickname of "Mad Harry."

Harry Kendall Thaw, then thirty-one years old, was an heir to an estate estimated to total forty millions. Physically he was anything but prepossessing, with a round puffy face, blank staring eyes and a rather idiotic grin. Friendship had always been something he had to buy with drinks or money. Even the thirstiest bar flies could barely tolerate his company. "Thaw's peeled-turnip face held stupid, glaring eyes," as Robert Dunn remembered him from barroom encounters, "and he had a touchy bluster that stemmed from frustrated snobbery."

Withal he was overwhelmingly conceited, and would announce himself grandly, "I am Harry Thaw of Pittsburgh," as though expecting a blare of trumpets and a bowing of heads.

Even in 1902 he was no stranger to the headlines, for he delighted in any kind of escapade that would attract attention. He preened himself on being pointed out as the man who rode a cab horse pell-mell down Broadway, who rode another horse up the steps of the Union League Club, who lighted his cigarettes with five-dollar bills, who gave a dinner for a hundred actresses and chorus girls which was said to have cost $400 a plate. Once he assaulted a police officer in the Tenderloin, and was soundly thrashed before anyone could inform the cop that he was operating on a Pittsburgh millionaire.

In those days the Pittsburgh millionaire was as ubiquitous, free-spending and uninhibited as the standard Texas oilman is today. Encumbered with inherited millions from coal, iron, steel and railroading, they roamed the pleasure spots of the world, spent money wildly and lived it up like latterday Romans with the Goths at the city gates. Their antics in Montmartre and the Tenderloin wrote a new chapter in the history of human folly.

Just after Andrew Carnegie sold out to J. P. Morgan and U.S. Steel for almost half a billion dollars, making thirty Carnegie princelings millionaires overnight, Pittsburgh was the parvenu capital of the world. In that city's Duquesne Club, new members had to be instructed not to tuck their napkins under their chins. A steward observed one new member covering sheets of club stationery with figures and explaining, "I'm trying to figure out whether I'm worth six million or eight million." Architectural nightmares were were erected on Sewickley Heights. One new millionaire engaged genealogists to trace his lineage back to Geoffrey Plantagenet, and another had his crest engraved on his cigar bands. Some of their parties turned into Neronian routs. One expansive host took six floors of a downtown hotel for a wingding, and when eight hundred guests showed up the brawl overflowed to the Pittsburgh Natatorium, where many drunkenly disrobed and frolicked in the nude, men and women alike. But one of Carnegie's overlords outdid them all by buying four gold-plated pianos, and kept them guarded behind gates so massive they had to be rolled back on wheels.

Newspapers of other cities, with some reason, began comparing Pittsburgh with one or another of the old Biblical hellholes. The very name Pittsburgh, it was observed, was "anathema in thousands of American homes."

Around the time of the Stanford White murder, Harry Thaw

was merely one of many Pittsburghers who were scandalizing the nation. Augustus Hartje ($6,000,000) was suing his wife for divorce, naming their coachman as correspondent; Lawrence Phipps ($10,000,000) had divorced his wife, kidnaped their children and remarried a former wife; W. E. Corey ($10,000,000) was divorcing his wife to marry New York actress Mabel Gilman; James K. Clarke ($4,000,000) quit his bride of three days in a flurry of nasty accusations, and J. Alston Moorhead ($3,000,000) married his mother's French maid.

Socially speaking, the Thaws were entitled to look down their noses at these new millionaires. The first Thaw had moved to Pittsburgh from Philadelphia in 1804. Harry Thaw's father, William, was largely a self-made man but no illiterate, ham-fisted puddler from an up-valley ironworks. At sixteen, he had traveled up and down the Ohio Valley making collections for the Bank of the United States; later he pioneered in railroading and other forms of transportation and became a vice president of the Pennsylvania Railroad, and before his death in 1889 had multiplied his millions through investments in coal and iron.

William Thaw had married twice and sired ten children, five by each of his wives. His second wife, Mary Copley, was Harry's mother. She had married the elder Thaw when he was fifty and she was in her twenties, and from all the evidence she was one of the most headstrong and foolishly indulgent mothers who ever lived. In any contest for worst mother of the century, Mrs. Thaw would have run a close race with her fellow Pittsburgher, Mrs. Nesbit.

Harry's father died when he was only eighteen, but the boy had already given such unmistakable indications of imbalance that the father stated in his will that "with great regret and reluctance and solely from a sense of duty, I hereby cancel and revoke any and all provisions of my said will directing payment of money or property to my said son, Harry Kendall Thaw." He directed that Harry was to be paid "for and during his natural life, the sum of $2,400 per annum, in monthly payments." Disregarding the wishes of her late husband, Mrs. Thaw saw to it that Harry had all the money he needed to complete the ruin of an already troubled life. Only the vagaries of mother love could account for Mrs. Thaw's doting defense of all of Harry's actions, her blindness to their consequences and her stubbornly held belief that the young man was merely sowing a wild oat or two while he showed every sign of a psychopathic personality. She was so proud of her family, it seemed, that she refused to believe that any offshoot could go wrong; hadn't one of her daughters married George L. Carnegie and wasn't another the Countess of Yarmouth? What anguish it must have caused Mrs. Thaw when lawyers for her son's defense stated in open court that Harry came of "tainted stock" and that there had been "insanity on both sides of the family" can only be imagined.

Almost from birth, Harry had been a problem child. In those days scientific exploration of the human psyche had barely begun; there were no psychiatrists or psychoanalysts as such, and the men who testified as experts on insanity were known as alienists, who usually doubled as keepers of asylums, but it was apparent even to family doctors, tutors and others who observed Harry as a child that he was abnormal.

He was subject to frequent tantrums, and even as an infant often went sleepless. A tutor testified at a subsequent sanity hearing that "He was excessively nervous . . . was frequently subject to outbursts of uncurbed animal passion . . . had St. Vitus Dance and used baby language as late as seven . . ." No one except his exasperated father, occasionally, tried to discipline him.

Signs of mental aberration only increased during his youth. Charles Koehler, an instructor at Wooster University, where Harry was sent at the age of sixteen, recalled that he often "walked in a zig-zag manner . . . his capacity for concentration was weak . . . frequently asked irrelevant questions." A butler employed by the Thaws said Harry frequently amused himself by "pulling the cloth off the breakfast table and booting the food into the fireplace." At least once, during a European tour early in his youth, he was committed to a private sanitarium following a suicide attempt. He was admitted to Harvard but expelled in short order for "immoral practices," the nature of which were unspecified. Even when he was well into his twenties, his mother said, he would weep bitterly for no apparent reason, would "settle into gloom and absent-mindedness."

To the madams of the Tenderloin, particularly those specializing in a clientele with unorthodox tastes, Harry was one of those "Pittsburgh queers" who had picked up strange ideas in the bordellos of Paris. Susie Merrill, the keeper of a house of assignation, later testified that Thaw rented rooms from her under the name of "Professor Reid." She said:

"He advertised for young girls to train for the stage — ages fifteen to seventeen. He had two whips, one like a riding whip, the other like for a dog. On one occasion, I heard a young girl's screams. Then I saw her partly undressed, neck and limbs covered with welts. I found others writhing from punishment."

Mrs. Merrill estimated that Thaw paid out $40,000 to two hundred and thirty-three girls he lured to her establishment for "stage training," with one of them, a Mrs. Reid, receiving seven hundred dollars for her lessons.

In later life, too, Thaw gave plentiful evidence of sadistic tendencies. Dr. John Holland Cassity, presently chief psychiatrist at Bellevue Hospital in New York, believes that Thaw considered himself "chosen to be a protector of girls being ravished by perverts . . . Thaw's delusion was nature's method of assuaging his unconscious guilt," a delusion that led him to kill White, over his own vicious and perverted approach to sex. Dr. Cassity, in his study of the records of the Thaw trials, concluded that Harry was incurably insane, or, as he puts it, "His type of per-

sonality disorder does not respond to any presently known psy-
chotherapeutic treatment."*

Obviously, if the young man's mother had seen her son as
clearly and unsentimentally as his late father, Harry Thaw would
not have been loosed on the world with all the money he needed
to carry out the fantasies of a sick mind.

3

AT THE OUTSET District Attorney Jerome seriously underestimated
the implications of the case. Perhaps this was because he was
not fully informed of all its circumstances; he was on vacation,
and whatever he knew of the background to Stanford White's
murder came from the newspapers and hurried telephone calls
to his office in New York, where Acting District Attorney Nott
and one of his ablest assistants, Francis P. Garvan, were in charge
of the investigation.

His initial attitude toward the case, one of studied disinterest,
may also have been conditioned by the facts of his private life.
He was in love with a woman twenty years younger than himself, and to the uninformed observer it might have seemed that
there was a suspicious parallel between his extra-marital life and
that of the murder victim — not that Jerome himself would have
considered that there was any comparison between his still tenta-
tive romance with Mrs. Elliot and White's notorious explora-
tions of the primrose path. His enemies, journalistic and otherwise, would have been delighted to expose his interest in Mrs.
Elliot and elaborate on that parallel. Colonel Mann, in particular,
would have known how to exploit even a few shreds of gossip
on this subject in *Town Topics*.

If his affair with Mrs. Elliot came to public attention, it would
certainly have aroused widespread suspicions that he was not
entirely objective in his conduct of the prosecution, coupled with
the fact that White was an acquaintance of his, both belonged to

* In his *The Quality of Murder*, New York, 1958.

the same clubs and social circles, and had many mutual friends. Without that private factor in his consideration of the case, it would be difficult to regard his first comments as anything but obtuse.

Reporters caught up with him in Atlanta several days after the murder, and one of them asked if he considered the case any more important than any other homicide.

"Important?" he was quoted as saying. "Why? What is there important about one man killing another for jealousy? It happens nearly every day in the week. In this case the defendant happens to have money; but, in the eyes of the law, that does not add luster to his situation.

"The romance is a product of the newspapers. As you know, the witnesses so far — most of them — have not been gifted with reticence. These women love to talk. Miss Doris So-and-so, or Miss Irene Such-and-such, will come down to the office and tell Mr. Garvan or another of my assistants what she purports to know. But the matter doesn't end there. Just outside the office there will be a newspaperman lying in wait. He takes Miss Doris or Miss Irene in charge, and carries her off to some café. Then comes a bottle of wine. Over the wine they talk. Naturally what the young lady has to say becomes somewhat embellished. Yet when finally it gets into print it appears somehow to come from the district attorney's office. Miss Doris and Miss Irene have — so the reader supposed — testified to such and such to Mr. Garvan or myself. And there you are. It's a great game. But important? Why, it's just an everyday police court story."

Hardly anyone else could see anything "everyday" about the case. No murder in American history attracted more attention. For one thing it happened at a time when people were just beginning to suspect that the upper classes were upheld, not by any superior morality, but simply by their money; it was the time of the insurance scandals and President Roosevelt's war on the trusts, when the happy old nineteenth century assumption that

wealth was conferred by God on those who deserved it was being destroyed forever. The moral superiority of the rich had
been unquestioned until various investigations revealed many of
them to be common cheats on an uncommon scale; then the
record of the Thaw trials, every grimy detail of which was spread
out in the newspapers from coast to coast, showed their private
lives to be as disorderly as the Jukeses' and Kallikaks'. Never have
so many skeletons tumbled out of so many closets in public view.
As Irvin S. Cobb has pointed out, the story had everything,
"wealth, degeneracy, rich old wasters; delectable young chorus
girls and adolescent artists' models; the behind-the-scenes of
Theaterdom and the Underworld, and the Great White Way, as
we called it then; the abnormal pastimes and weird orgies of
over-aesthetic artists and jaded debauchees. In the cast of the
motley show were Bowery toughs, Harlem gangsters, Tenderloin panders, Broadway leading men, Fifth Avenue clubmen,
Wall Street manipulators, uptown voluptuaries and downtown
thugs — a bedaubed, bespangled Bacchanalia . . ." And the whole
country was yearning to learn just what went on in wicked New
York among the rich and beautiful and famous.

From the beginning the character of Stanford White was besmirched beyond recognition. He was pictured, particularly in
the more sensational papers, led by Hearst's *Journal* and *American*,
as a monster of depravity, and Bennett's *Herald* was not far behind after its absentee publisher cabled his editors from Paris:
"Give him [White] hell."

No one paid much heed, certainly not the newspaper editors
with their circulation figures leaping by the hundreds of thousands, when Assistant District Attorney Garvan cautioned that
"It is ridiculously easy to besmirch the character of a dead man
who cannot reply or institute a suit for libel."

Instead the newspapers splashed all over their front pages the
dubious recollections of a Broadway butterfly named Katherine
Poillon, who was all too willing to tell of "scenes that took place

on board a certain yacht owned by one of White's intimate friends, which baffle description . . . The scenes that I witnessed on the boat that night will forever remain in my memory . . . The nest of moral lepers who to my knowledge have infested upper Broadway for years cannot be too soon wiped out."

The outpouring of denunciation and innuendo on White was almost incredible. "Why," demanded the New York *American*, "did Stanford White need the finest studio in New York in the Madison Square Tower? He did not paint or make sculpture. He was an architect, whose work consisted principally in getting orders from rich men and in copying European buildings . . . If he ever needed to draw an architectural plan he had unlimited room in a big office, and he also had a great house of his own only three blocks away from Madison Square Garden. He needed the studio for the purposes that have been so abundantly revealed in the disclosures following his tragic end." The New York *Tribune*, a much more conservative journal, reported that "along Broadway there were but few expressions of regret for White's death. In the vernacular of Broadway 'Stanford White only got what was coming to him.' Many unsavory stories concerning him were recounted. Even Tenderloin cabmen spoke harshly of his reputation. One of them said to a *Tribune* reporter: 'I knew that fellow would be killed sooner or later, but I thought it would be a father who would do it, not a husband.' " Just how much a man who drove a hack in the Tenderloin could possibly know of White's private life was not explained.

Day after day the newspapers kept the story on their front pages, pounding away at the popular theme of "moral lepers in high places," while the thundering from pulpits across the land grew positively deafening.

Of all the personal and professional friendships he had formed — and friendship was practically a religion with White — only one prominent person publicly defended him.

That friend was Richard Harding Davis, war correspondent, novelist and apostle of clean living, who condemned (in an article in *Collier's*, August 8, 1906) the tactics of the "yellow press" in presenting an image of White that was "hideous" and "misshapen," in launching an attack on the dead man that "left those who were supposed to be his friends stunned and silent." He continued:

Since his death White has been described as a satyr. To answer this by saying that he was a great architect is not to answer it at all. He was an architect. But what is more important is that he was a most kindhearted, most considerate, gentle and manly man, who could no more have done the things attributed to him than he could have roasted a baby on a spit. Big in mind and body, he was incapable of little meannesses. He admired a beautiful woman as he admired every other beautiful thing that God has given us: and his delight over one was as keen, as boyish, as grateful as over any of the others. Described as a voluptuary, his greatest pleasure was to stand all day waist-deep in the rapids of a Canadian river and fight it out with the salman . . ."

For the truth about White's relations with the young females he admired Davis recommended a reading of the remarks of a girl who danced in the chorus of *Mamzelle Champagne*, who said, "Most chorus girls considered it a great feather in their caps to be seen with Stanford White or his associates. He was generous to an extreme. If he had a pet in a show she could entertain the entire company at his expense. He paid doctors' bills for chorus girls he never saw; he paid hundreds of dollars for cabs for girls and their friends. Temptations? Nonsense! They are hunting for such temptations. Chorus girls run no more risk of being led astray than girls in any other walk of life."

Until he dared to defend White, Davis was regarded as a sort of Sir Galahad of the literary world. The reaction to his article was all the more explosive for that. A New Jersey librarian gathered all his books from the shelf, marched ouside and dumped them in the gutter. The headmaster of a prep school warned his charges not to read the "foul emanations of a depraved romancer," meaning Davis.

The Nation, too, was courageous enough to suggest that the truth about White's private life had not been, and probably never would be developed this side of the Judgment Seat, but was critical of the way he had wasted his talents in catering to his wealthy patrons: "He seems to have been in a large degree the victim of the society which he sought above all else to please, to which he was the titular arbiter of taste."

Only a few weeks before everyone was praising him as "the modern Benvenuto Cellini" but, as one old friend wrote, "now that his life has ended in a shocking tragedy, America seems likely (if not eager) to forget the debt we all owe him."

Solely on the charges of an obviously unbalanced young man seeking to justify himself and escape the electric chair, carried along by a tidal wave of sentimentality and near-hysteria, public opinion was all but unanimous in condemning not the murderer but his victim. It went along wholeheartedly with Thaw's claim that he had invoked the "unwritten law" in defense of his wife's honor, and was not at all influenced by the occasional voices of reason which pointed out that Thaw had avenged himself for an alleged offense against his wife which had occurred months before the Pittsburgh heir even met her. Behind all this there was a certain amount of manipulation. Irvin S. Cobb, covering the story for the *World*, observed that money was "poured out by the Thaw family, and sucked up, like water in a sand bed."

People in general were convinced that the Thaws were a couple of naïve kids menaced by a suave and insistent seducer intent on wrecking their home.

Indications to the contrary, such as those published in the studiedly impartial New York *Times*, were brushed aside, yet they gave a considerable amount of insight into the kind of people Harry and Evelyn Thaw really were.

Item: In October of 1904, when they returned from a pre-honeymoon trip to Europe, they were thrown out of the Cumberland Hotel for "refusing to register as man and wife."

Item: A girl named Ethel Thomas filed suit against Thaw for $30,000 charging that, as "Professor Reid," he had whipped her.

Item: Evelyn's mother, now Mrs. Charles J. Holman, announced in Pittsburgh that she had collected ten shirtwaists which Thaw had ripped from her daughter's body at various times in sadistic paroxysms. To each shirtwaist, she said, was affixed the date of the incident. It was quite clear that Thaw had not lived up to her expectations of what a wealthy son-in-law should do.

Item: It was revealed that George Lederer, producer of *The Wild Rose*, was divorced by his wife Adele on charges of misbehaving himself with Evelyn Nesbit in various New York hotels between October 1, 1902 and March 25, 1903 . . . two years before her marriage. (When reporters interviewed Lederer shortly after the White murder, the producer characterized Thaw as a "cigarette fiend" — a pretty serious charge in those days — who "always seemed half-crazed.")

Item: When she was only seventeen, in the summer of 1901, before she met Barrymore, White or Thaw, she went yachting with a married man, James A. Garland, who was subsequently divorced by his wife.

Item: Friends of the Thaw family in Pittsburgh recalled that Mrs. Thaw was so opposed to her son's marrying Evelyn Nesbit that she threatened to cut off his $80,000 a year allowance.

None of these revelations, however, could prevail against the tides of treacle loosed by the sob sisters, to whom Evelyn was "that Angel Child." There were no protests when it was disclosed that Thaw, in his cell in the Tombs, was having his meals sent in from Delmonico's and that the kindly prison doctor had been persuaded to prescribe a bottle of champagne daily for the prisoner for "medical reasons." Every time his "widowed mother" and his "faithful wife" visited him in the Tombs the occasions were described in threnodic prose.

By now Thaw, it was reported, considered himself a hero. Evelyn later said that the shadow of the electric chair impressed him less than "the sudden fame which had come to him." And for once Thaw's opinion of himself and that of a formerly scornful and hostile world coincided: he was indeed a hero.

One of the few newspapers in the world to see the case in all its pathetic and ludicrous aspects was *La Vita* of Rome, which observed that "justice is equally as great in comedy in America as it is in Italy," and added in a fine display of acidulous common sense:

Indeed with all the public stir this case is causing in the fantasy of the star-striped race we seem to be transported into one of our own turreted towns amidst the babble of our fellow citizens. Nor shall we be astounded if Roosevelt instead of sending a message to Congress apropos the cause, should dash off a magazine article on the subject in the best Presidential prose, or if Mrs. Alice Roosevelt Longworth proceed amidst queenly honors to the assize court to grace the debates, which instead of centering on the crime and the criminal or the problem of responsibility, will likely enough seek to discuss whether the victim did not really provoke his aggressor to madness.*

La Vita came perilously close to the mark in its sardonic essay.

4

ONE OF THE fondest illusions concerning the Anglo-American system of trial by jury, and undoubtedly a necessary one, is that it is quite possible to impanel twelve good men and true, and free of prejudice about the case they are trying. This, of course, is impossible in many cases. Almost any juror selected to a case which has attracted considerable attention is prejudiced by what he has read and heard. In many instances twelve deaf and illiterate hermits might be the only unprejudiced jury that could be placed in the box.

This was especially true of the Thaw case, coated as it was

* Quoted in Frederick Collins' *Glamorous Sinners*.

with so many layers of sentiment by professional or self-appointed commentators.

It stirred deep currents in this country, prodded awake that "ape behind the mask" who has lumbered on the scenes of lynchings, witch-burnings, riots and other rebellions against reason. It aroused all the latent American suspicion of the intellectual, the artist, the noncomformer.

This deep-seated expression of inferiority was knowingly catered to by the press, perhaps unwittingly by the pulpit, unthinkingly by the professional moralists.

A climate of unreason was created which made it impossible for Harry K. Thaw to have been impartially tried by his peers anywhere in the United States.

5

IF REASON HAD prevailed even closer to the heart of the case, Harry K. Thaw would have been disposed of with a few brisk formalities, the state would have been saved the expense of two trials and the public would have been spared such a washing of dirty linen as could be found only in the casebooks of Krafft–Ebing. Everyone connected with the case knew that Thaw was insane — everyone but Thaw and his doting mother. Most members of the coroner's jury which heard the first evidence presented on the case considered him irrational.

His mother, on the advice of the family attorney, engaged Judge William M. K. Olcott as the first of many criminal lawyers brought in to defend her son. It was Olcott and his aides who so skillfully succeeded in presenting Thaw to the public as a "crusader" who slew a lecherous monster threatening his home. Olcott, however, soon realized that his client was not mentally fit to stand trial.

He sent a leading expert on mental diseases, Dr. Allen McLane Hamilton, to examine Thaw in the Tombs. Dr. Hamilton reported that, medically and legally, Thaw was insane.

District Attorney Jerome was of the same opinion, and sought to have his own experts examine Thaw. But Thaw refused to see them, and without his cooperation nothing could be done.

Even so, a lunacy commission could have been appointed to decide the case; Thaw could have been committed to the Matteawan state hospital for the criminally insane; his victim's memory could have been spared the additional besmirching essential to a defense bent on proving that he deserved to be killed. It would obviously have been better all around, even from Thaw's standpoint, had he been capable of reasoning; for his lawyers were convinced that eventually the only way they could save him from the electric chair would be to plead insanity.

To this sensible disposition of the case, however, there were two stumbling blocks. Thaw himself was enjoying the role of hero, a pose that would have been ruined by any admission that he was insane. And Mrs. Thaw, with her immense family pride, hoped against hope that Harry could be freed, that she and all the other members of her family would not be tarred by the brush that depicted her son as a hopeless lunatic.

A revealing glimpse of Mrs. Thaw's lofty estimate of her social position, undiminished by the maternal anguish she must have been enduring, was provided by her daughter-in-law. Evelyn Nesbit Thaw, in her otherwise opaque memoir *The Story of My Life*, told of an incident that occurred during one of their visits to the Tombs. Their automobile was halted by a traffic jam and Evelyn exchanged pleasantries with a policeman on duty at the intersection. Out of the corner of her eye Evelyn noticed that Mrs. Thaw was "sitting with frigid face and stiff back in the corner of the automobile." She quoted her mother-in-law as saying, "Evelyn, how can you speak with these people? Don't you realize the social position you hold?"

Evelyn, wondering exactly what was the social position of a murderer's wife, recalled that she asked Mrs. Thaw, "What kind of story do you imagine it would make if I turned up my nose at men whose social position is, at the moment, infinitely superior to Harry's?"

Already Evelyn was beginning to rebel at her assigned role of the wronged wife — wronged, that is, by White — but she was being given a "handsome" allowance by Thaw's mother, according to the newspapers, to insure that she would behave and eventually testify in such a manner as to "get Harry off."

The elder Mrs. Thaw, in any case, allowed herself to be persuaded by Harry that Judge Olcott, Dr. Hamilton and everyone else was wrong. Both the Thaws were determined to base the defense only on a plea of "temporary" insanity, which, if the jury were sufficiently impressed by it, would allow Harry to go free.

With his mother's approval and support Harry therefore dismissed the capable Judge Olcott and replaced him with relays of other legal advisers. There would be no lunacy commission to decide Harry's fate with whatever cold logic and scientific evidence it could muster for the task. Harry would rely upon the more malleable motions of a jury.

And so that tragedy, of which Harry Thaw was as much a victim as the man he slew, was needlessly and foolishly prolonged . . . extended not only through two laborious trials but almost a score of subsequent legal actions, including sanity hearings, attempts to obtain writs of habeas corpus and appeals to higher courts. The Thaw case, in fact, was to be dragged out for nine exhausting years.

8

A Crime of Many Passions (II)

> Apparently there is a higher law in
> hiding behind a woman's petticoats.
> — William Travers Jerome.

IN PREPARATION for the Thaw trial, District Attorney Jerome
put himself through a cram course in abnormal psychology
that enabled him to debate with the experts, real and self-
proclaimed, on their own ground. He spent six months reading
every available authority on mental diseases, especially those
dealing with paranoia, and all the legal precedents bearing on the
case. Later, several of the experts agreed that Jerome knew as
much about their subject as they did. He had already taken a
private oath that Thaw would be placed where he could do no
more harm, to himself or anyone else.

The odds, as everyone knew, were against him. The Thaw
millions, and all the legal and medical talent they could buy,
were arrayed in opposition. Public opinion, which for some years
had supported him unfailingly and sympathetically, now was
ranged against him. Not Harry K. Thaw but Stanford White
would be on trial, and it would take the most skillful maneuvering
to refocus guilt and responsibility where it belonged. Worst of
all, he had to contend with the widespread belief that there was
such a legally recognizable thing as an unwritten law which per-

mitted a man to start shooting whenever he considered the sanctity of his home endangered.

Ill-chosen though the field, this was where Jerome intended to stake his prestige and his career, in the determination to prove the cynics were wrong when they said any millionaire could escape the consequences of his crime, to undergo his first major test as a prosecutor, to uphold the dignity of the State in what was certain to be an extravaganza and to guarantee that, one way or another, society would be protected from Harry Thaw.

In his preparations, Jerome's task was complicated by the fact that he had to contrive a sort of two-way, all-purpose case against the defendant. Under New York law it was not necessary for Thaw's lawyers specifically to enter a plea of not guilty by reason of insanity; that possible defense was included under a general not-guilty plea. Jerome, as Arthur Train said, had to prepare to prosecute the case "not only upon its merits, but upon the possible question of the criminal irresponsibility of the defendant."

But the greatest complication facing the district attorney was public opinion as it reflected itself in the minds of the talesmen summoned to qualify for the jury. There was nothing Jerome could do to persuade the public that it was being flimflammed in accepting Thaw's concept of himself as a hero and White as a monster. White's rich and famous (and cowardly) friends, Richard Harding Davis and one or two others excepted, had betrayed the slain man by their silence; none had attended his funeral, and almost without exception, since his death, they had refused to be interviewed on the subject of White or his private life. The inference everyone drew from this was that they feared they would be accused of sharing White's proclivities, the unwholesomeness of which no one but Davis had attempted to deny.

For all Jerome knew, or could ever know, the case had already been decided in the minds of jurors yet to be chosen, and for all his elaborate preparations he might be hammering at closed minds.

2

ON JANUARY 27, 1907, the "trial of the century," as the newspapers called it, opened in Part I of Supreme Court, Justice Fitzgerald presiding, in the Criminal Courts Building. The courtroom, the corridors outside, even the streets below were thronged with the curious. Present also were such journalistic stars as Irvin S. Cobb, *Evening World;* Samuel Hopkins Adams, *Morning World;* Roy Howard, Scripps–McRae newspapers, and Alfred Henry Lewis, the color-story and sidebar specialist for the Hearst papers, plus such representatives of circus journalism at its worst as the *Herald's* all-too-well-informed commentator, Roland B. Molineux, who had recently been acquitted of a murder charge. In addition there were dozens of other temporary correspondents, actresses and clergymen mostly; sob sisters and sketch artists avidly studying the faces of the principals and hoping to capture the slightest indication of stress or emotion on their pads. "Des'prit journalists," as Finley Peter Dunne's Mr. Dooley would say, "that had pledged their fortunes an' their sacred honors, an' manny of thim their watches, to be prisint an' protect th' public again th' degradin' facts."

Justice Fitzgerald was fat and ponderous, at first glance, but demonstrated that he was also strong-minded, quick-witted and objective.

The defense, if nothing else, was numerous; the most, if not the best that money could buy. It included the stout, benevolent and bumbling John B. Gleason, whose specialty was supposed to be the examination of witnesses; the tall, athletic Clifford W. Hartridge; Hemple McPike, A. Russel Peabody, Dan O'Reilly, and last but far from least, Delphin Michael Delmas, of San Francisco, "the Napoleon of the Pacific bar." And others were added from time to time, until the defense table seemed to be a mass of beards and elbows. Of this aggregation, Delmas was indisputably the celebrity and the star performer; he had been imported for a fee of $50,000 to deliver the closing argument, which was expected to be a new high in courtroom oratory. The short, round, dapper Delmas, whose pudgy fingers glittered with huge seal rings, was an organ-toned orator of the old school, full of sonorous clichés and opulent gestures. "His fashion was so outmoded," Cobb observed, "that almost you could see the lichens forming at the back of the neck"; his vocalizing ranged from "the gusty roar of a Nubian lioness yearning for her mate" to the "softly plaintive notes of the lowing herd." Among his other distinctions, he had nominated William Randolph Hearst for the Presidency at the Democratic National Convention, and he did not discourage rumors than he had been sired, out of bounds, by the late Napoleon III.

Of all the gentry ranged against him at the defense table, Jerome bore only one of them — Dan O'Reilly, the "Irish Cupid of Park Row" — a personal grudge. The handsome, debonair O'Reilly was a member of the old Tammany crowd which had once hung around the portals of the district attorney's office, a fixer and a wire-puller, who had been engaged to look into the backgrounds and prejudices of the jury panel and to ferret out any surprise witnesses the prosecution might be planning to present. According to the story told around Park Row (and related by Cobb in his autobiography), O'Reilly was responsible for saving Nan Patterson's pretty hide. O'Reilly got to her first after the shooting in the hansom cab, interviewing her briefly at the precinct house and secretly carrying away with him her long white gloves, one of which had powder burns on the palm. That glove would have convicted Nan beyond doubt. Jerome, Cobb said, "picked at his sores and swore to get even." He found no opportunity to fault O'Reilly in the Thaw case, tricky as some of his maneuvers were behind the scenes, but a short time later the district attorney trapped him in professional misconduct, had him disbarred and sent to Blackwell's Island.

Thaw's legal battery was so large and at times so vociferous in trying to prove they were earning their handsome fees that on one occasion, while several of them were shouting across the courtroom at Jerome, the district attorney eyed them scornfully and snarled, "How many counsel are in this case? I believe I have a right to know whom I should address."

At the prosecution table sat only two men — Jerome and his silent but exceedingly able partner, Assistant District Attorney Francis P. Garvan.

Jerome was a trifle malicious about pointing up the numerical superiority of the opposition while questioning a prospective juror.

"Do you know any of the defendant's counsel?"

"Is that all of them?" the talesman asked.

"I hope so!" Jerome retorted.

The Thaw family contingent was equally large: Mother Thaw, in widow's black, with her strong jaw concealed by a heavy veil, seated between her two daughters, the plain-featured Countess of Yarmouth, who was separated from her husband, and the shy, birdlike Mrs. George L. Carnegie, who had married into Pittsburgh's First Family. Harry himself, at the outset of the trial, was calm and self-contained. Seated apart from her in-laws, at a distance and in a manner suggesting estrangement, was Evelyn Nesbit Thaw. Her beauty, her demure sex appeal still caused reporters to gush whenever they came to describing her, which was often. Her companion, day after day, was a twittering little chorus girl named May McKenzie, with whom she had taken shelter the night of the murder. May, the "Broadway sparrow," as the newspapers called her, was perfectly cast for the role of the heroine's friend. The *Herald* described her as always being "cheerful, almost chirpy." Stanford White had once paid her hospital bills, just as he had befriended Evelyn and her family but with less dire results.

The victim, whose presence in that courtroom was to become almost palpable at times, was given no visible support from that glamorous world which he had enhanced so long. None of his friends or relatives showed up — only his secretary, Charles Harnett.

But the reporters, particularly that new phenomenon of the metropolitan press, the female reporter specializing in "sob stuff," had plenty of material to work with in the Thaw family. "The Pity Patrol," as the dignified and disdainful New York *Sun* called them, reported daily that one or another member of the Thaw family was "on the verge of collapse." As the *Sun* observed, "The diagnosticians of the Thaw family have got it all plotted out, and the days for being on the verge of collapse are now being arranged as follows: Mondays, Mrs. Evelyn Nesbit Thaw; Tuesdays, the Countess of Yarmouth; Wednesdays, Mrs. George L. Carnegie; Thursdays, Mrs. William Thaw, and Fridays, Harry Thaw."

Sensation-hungry though they were, press and public had to endure a lengthy and exhaustive process of jury selection. Both sides were very choosy, hurling peremptory challenges at the jury box like blasts of birdshot. District Attorney Jerome was insistent that each prospective juror demonstrate that he wouldn't be swayed by pleadings of the "unwritten law" but would be guided by Justice Fitzgerald's pronouncement that "There is only one law, the law of the State of New York."

And the prospective jurors themselves started shying away from their duty when Justice Fitzgerald made known the special conditions under which they would have to serve. Throughout the trial, he announced, the jurors would be isolated from all influences which might possibly mitigate against an objective consideration of the evidence; each night deputy sheriffs would lead them in a column of twos across City Hall Square to the

Broadway Central Hotel, where they would be kept in separate rooms, each with a deputy on guard outside. Nobody, he indicated, was going to tamper with this jury.

Such a groan of protest went up from the two hundred waiting talesmen that Justice Fitzgerald had to command silence. An astonishing proportion of the panel thereupon confessed to having formed an opinion of the case from reading the newspapers, or presented certificates from their physicians indicating their health would be ruined by serving on the jury, or claimed they'd known Stanford White.

One member of the panel, having wriggled off the hook, left the witness stand humming "Praise God from Whom All Blessings Flow."

It wasn't until February 4 that twelve men were selected and seated in the jury box.

Next day John B. Gleason, for the defense, declared in his opening statement that it would be proven that Thaw slew White in a fit of temporary insanity. It was not an auspicious opening. "I have attended many murder trials during the past fifteen years," wrote Samuel Hopkins Adams in the *Morning World*, "but in none have I heard a forecast by the defense so wandering, so purposeless, so lame, so halt and straggling as the opening address of Thaw's counsel. Hint and innuendo, cross-purposes of insanity, mania, justification and self-defense were whelmed in a jargon of words struggling to express a jumble of ideas."

Worse was to follow. Gleason's first witness was Dr. Charles Chase Wylie of Pittsburgh, one of a herd of domesticated head doctors who now outnumbered the attorneys in the courtroom. In addition to the defense's line-up, Jerome had three alienists of his own choosing present to study Thaw's behavior and try to determine whether he was sane. They were a highly flexible lot on both sides, Cobb observed, terming their testimony as a whole as a "scurvy, sweated smear of pseudo-scientific poppycock which was spread . . . all over the fraud-tinged transcript" of the trial. Cobb also claimed that these "former Poo Bahs of the popular lunatic asylums along our eastern seaboard" avoided each other's gaze "for fear of a betraying giggle."

Hardly had Gleason finished attempting to qualify Dr. Wylie, who was assistant superintendent of the York County (Pa.) Almshouse for the Insane, as an expert witness, than Jerome rose to his feet and proceeded to rip his credentials to pieces. As one observer wrote, Jerome showed himself to be "quick as a panther to spring and as ready to strike as an adder; always keeping an eye skinned for the advantageous main chance and having the probing, boring abilities of a crawfish to undermine his adversary's strained and weakening levees."

A stretch of cross-examination shows just how Jerome left Dr. Wylie torn and bleeding on the witness stand:

"Do you know anything about the Romberg test for physical evidences of mental unsoundness?" Jerome demanded.

"I don't recall," Dr. Wylie confessed, "reading anything about the Romberg test."

"How many supposed lunatics have you professionally examined in your life?"

"About eight hundred I should say."

"Did you apply the Romberg test to any of these eight hundred?"

"I think not."

"Did you discuss the Romberg test for epilepsy during the lunch hour?"

"Yes, I discussed the matter with several gentlemen."

"What gentlemen?"

"Why, some of the attorneys for Mr. Thaw."

"Were any of the alienists for the defense present?"

"No, I think not."

"Have you heard of the coccyx?"

"No."

"Do you not know that it is at the extremity of the spine?"

"I don't recall."

"Are you prepared to say that there is no such thing as the coccyx in the human body?"

"No."

"Have you ever read Dr. Hammond on *Nervous Diseases?*"

"I don't remember."

"Do you know the difference between the cardiac nerve and the pneumogastric nerve? Do you know that they are one and the same thing?"

"I do not."

"Do you undertake to treat nervous diseases without knowledge of the nervous system?"

"I do not."

"Do you know whether the cardiac nerve enters the brain or the spinal column?"

"I am not prepared to say at this time."

"What is the principal nerve in the body?"

"I should say the cardiac nerve."

"Are you prepared to say that the cardiac nerve and the pneumogastric nerve are not synonymous?"

"I am not prepared to say."

"What nerve controls the spleen?"

"I can't say."

"What nerve controls the kidneys?"

"I won't say positively."

"Do you know of any nerve that doesn't have its direct connection with the spine?"

"I think possibly the auditory nerve doesn't connect."

"Do you know the name of a single vital nerve that does connect with the spinal column?"

"I am not prepared to say."

"Will you name a single *unimportant* nerve that connects with the spinal column?"

"I think of none now."

"Is not the pneumogastric nerve the main nerve of the body?"

"I won't be positive."

(All this time Jerome was firing his questions without letup, rapid-fire style, while the good doctor wriggled as though he were being barbecued.)

"Can you name a single nerve that performs an important or vital function?"

"Oh, yes."

"What nerve do you know best?"

"The optic nerve I should say."

"Do you know what alienists mean by the Aigile Robertson symptoms?"

"I don't remember, exactly."

"Now, Doctor, are you prepared to say whether Aigile Robertson was a real person or whether he is merely a creature of my fancy?"

"I have seen the name in a textbook."

"What textbook?"

"I can't say."

"Can you name any textbook on God's green earth where such a name is used?"

"I guess I can't. I only came here to testify. You have tried to convert me into an expert."

"Do you think the conversion will last?" Jerome turned from the witness stand without waiting to hear Dr. Wylie's reply.

His cross-examination of the defense's first "expert" witness had been so destructive, a *Times* reporter noted, that Harry Thaw was in a "mingled state of rage and terror."

That evening the Thaw family and all their attorneys held a meeting to consider the disastrous first day of testimony. Obviously the earnest but lackluster Mr. Gleason would not be able to cope with Mr. Jerome. After hours of wrangling, it was decided that Delphin M. Delmas, in addition to delivering a stemwinder of a closing argument, would conduct the defense's case; perhaps his Napoleonic presence and California reputation as a defender of the damned, etc., would tend to make the district attorney more respectful. The printed rumor in the newspapers had it, in fact, that Delmas served notice on his colleagues that he would withdraw from the case unless he was allowed to take over. If so, it was a decision that ranked in foolhardiness with his putative papa's war with Prussia.

3

ON THE MORNING of February 7, Evelyn Nesbit Thaw took the witness stand to tell the court and the world why her relations with Stanford White should have prompted her husband to murder. In doing so, in attempting to save her husband's life, she had to "lay bare her soul," as the sob sisters expressed it. In the "most astonishing narrative ever heard in a New York court," both White's and her husband's reputations suffered almost equally.

Evelyn, in her autobiography published some years later, was frankly bitter about the whole experience, which she regarded as above and beyond the bounds of wifely duty. "Nobody doubted that I would hesitate to lay bare my soul," she wrote, picking up a phrase from the ladies of the press.

The Thaws took it for granted that I should be pleased to have this opportunity. It shows Harry in the light of a saint; and that is enough. I hinted that the evidence might discover him to be something else — but was "s-s-sh-ed" out of a hearing by his relatives . . . It is a question whether any human being should suffer as I must suffer, on the witness stand, however momentous the issue. I have read in books of heroic prisoners who have risked death rather than the honor of their wives should be questioned. Harry's heroism is not of that variety.

As she walked to the witness stand that morning, she recalled thinking, "The worst they can do is to kill me — so here goes!" So many an actor has thought to himself as he stepped out of the wings. And if Evelyn inwardly regarded her testimony as a sort of dramatic performance, it was admittedly a good one. Her demeanor was variously demure, shamed, naïve, hesitant, apparently candid. Her voice was appropriately low-pitched, with an occasional effective tremolo. To emphasize her self-portrait of innocence betrayed, she wore a short, dark-blue schoolgirlish dress with a broad white collar, and a black hat with artificial violets on the side. "That lovely child," District Attorney Jerome always called her, merciless though he was in cross-examination. To cap it all, she spoke with a touching lisp, and even though she was now in her twenty-third year she could easily have passed for a teen-ager.

In guiding her through her testimony, the new chief of defense counsel adroitly suggested that she tell the jury not what her relations with Stanford White had been, which Jerome could have blocked off with objections, but what she told Thaw those relations had been. According to Evelyn, she revealed her seduction by White to Thaw in Paris, in June, 1903, almost two years before her marriage. By this method the defense was able to introduce much evidence that would not otherwise have been admitted to the record; also the prosecution could not question the accuracy of her account, for the issue was not whether she was telling the truth but whether she had made such a confession to Thaw.

Evelyn's story as developed under direct examination was that she first met White in August, 1901, when she was seventeen. An actress named Edna Goodrich took her to lunch with the architect and a man from Wall Street at White's apartment over a toy store at 22 West Twenty-fourth Street. (On tour with Nat Goodwin's company, Miss Goodrich denied to reporters in Meridian, Mississippi, that she introduced Evelyn to White, but she subsequently dodged service of a subpoena which would have called upon her to testify to that effect for the state.) Evelyn testified that she first met White — a "very big man" whom "I thought very ugly" — in a "gorgeous" room hung in velvet with "divans and pillows everywhere."

After lunch White's friend left him with the two girls, who were then taken to the celebrated room with the red velvet swing. "Mr. White would put us in this swing and we would swing up to the ceiling . . . There was a big Japanese umbrella on the ceiling, so when he would push us he pushed us so our feet would crash through." Then "after a while Mr. White said that he had to go back to his business, much as he would like to stay all day to swing us . . ." He took the girls on a ride around Gramercy Park in his electric hansom, then returned Evelyn to her mother.

Mrs. Nesbit encouraged White's apparently paternal attentions, Evelyn recalled, because he was "in New York society." Not only that, but Mrs. Nesbit allowed herself to be persuaded to take a trip back to Pittsburgh at his expense and with his promise to "look after your little girl."

Mrs. Nesbit was hardly packed off on the steamcars before White had lured Evelyn to still another of his hideaway studios, this one at 122 East Twenty-second Street, on the pretext that she would be one of a number of guests at supper. Instead she found White awaiting her alone. After they had supped, he suggested a tour of the premises. White led her to a bedroom, where there was a table with a bottle of champagne and one glass. Pale and tense, Evelyn continued:

"Mr. White picked up the bottle and poured the glass full of champagne. I paid no attention to him because I was looking at a picture over the mantel, a very beautiful one that attracted my attention, and asked him who painted it and he told me. Then he told me that he had decorated this room himself and showed me all the different things about. It was very small.

"Then he came to me and told me to finish my champagne. I didn't care much for it. He insisted that I drink this glass of champagne, which I did. It was bitter and funny tasting and I don't know whether it was a minute after or two minutes after, but a pounding began in my ears, a pounding and pounding. Then the whole room seemed to go around and . . . everything got . . . very . . . black."

Evelyn buried her face in her hands and wept. When she raised her tear-stained face, Delmas insisted that it was her duty to go on, and Evelyn did:

"When I woke up all my clothes were pulled off me and I was in bed. I sat up in the bed and started to scream. Mr. White was there and got up and put on one of his kimonos. The kimono was lying in a chair, and then I sat up and pulled some covers over me. There were mirrors all around the bed; there were mirrors on the side of the wall and on the top. Then I screamed and screamed and screamed, and he came over and asked me to please keep quiet, that I must not make so much noise.

"He said 'It is all over now.' Then I screamed: 'Oh, no!' And then he brought a kimono over to me and went out of the room. Then as I got out of bed I began to scream more than ever."

Delmas then elicited the information that Evelyn had been a virgin before she entered that mirrored bedroom.

His thirst for details, however, was unquenched. He wanted to know where White was when Evelyn regained consciousness.

"He was right there beside me," Evelyn said.

"Dressed or undressed?"

"Undressed."

"Completely so?"

"Yes."

And the next day, Evelyn testified, White "came to my home . . . I was quiet now and sat staring out the window . . . After a while he said, 'Why don't you look at me, child?' I said, 'Because I can't.' Then he began to talk to me. He said I had the most beautiful hair he had ever seen. He would do many things for me.

"Then he told me that only very young girls were nice, and the thinner they were, the prettier they were, that nothing was so loathsome as fat, and that I must never get fat.

"He said the greatest thing in the world was not to be found out. He said that all women did this kind of thing, but the wise ones were not found out . . ."

Jerome protested with all his vigor at Evelyn's story "told when Mr. White is dead and in his grave."

Pacing before the bench and the jury box, he almost shouted, "Are there no limits to this? There is no way in which we can controvert a single bit of this testimony."

It was, Jerome fumed, "all gossip of the Tenderloin," unworthy of credence by any thinking juror.

"Gossip of the Tenderloin?" Delmas archly inquired, raising his tufted eyebrows. "I have heard it mentioned, the Tenderloin, I do not know what it means. I assume he refers to the gossip of a disreputable part of the city."

This bit of repartee convinced the *World's* Samuel Hopkins Adams that Evelyn's "innocence is far surpassed by that of Lawyer Delmas . . . This is the first intimation on record that the Yale Club, where Mr. Delmas has been staying for some weeks, is either a monastery or a deaf-mute asylum."

4

FEW WORDS IN American history, including much more important documents, though possibly not the Gettysburg Address, have been studied with such intensity as the newspaper accounts of Evelyn's testimony of February 7.

Congress practically halted its deliberations on a vital piece of legislation providing the Navy with more and bigger battleships until every Honorable Member had read through her testimony the following morning. Speaker Nicholas Longworth, a gay dog in those days, read it word for word to a circle of his followers on the platform of the House of Representatives.

A great uproar arose over publication of the testimony. Some newspapers, like the New York *Sun*, expurgated their accounts, referring to "conditions which cannot be described in a family paper." Most, however, made their circulation managers happy and gave it the works.

"It is easy enough," the New York *World* commented, somewhat defensively, "to rail at the newspapers for printing stenographic reports of the case, but what ought they to do? Garble the testimony? Suppress the evidence upon which Thaw's life depends? Or print without color and without elaboration the verbatim testimony of the material witnesses, as English newspapers are compelled to do by law, if they undertake to print anything at all?"

Several ministerial associations, oddly enough, voted in favor of printing all the testimony as an "object lesson." Just what a curious adolescent might learn from it, aside from a short course in the art of seduction, the men of the cloth did not make plain. *The Nation*, however, warned the press that it was in danger of becoming "a purveyor of salacious and demoralizing minutiae of vice."

President Roosevelt professed himself so disturbed by the fullness and frankness of many newspaper accounts of the trial that he asked the Postmaster General if it wasn't possible to exclude from the mails, as Canada had just done, the newspapers which felt it their duty to tell all. Which caused the Brooklyn *Standard-Union* to wonder if "the President of the United States has undertaken publicly to edit the newspapers."

For once Jerome was inclined to agree with Roosevelt. That the press should publish all the "revolting details" seemed to him more shocking than the details themselves, he said. Subsequently he was to move, unsuccessfully, that newspapermen be ordered out of court during the presentation of certain evidence.

5

WHEN SHE HAD finished testifying under direct examination, Evelyn Nesbit Thaw impressed almost everyone with a picture of herself as the wronged maiden whom a man old enough to be her father had taken advantage of with such trappings as velvet draperies, drugged champagne, electric hansoms and mirrored rooms. Hardly a prop in contemporary melodrama was missing. It was all so believable because people had seen it all before, acted out almost as convincingly by the local stock company at the local opera house. Little Evelyn was the perfect ingénue, down to the last fluttering eyelash, the last trembling syllable.

On this demure, pastel-tinted self-portrait Jerome proceeded to operate with sweeping brushstrokes, and from his cross-examination a much less innocent Evelyn emerged, though reluctantly.

Just before she succumbed to the drugged champagne, she admitted to posing for White and a photographer, clad in a kimono and stretched out on a polar-bear rug. Just after it, she continued to receive money from White for support of herself and her family, briefly for her education and that of her brother, for medical and dental bills. Was that the attitude of outraged maidenhood? Jerome demanded. Evelyn's replies to his questions were composed and sure-footed; she was a first-rate witness.

"What I am trying to get is this," Jerome pounded at her, "did not your act through drugs make a profound and terrible impression on your mind as an outrage to every maidenly decency?"

"I did not remember the occurrence myself; all I remember is what I felt like when I woke up and I remember that distinctly."

Jerome's eyebrows shot up in wild surmise: didn't the girl know she'd been sexually molested?

"Do you mean," he continued, "that when you met Thaw in

Paris in 1903 you didn't understand what had taken place?"

She related that she and Thaw sat up all one night in Paris when he proposed to her and she "confessed" to the drugged champagne incident. She felt that because of it she couldn't accept his proposal. Thaw, she said, was wild with grief and rage. Until he explained just what White had done to her, she insisted, she didn't quite understand the enormity of White's act. For the first time she felt "intensely bitter" toward White. Yet Jerome forced her to admit that she wrote White a few days later from Boulogne.

"You felt more kindly toward your betrayer," Jerome demanded, "when you got to Boulogne than you had in Paris?"

"No, sir."

"Did you feel just as bitterly against White when you wrote him from Boulogne as you did when you discovered the full significance of his acts?"

"I felt the same about it all along."

"Why did you write a letter from Boulogne to the man who had ruined your life after the wickedness of his acts had been exposed to you by the man who loved you and whom you loved?"

"Because my mother gave me no peace until I did."

"You were coerced into writing?"

"I was."

"What did your mother say to you?"

"That I was ungrateful not to have written to Stanford White more than I had."

"It did seem horrible to you that 'a big yellow brute of a man' had drugged you, a young girl?"

"It did."

"You thought your mother was a good woman, and you were on friendly terms with her?"

"Yes."

"Why didn't you turn to her and tell her these things?"

"Because I couldn't."

"You preferred to write to this brute, as you esteemed him — the monster, as you called him — than to tell your own mother, who had been good to you, and brought you up?"

"Yes. I would rather have died than tell her."

Evelyn was also forced to admit that she took a letter of credit from White when she went abroad with Thaw in the spring of 1903, and that White's money was used to buy clothes for Mrs. Nesbit while Thaw himself paid their bills.

Jerome also drew from Evelyn the admission that she continued to have sexual relations with White "for a short time" after the drugging incident.

For three days he kept the young woman under the most searching cross-examination, and managed to make only a few dents in her composure.

Once was when Jerome persuaded her to tell exactly what her feelings were for Stanford White. Into her voice and manner, unbiddingly perhaps, crept a genuine respect, admiration, almost awe; everything about that statement was warmer in tone than anything she said about her husband.

"I say outside of this one terrible thing about Stanford White," she testified, "he was a very grand man, and when I told this to Mr. Thaw he said that only made him more dangerous, because when Stanford White came to see me he always talked as my father, and he had never made love to me up until that night; he had professed his admiration for me only in the most fatherly manner. Everybody says the same thing about him that knew him. He was kind and considerate and exceedingly thoughtful — much more thoughtful than most people. He had a very peculiar personality. People liked him very much. He made a great many friends and always kept them . . ."

No one could have paid White a warmer tribute than this young woman who had deliberately and definitively destroyed his reputation; never was his spirit more palpably present in the courtroom than at this moment.

The spell these words evoked, the reminder of what the world lost when her husband killed White, was broken by Evelyn herself, with the curious ambivalence of her testimony, as she quickly added that people were "unwilling to believe the bad things" about him and that Thaw convinced her White "would get worse in this terrible passion he had for young girls."

If Evelyn was visibly embarrassed during her three days on the witness stand under cross-examination, it was when Jerome ungallantly probed at her relations with the young man who had preceded both White and Thaw. He was identified in the newspapers as "Jack Barrymore, an actor," surely the most casual billing he was to receive in a long and spectacular career. Around Broadway, the wise guys and insiders and curbstone commentators cracked that "Thaw shot the wrong man" — meaning that the frenzied young man should have aimed his revolver at Barrymore. The Broadway observers were dead certain that of the three men, Evelyn cared only about the brilliantly shiftless Barrymore.

Early in the trial Jerome had Barrymore subpoenaed, and since he appeared to be a reluctant witness he was brought to court in custody of a detective sergeant. Reporters described him as "gnawing nervously at his mustachios" and quoted him as saying, "I really don't know why the District Attorney insists on my presence here. I dislike this notoriety exceedingly . . . I can't see why I should be dragged into it." Jerome insisted that Barrymore be seated close to Evelyn. The purpose of the tableau was obviously to raise certain questions in the jurors' minds. Hadn't Evelyn really lost her innocence before she met Stanford White? Wasn't this the man Thaw should really have been jealous of? Wasn't it possible that Evelyn, in her confession to Thaw before their marriage, threw the blame on White to spare the man she really loved, the handsome young actor seated close to her?

Barrymore cared so little for this kind of real-life drama that he fled town and stayed out of reach of subpoena servers until the trial was over.

But that didn't prevent his name from being "dragged" into the trial record. Under Jerome's cross-examination Evelyn admitted that White objected to her seeing so much of Barrymore.

"He said he [Barrymore] did not have any money," Evelyn testified; "that I did not have any money. He asked what we could expect to live on."

Evelyn said that White was "purple with anger" over Barrymore's attentions during a supper party in the Madison Square Tower apartment.

Jerome asked whether Barrymore had asked her to marry him.

"He had," Evelyn replied.

"How did Stanford White know about it?"

"Mamma told him."

"Did Stanford White endeavor to get you to make a complaint against Barrymore?"

Defense objections cut off this line of questioning. If there was one thought Delmas wanted to keep out of the jury's mind, it was the suspicion that Thaw, after all, had shot the wrong man.

With some emphasis Jerome asked whether she hadn't once gone to visit a doctor with Barrymore, but Evelyn said she couldn't remember.

The high point of the state's counterattack on Evelyn's testimony came with the introduction of a photographed copy of an affidavit which, the state charged, she made out in Abe Hummel's office at Stanford White's suggestion, part of the constant skirmishing between White and Thaw that extended from early in 1903 to the night White was murdered. Hummel had turned over the copy of the affidavit to Jerome, which may have explained the rather light sentence he received in the Dodge–Morse case.

Evelyn evidently had placed herself under White's protection again after returning from the European tour with Thaw in the autumn of 1903. The affidavit she swore out was designed to protect both her and White from Thaw's unbalanced rages. It told of several occasions on which Thaw had whipped her in a sadistic frenzy. The first took place in a Tyrolean castle at which they were staying. She related in the affidavit:

After breakfast the said Thaw said he wished to tell me something and asked me to step into my bedroom. I entered the room, when the said Thaw, without any provocation, grasped me by the throat and tore the bathrobe from my body.

I saw by his face that the said Thaw was in a terrific excited condition and was terrorized. His eyes were glaring and he had in his right hand a cow-hide whip. He seized hold of me and threw me on the bed. I was powerless and attempted to scream, but the said Thaw placed his fingers in my mouth and tried to choke me.

He then . . . began to inflict on me severe and violent blows with the cow-hide whip. So brutally did he assault me that my skin was cut and bruised. I besought him to desist, but he refused. I was so excited that I shouted and cried. He stopped every minute or so to rest, and then renewed his attack upon me, which he continued for about seven minutes . . .

Next day Thaw whipped her again, until she lost consciousness. "It was nearly three weeks before I was sufficiently recovered to be able to get out of bed and walk."

Several weeks later, in Paris, Thaw assaulted her, she affirmed, "with a rattan cane for an entire day, at intervals of half an hour or an hour, striking me severe blows on the body as a result of which I fainted."

She also told of finding a hypodermic syringe among Thaw's possessions and said he tried to make her take cocaine with him, that drug being a notorious sexual excitant.

And she added:

I have received a number of cablegrams from the said Thaw, which I have delivered to my counsel, Mr. Abraham Hummel. I have been repeatedly told by the said Thaw that he is very inimical to a married man whom he said he wanted me to injure, and that he, Thaw, would get him into the penitentiary, and the said Thaw has begged me time and again to swear to written documents, which he had prepared involving this married man, and charging him of having betrayed me when I was fifteen years of age. This was not so and I told him, but because I refused to sign these papers, the said Thaw not only threatened me with bodily injury, but inflicted on me the great cruel injury which I have herein described.

Despite all this, Evelyn went back to Thaw when he returned from Europe. The affidavit was sworn in November, 1903. On Christmas Eve she had promised White to attend a party with him, but instead she went off with Thaw on a round of the cabarets and spent the night with him at his hotel. A few days later she moved into his quarters and became his mistress. On April 4, 1905, in Pittsburgh, she married Thaw when he finally obtained his mother's consent.

Evelyn's yoyo-like bouncing from White to Thaw, her deliberate course of betraying both men, neither of whom she loved, was perfectly reflected in her testimony under cross-examination.

At first she repudiated the affidavit. Then Abe Hummel was called to testify to the veracity of the document, and her brother Howard, also a prosecution witness, declared that Evelyn had told him of the times Thaw whipped her.

Then Evelyn, recalled to the stand, considerably weakened her repudiation by admitting to the truth of many of its statements.

Under Jerome's questioning, she testified to receiving a letter from Thaw in November, 1903, which discussed practices of a degenerate nature. She also told of being warned by a friend that Thaw had once poured scalding water over a girl in a bath-tub, that he "was in the habit of taking girls and tying them to bedposts and beating them," and that he was a drug addict. When she taxed Thaw with these accusations, she said, he merely shook his head and remarked, "Poor little Evelyn, I see that they have been making a fool of you."

When Evelyn finally departed the stand, she left the impression of a witness with emotions as conflicting as some of her statements. Jerome had succeeded in pointing up that conflict but not in shaking her story that Stanford White's seduction of her — four years before her marriage and five years before White was slain — and her recital of its details had inflamed Thaw's mind to the flash point of murder.

Little Evelyn had conducted herself admirably as the defense's star witness.

Certainly the jury box seemed to be impressed, even though the *Times* labeled her story "preposterous" and the *Sun* commented that the picture of Mr. and Mrs. Thaw as a pair of young innocents wronged by White was ridiculous, considering that "she travelled in various parts of Europe with Mr. Thaw and passed many weeks of an informal honeymoon in the Austrian Tyrol with this refined Sir Galahad . . . The sanctity of Thaw's home was never invaded by White. At the time of the alleged 'ravishment' — as it is now dramatically called — Evelyn Nesbit (Mrs. Thaw) was a chorus girl and not married to anyone."

Now Jerome had to train his heaviest guns on the contention of the defense that Evelyn's story had caused a *temporary* fit of insanity in her husband. The ablest and nimblest of the alienists testifying to this effect was Dr. Britten D. Evans, director of the Morristown (New Jersey) Insane Asylum and a veteran expert witness at murder trials. Day after day Jerome hammered at the men he sometimes sarcastically addressed as "Mr. Scientific Expert," slashed his way through verbal jungles of professional jargon and labored to pin them down on exactly what they considered Thaw's past and present mental condition.

Dr. Evans distinguished himself by coining the phrase "brainstorm" to describe Thaw's essay in murder, a coinage which many observers credited with bolstering the defense's case considerably. A piece of cross-examination will illustrate Jerome's difficulty in coping with a very expert witness.

"From your observation of him [Thaw] are you of the opinion as a scientific man that he ever was afflicted with that form of insanity which you group under the class of melancholia?"

"That is not only impossible for me, but impossible for anyone to tell whether he ever had melancholia by looking at him from the witness stand."

"Do you understand that is what I asked you?"

"That is as I understood your question. I cannot say. I have no opinion today by looking at him whether he ever had it. You might as well ask whether he had pneumonia or typhoid fever."

"I have not asked you anything about looking at him today; I ask you, as a scientific man, from your varied examination of this defendant, have you the opinion that he ever belonged among that class of insane persons whom you group under the heading of melancholia?"

"That cannot be answered by yes or no, so as to give any intelligent expression of opinion."

"I am not asking you for either an intelligent or unintelligent expression of your opinion. I am asking simply whether you have such an opinion, whether intelligent or unintelligent. Have you?"

"He is in a melancholia state of mind which brings him for the time being under the head of melancholiacs. I am of that opinion."

"Then you are of the opinion from the examination and observation you have made of this defendant that at some period he was afflicted with that form of insanity which you group under the head of melancholia?"

"Yes. He was in that state which comes under the general heading of melancholia."

"An insane state I am asking you?"

"Yes."

"An insane condition of mind that you classify under that heading?"

"I have plainly and clearly not said that. I — "

"If you would say yes or no, I would understand you."

"I decline to do so."

On March 1, the third and last day Dr. Evans was under cross-examination, Jerome finally forced him to admit that, in his opinion, Thaw was suffering from paranoia, regarded as an incurable form of insanity. Dr. Evans quickly qualified this by adding that Thaw suffered from "a paranoiac form of adolescent insanity" — whatever adolescent insanity was supposed to be. He insisted that Thaw was not "permanently insane."

It was generally agreed that Jerome's highly informed assault on the credibility of the alienists had "shown them up." The medical profession itself, in fact, was disturbed by the display of ineptitude and pettifoggery so widely reported from the Thaw trial. One authority suggested that henceforth alienists be appointed by the court and that "they should be men who could neither be purchased by wealthy criminals nor moved by public comment, men who are as judicial as the judge himself."

The same day on which Dr. Evans ended his testimony reporters covering the trial observed that Thaw's behavior was increasingly erratic. "Thaw acted more like a child than a man," the *Times* reported the next morning. "He had his big bundles of papers and he spread them out and played with them all day." That day, too, Thaw tried to pass a note to reporters which one of his lawyers intercepted before it could be read.

On March 8, the defense closed its case, and ten days later the state did likewise. Before the final arguments could be

delivered, however, Jerome unexpectedly submitted seven affi-
davits from doctors who had observed Thaw in the courtroom
— but had not been allowed to examine him — stating that they
believed he was incurably insane. The district attorney then
moved that a lunacy commission be appointed to determine
whether Thaw was mentally responsible enough to stand trial.
Obviously he had decided that Evelyn's testimony, which he
was unable to contradict in its essential phases, would sway the
jury toward an acquittal. The ruling of a lunacy commission
that Thaw was not fit to stand trial would at least prevent him
from going free. Justice Fitzgerald agreed to Jerome's motion,
and appointed a commission consisting of Peter B. Olney, David
McClure and Dr. Leopold Putzel.

Eight days later, on April 4, the commission returned its
findings: Thaw was mentally capable of consulting with his
attorneys and understanding the proceedings. Continuation of the
trial was recommended. The issue of whether or not Thaw was
insane thus was dodged. Jerome was faced with the necessity
of contending that if Thaw was sane when he killed White, he
was sane now and should be convicted of first-degree murder.

Both sides proceeded with their final arguments, providing
more heat than light, perhaps, but an interesting contrast in
forensic styles. Pitting Delmas against Jerome was, in Irvin S.
Cobb's opinion, a contest of "rusted rapiers against the very
newest in the line of Gatling guns." Jerome "preyed on his
cornered but still gallant adversary as a famished tramp might
prey on an unguarded free lunch . . . ate him alive, bite by
wriggling bite. Jerome always was like that. Once let him taste
blood and he'd turn tigerish and have no mercy." Inadvertently,
Cobb believed, Jerome created sympathy for his opponent; and
not logic but emotion often rules a jury chamber.

Delmas, his "educated forelock" fluttering on a Napoleonic
brow, pulled out all the stops. It was an oratorical set piece
reminiscent of the late William F. Howe. "If Thaw is insane,"

he shouted at the jury, "it is with a species of insanity that is known from the Canadian border to the Gulf. If you expert gentlemen ask me to give it a name, I suggest that you label it *dementia Americana*. It is that species of insanity that inspires every American to believe that his home is sacred. It is that species of insanity that persuades an American that whoever violates the sanctity of his home or the purity of his wife or daughter has forfeited the protection of the laws of this state or any other state . . .

"Oh, better for Stanford White if he had never been born, rather than that he should have seen that day," Delmas ranted on, referring to the seduction related by Evelyn. "Far better that his ears had never been opened than that they should have heard the shriek of horror and anguish of the victim that lay mangled and devoured before him! For what had he done? He had perpetrated the foulest, the most cowardly, the most dishonorable of the sins and crimes that can stain or deface the image of God. He, the strong, the powerful, had lured a poor little child to her undoing and to gratify a moment of passion and lust had crushed the poor little flower that was struggling toward the light and toward Heaven."

As for the defendant, he "struck for the purity of the American home. He struck for the purity of the American maiden." Delmas suggested, in fact, that his client was "an instrument of God and an agent of Providence."

It was a speech calculated to make a mining-town jury snuffle into their beards, not to sway sophisticated New Yorkers; yet it was observed that Thaw's jurors were strongly affected.

Jerome, in his closing argument, paid the jury the undeserved compliment of considering them men capable of reasoning. Thaw himself, of course, had not been placed on the stand, so he had to aim his shafts at Evelyn's story, at Delmas's "*dementia Americana* plea." Coolly and reasonably he pointed out that White was dead and could not defend his own reputation; that Evelyn could not be pinned down on the exact date of her seduction, so the state might introduce evidence to show White was elsewhere on that alleged occasion; that no known drugs could produce the effect which Evelyn claimed the drugged champagne had on her, and finally that Thaw had taken his revenge long after the incident, the telling of which had so inflamed him.

This was no American Tragedy, Jerome declared, but "a vulgar, sordid, common murder of the Tenderloin." As for the phrase Delmas concocted: *"Dementia Americana!* That is not the kind of insanity you have sworn to take into consideration."

"Justifiable homicide," he continued, "does not mean *dementia Americana.* Justifiable means self-defense, and when a man sits with his head in his hands, quietly looking at a play . . . and is shot down by an enemy with a revolver, held so close that his very features are so disfigured that his brother-in-law does not recognize him, even the wildest stretch of the imagination will hardly picture that to a jury east of the Mississippi River as a case of self-defense."

He struck hard at the story told by "the angel child," as he referred to Evelyn with enormous sarcasm, "the girl whose great love was undermined in twenty-four hours," the girl whom Thaw "flaunted through the capitals of Europe as his mistress." He begged to differ with Delmas as to Evelyn's representing the "purity of the American maiden." Thaw had found a higher law, he said, not in the so-called unwritten law but in "hiding behind a woman's petticoats."

The *Tribune,* not one of his greatest admirers, praised him for his "hard-headed riddling" of Thaw's blatantly mawkish defense.

But it was all in vain. The jury went out April 10, spent forty-seven hours in deliberation, and finally reported itself hopelessly deadlocked. Justice Fitzgerald dismissed the jurors — seven of whom stood for conviction, five for acquittal — on April 12. After a trial lasting three months and costing the Thaw family a reported third of a million dollars, the process would have to be repeated. Evelyn's unassailable story, with its vagueness on certain critical points, its curious switchbacks and betrayals of admiration for her husband's victim, had turned the trick. Her testimony, said the *Tribune*, was "a triumphant bit of malignity," which, under the rules of evidence, could not be contravened.

As for Jerome, exhausted after the three-month struggle, the *Times* reported that "persons close to him believed him elated" by the mistrial. "It is pointed out . . . a conviction would have placed the District Attorney in the unenviable position of having successfully prosecuted for murder in the first degree a man whom he himself believed beyond the pale of the law."

Perhaps so, but he was still determined that Thaw would be taken out of circulation, if not permanently by the electric chair, which he was now convinced would not have been justified after observing him in court and considering the opinions of doctors he trusted, then just as effectively through hospitalization for the rest of his life.

6

JEROME'S CHIEF OPPONENT at the second Thaw trial was a younger, abler and steelier man then Delphin M. Delmas, who went back to California with his $50,000 fee and bittersweet memories. Delmas's replacement was the curly-haired and eloquent Martin Littleton, whose admirers said he looked like Stephen Douglas in his youth and who was accounted Jerome's peer at razor-edged repartee.

Littleton's stirring recital of the achievements of Colonel William D'Alton Mann as a Union Army paladin — though delivered in a ripe Southern accent — had won an acquittal for the publisher of *Town Topics*. It didn't pay to take liberties with him. Once he was invited to make an after-dinner speech before one of the Southern societies in New York, and arrived late and somewhat tipsy. The toastmaster, noting that he was dozing off during his introduction, made a number of sarcastic remarks about Littleton, concluding with "And now we are to hear this gifted friend of ours who is never at a loss on an occasion like this. The formula is simple: Down goes his dinner and up comes a speech." Littleton sprang up, suddenly clear of head and sharp of tongue. "How different from your toastmaster," he said. "Down goes *his* speech — and up comes your dinner."

Jerome could expect a far brisker performance from Littleton, who immediately on accepting the Thaws' retainer informed the family that he would assume full responsibility for the strategy of the defense, would not permit any interference from them, and would save Harry's life the best way he knew. In the months since the first trial, the panic of 1907 had sobered the country and made people much less tolerant of wealthy playboys with homicidal tendencies. Bearing in mind that the previous jury had voted seven to five for conviction on first-degree murder, he would not shilly-shally around with attempts to prove temporary insanity. It must be admitted that Harry was insane, and conceded that he would have to be hospitalized.

The second trial began January 6, 1908, with the *Times* expressing the hope that in the repeat performance "the lawyers will soon be as tired of the case as a suffering public has been for a year or more." Actually the public was still fascinated; the courtroom and corridors were as crowded as before, and when Evelyn arrived in a new electric brougham, presumably part of her bounty as the star witness for the defense, there was a mob scene in the streets around the Criminal Courts Building. She disclosed that she had received one hundred and twenty-two proposals of marriage in the event that Harry was sentenced to the electric chair. She denied having been paid $300,000 by the Thaw family. She smiled dutifully across the courtroom at her husband, and was ready to play her role once more. The newspapers again splashed the trial over their front pages, although at the outset the story had to compete for space with the case of a Wall Street broker who had despaired over the financial panic and took illuminating gas and the Black Hand (Mafia) bombing of a Greenwich Village tenement.

District Attorney Jerome again took charge of the prosecution, although other matters clamored for his attention. He was under heavy fire for not having prosecuted certain street railway magnates with sufficient vigor — a matter to be expanded on later — and his office had renewed its intermittent feuding with the New York Police Department. The police, he charged, were nothing but "an army of crooked cops," and the gambling laws were being violated in "every precinct." Furthermore, he told the newspapers, his investigators were being shadowed by police detectives determined to abort raids on houses where gambling and prostitution flourished. In addition to these outside distractions, Jerome suffered from a heavy cold throughout the second trial and kept himself going, reporters observed, by sniffing constantly at a menthol preparation.

Justice Dowling, presiding at the new trial, announced that the proceedings were to be conducted at a brisk pace and ordered three sessions daily instead of the customary two. Every night the court reconvened from eight to ten o'clock.

In his opening statement for the defense, Littleton revealed that Thaw had tried to kill himself by taking laudanum in Paris just after Evelyn told him how White had drugged and seduced her. With the defendant's mother absenting herself in Pittsburgh, Littleton, determined to prove that his client came of "tainted stock," dragged out every skeleton in the family closet, a pitiable and depressing tale of mad uncles and ancestral lunatics of all sorts on both sides of Harry's house. Jerome, however, successfully objected to the introduction of records from the asylums where various Thaws and Copleys had been kept under restraint.

Evelyn took the witness stand again as the main prop of the defense, this time with a much less detailed version of her comatose downfall. There were fewer sentimental hesitations about her

testimony this time. Like any competent actress, she realized
that her story was beginning to go flat. As Irvin S. Cobb wrote,
"It nearly always was drugged champagne in those days when
seduction seemed to require more apologizing for than it does at
present." The *Times* reporter remarked that her "composure
smacked of the well-trained ingénue furnishing the gayety in a
somber play." One of the few new details she added was that
White had sent her to a finishing school in New Jersey, briefly,
for the purpose of breaking up her "attachment" to Jack Barrymore.

On January 22, she faced two hours of cross-examination by a
hoarse but determined Jerome, who bitterly allowed that he was
now prepared to believe that Evelyn had been "wronged" by
Stanford White but that White hadn't needed any drugs to
achieve his purpose. The courtroom was filled with gasping and
clucking at this remark.

Littleton sprang up to denounce Jerome for the "savagery" of
his cross-examination, and complained of the district attorney
"pacing this clearing like a lion in a den."

When the ordeal was over, Evelyn smiled impishly and remarked to reporters, "All that is left for Jerome to do is to tear
my little Buster Brown collar to pieces."

This time it took only three weeks for both sides to present
their evidence, with Littleton briskly marshaling his witnesses,
mainly English and American doctors who expressed the opinion
that Thaw was a manic depressive with "reformatory delusions"
— that is, he "believed it his duty to punish people for their
misbehavior."

Jerome, in his closing argument, shook his fist under Thaw's
snub nose and referred to him as "this miserable man," once again
cast doubt on Evelyn's "purity," but he was much less forceful
than at the close of the first trial. He even hinted to the jury
that he would be satisfied with a manslaughter verdict.

But the jury, after deliberating for twenty-five hours, returned to the courtroom on the afternoon of February 1 with a verdict of not guilty by reason of insanity. The verdict, Arthur Train commented, could have meant one of two things, "(a) that they had a reasonable doubt in their own minds that Thaw knew that he was doing wrong when he committed the murder — something hard for the layman to believe, or (b) that, realizing that he was undoubtedly the victim of mental disease, they refused to follow the strict legal test."

Jerome, according to the *Times*, "seemed well satisfied with the verdict." Perhaps he was even more satisfied with the swiftness of Thaw's dispatch to confinement in the State Asylum for the Criminal Insane at Matteawan, near Poughkeepsie; just three hours after the verdict was returned, he was being placed aboard a train at Grand Central Station. Evelyn saw him off, the *Times* said, "with no sign of regret."

Just as he was being put aboard the train, Thaw protested to his lawyers, who also saw him off, "I will not go there; I don't want to go to Matteawan."

"You've got to go," Martin Littleton told him.

"Where did you expect to be sent?" Dapper Dan O'Reilly asked. "Rector's or Martin's?"

The *Times* warned that "to set him free again would be in itself a monstrous crime against society." Jerome was even more determined to keep him locked up where he could do no more harm with his delusions of being an avenging angel, armed with whip and gun, with a mission to punish the wicked. Yet the Thaw family, with all the horrors that had been placed on the record, was still convinced that Harry should be free. Perhaps Mother Thaw and her advisors believed that Harry was cured, now that the shadow of Stanford White had been lifted from his psyche, and he would never again feel called upon to correct matters personally outside the law. In little more than three months after he was committed, they were trying with all their might, main and millions to have him released . . .

A new shift of legal and medical advisers was employed by Mrs. Thaw, and on May 6 they went into action, starting writ of habeas corpus proceedings in the Poughkeepsie court. Upriver for the latest round went Jerome, a batch of his own alienists and a sizable entourage of newspapermen, photographers, sketch artists and other outriders.

The Thaws moved to have Harry released on the grounds that, whatever his mental condition when he killed White, he was sane and responsible now.

After the family's alienists testified along expected lines, Harry himself took the stand, the first time he had been permitted to do so since the murder. Obviously both Delmas and Littleton had been well advised to keep him under wraps. His testimony, according to one observer, consisted of "semi-coherent answers to a few cautiously framed questions."

From Monday morning to Saturday afternoon of that week in Poughkeepsie, Jerome allowed the Thaw faction to present their evidence and arguments for Harry's release. He hardly entered an objection. Mr. Jerome, in fact, appeared somnolent through most of the proceedings. A night session of court was ordered Saturday, May 11, so the district attorney from New York could present his evidence against a writ which would mean Thaw's deliverance from Matteawan (where, incidentally, the therapy in his case seemed to consist mainly of letting him have all the vanilla éclairs he wanted).

To the general astonishment Jerome rose at the opening of the night session to announce that he would rest his case on the testimony presented by the other side; not only that, so confident was he that everything pointed to Thaw's continued lack of mental balance, he would also waive his right to make any kind of argument before the bench.

The court was equally crisp and laconic, disallowing the Thaw petition and ruling that Harry was unfit to be turned loose on society.

Jerome served notice, moreover, that he would oppose his release under any circumstances, whenever and wherever it was sought.

During the remainder of his term as district attorney, he might well have established a special Thaw Affairs Bureau in his office. If nothing else, the Thaws were persistent. Only a month after the first habeas corpus was denied, they were back in court, petitioning for Harry's transfer to a homeopathic hospital; on June 29, they demanded a jury trial to determine whether he had not recovered his sanity; on January 4, 1909, they appealed an adverse ruling on the petition; on July 14, they sought another habeas corpus; on August 26, they appealed the denial of the writ before the State Supreme Court, and on December 30, the day before Jerome left office, they lost their appeal to the United States Supreme Court.

In office, Jerome defeated every move they attempted.

Out of office, he would continue the struggle, year in and year out, until someone began spreading the canard that wealthy friends of the late Stanford White were secretly financing him.

9

"Pulitzer the First" on the Griddle

I've let King Pulitzer — and his
gang of sycophants — stew in their
own juice.
— William Travers Jerome.

IN THE YEAR 1908, following the second Thaw trial, Jerome
found himself under heavy fire. As a culmination of events in
the financial jungle of lower Manhattan, and the manner of his
response to them, his conduct in office was bitterly assailed and
he was forced to defend himself personally and professionally.
From then until the end of his second term, Jerome, once the
crusader whose integrity no one would think of questioning, was
placed on the defensive regarding his role in the insurance company and Metropolitan Street Railway scandals.

If that year had one satisfying moment, it came when he
was handed the opportunity of letting both President Roosevelt
and Joseph Pulitzer, then the mightiest of daily newspaper publishers, "stew in their own juice," as he put it, when those two
personages became involved in what might have developed into
the most noisome political scandal since the Credit Mobilier
affair.

Jerome not only disliked Theodore Roosevelt from their first
acquaintance in the New York reformist movement but envied
him for having accomplished the goal Jerome had set for himself.

Roosevelt had snatched away the banners of reform and marched behind them right into the White House.

As for Pulitzer, his round-the-clock editions of the *World* delighted in criticizing Jerome at every opportunity. Since both the newspaper and the district attorney were more or less independent Democrats and both had made their marks on the city as civic crusaders, Jerome could only conclude its publisher was opposed to him on personal grounds. The *World's* publication of a photograph of him sleeping at his desk, which it re-ran from time to time whenever the district attorney proved irksome, was, in Jerome's opinion, an act of pure malice. Much more damaging were the constant complaints in the *World* editorial columns that he was "soft" on "wealthy lawbreakers" — presumably excepting Thaw — and unduly harsh with gamblers and madams. It was the *World's* contention that Jerome was a tiger in the Tenderloin but an amiable pussycat in Wall Street.

Jerome's opportunity to thwart Roosevelt and harass Pulitzer burst into bloom when the *World* dug into and exposed some of the intrigue surrounding the negotiations which preceded the construction of the Panama Canal.

The Wall Street lawyer William Nelson Cromwell formed the New Panama Canal Company to take over the project from the De Lesseps company, which had gone bankrupt and swallowed up $260,000,000 in the savings of 600,000 Frenchmen. The canal was to have been cut through the narrow Isthmus of Panama, then a province of Colombia. Cromwell's associates in the newly formed company included such well-placed personages as Douglas Robinson, the brother-in-law of President Roosevelt; Charles P. Taft, brother of William Howard Taft, whom Roosevelt had picked as his successor to the Presidency; J. P. Morgan and Elihu Root, the Secretary of War, and others.

Cromwell's plan was to buy out the French company, then negotiate with Colombia to regain the rights to build the canal across the Isthmus of Panama. The Republic of Colombia, however, refused to cede the six-mile strip of land required for the project. And now President Roosevelt and his Secretary of State John Hay stepped in; two American cruisers were sent to the waters off Colon to prevent interference from Colombia while mercenaries paid by Cromwell fomented a revolution in the city and proclaimed an independent state of Panama. A few days later Washington recognized the new Republic of Panama. President Roosevelt did not ask the approval of Congress. As he later boasted, "I took the Isthmus, started the Canal, and then left Congress, not to debate the Canal, but to debate me."

After that coup of November, 1903 everything went smoothly. Congress appropriated $10,000,000 to be paid the new Panamanian republic for its strip of land and another $40,000,000 for the French rights to the project. This latter appropriation took a rather curious route: the United States Treasury presented J. P. Morgan and Company with the check for distribution, presumably to be performed by the French government. Cromwell later testified that "of the $40,000,000 thus paid by the United States Government, $25,000,000 was paid to the liquidator of the old Panama Canal Company under and in pursuance of an agreement entered into between the liquidator and the new company . . . Of the balance of $15,000,000 paid to the New Panama Canal Company, $12,000,000 have already been distributed among its stockholders and the remainder is now being held awaiting final distribution and payment."

Despite the best efforts of Mr. Cromwell and his friends rumors persisted that the canal deal had been a gigantic swindle, that they had paid French stockholders only $3,500,000 and pocketed the rest. The *World* kept worrying at it even while the public was rejoicing over the triumph of American know-how, the heroic feats of American engineers and doctors, and the eventual grand opening of the canal. Something about the deal reeked, and Pulitzer's nostrils were offended.

Even with the suspicious probings of the *World*, the Panama

Canal affair might have fizzled out harmlessly if President Roosevelt had not displayed so much energy in pushing the nomination of William Howard Taft as his successor in 1908. Among those offended by his tactics was Charles W. Fairbanks, who was not only a Presidential candidate himself but publisher of the influential Indianapolis *News*. The Indianapolis paper and the New York *World* joined in asking, as their editorials on the subject were headed, "Who Got the Money?"

"Why," the *World* asked, "did the U. S. pay $40,000,000 for a bankrupt property whose control could undoubtedly have been bought in the open market for less than $40,000,000?

"Who were the New Panama Canal Company?

"Who bought up the obligations of the old Panama Canal Company for a few cents on the dollar?

"Among whom was divided the $15,000,000 paid to the New Panama Canal Company?

"Whether Douglas Robinson, Mr. Roosevelt's brother-in-law, or any of Mr. Taft's brothers associated himself with Mr. Cromwell in Panama exploitation or shared in these profits is incidental to the main issue of letting in the light."

The *World* charged President Roosevelt, whose term was ending in a few months, with "flagrant untruths" and "reeking misstatements" in connection with the acquisition of the canal strip.

Teddy Roosevelt was not the man to take this kind of criticism lying down. In Washington it was reported that he had announced that he was "out to get old Pulitzer." This threat was taken very seriously by Joseph Pulitzer, then blind, ailing and nerve-racked but still actively concerned in the direction of his newspaper properties; he boarded his yacht *Liberty* and began cruising up and down the coast between New York and Charleston to place himself beyond the law's reach.

Pulitzer's hunch proved entirely correct. Under pressure from the White House federal indictments were sought against Pulitzer, two of his chief editors, and the company which published the *World* on charges that they had criminally libeled President Roosevelt, Elihu Root, Charles P. Taft, William Nelson Cromwell, Douglas Robinson and J. P. Morgan, despite an outcry that Teddy was using his vaunted big stick to restrict or suppress the freedom of the American press. A federal attorney resigned rather than press the indictments. The general opinion was that this time Roosevelt had gone too far, and the case against Pulitzer and the *World* would collapse in open court.

Then the word got around that Roosevelt and his friends were demanding that District Attorney Jerome proceed against Pulitzer under the state law governing malicious misstatement, that he have Pulitzer arrested and arraigned and harassed to the limit of the law.

Pulitzer was fairly confident that he could beat the federal charges of criminal libel, but the possibility that William Travers Jerome, with all his tenacity and ferocity, and his well-known taste for eating his revenge hot or cold, would take action against him thoroughly alarmed the publisher. He was back on dry land, holed up in his mansion on East Seventy-third Street, but he was reported to be quaking with terror that Jerome and his detectives would break down its doors and haul him off to the Tombs. One of his irreverent young reporters later wrote that Pulitzer was "on the verge of a complete collapse" and "his chamberlains and his chancellors were panting like lizards."

"My opinion," Pulitzer wrote Frank Cobb, his chief editorial writer, "is that if anything comes out of this Roosevelt–Panama matter it will be through Jerome. If they should go for me personally through Jerome it will be necessary to show Jerome's animus. I don't think I would be silent then. Show how the machinery of justice is prostituted. For years we have asked Roosevelt to send somebody to jail; so he begins on the editors of the *World*. We pitched into Jerome because he did not do

anything against wealthy lawbreakers; now he turns against the
World . . ."

Actually Mr. Pulitzer was underrating both Mr. Jerome's sense
of independence and his hearty dislike of President Roosevelt. The
pressure from Washington and Wall Street for action against
Pulitzer only annoyed Jerome and caused him to resist the whole
idea. Furthermore he was not eager for the role of cat's paw;
any time he went around raking chestnuts out of the fire, they'd
be his own. Precipitous action such as the Roosevelt group
craved would be a great mistake.

Jerome, at this moment, was undoubtedly enjoying himself to
the hilt. The situation appealed enormously to his taste for
sardonic comedy, and he was not so lacking in malice that he
could not enjoy keeping two men he heartily disliked dangling
while he dawdled. Anyone who knew him fairly well should
have realized that if Jerome dawdled it was not from indecision
or timidity but for a tactical purpose.

He had three alternatives to mull over. Charges could be
pressed against Pulitzer, but that would please Roosevelt. He could
announce that he would not proceed against the publisher and his
newspaper, but that would please Pulitzer. Or he could annoy
Roosevelt and worry Pulitzer by doing nothing and keeping his
own counsel. Obviously the last alternative was the most appealing. Jerome spent four delightful weeks doing nothing, throwing
out hints, enraging Roosevelt and harassing Pulitzer no end.

All he would say when newspapermen asked him direct questions about whether he intended to prosecute Pulitzer was that
"the matter is occupying my mind."

Pulitzer and his executives were so fretted by the district attorney's attack of coyness that they hired private detectives to
shadow Jerome and his chief assistants, to hang around the
Criminal Courts Building soaking up tips and rumors and to offer
bribes to Jerome's office help for information on what the district
attorney intended to do.

To you Bill,

Robert Carter's celebrated caricature of Jerome as an eminently self-satisfied tiger. The inscription below is to his son William Travers Jerome, Jr.

Harry K. Thaw and his mother, Mrs. Mary Copley Thaw, her pride and determination still intact

Stanford White in a photograph taken some years before he became involved with Evelyn Nesbit and

Evelyn Nesbit in the days when she was a photographers' and artists' model.

Evelyn Nesbit Thaw with Jack Clifford, her partner in a dancing act that thrived for a time after the Thaw trials.

Evelyn Nesbit Thaw as she settled down to write her memoirs, which were advertised as "an exposé of the pitfalls that imperil young girls."

Delphin M. Delmas, dramatic star of the first Thaw trial, his "educated" Napoleonic forelock in place.

Jerome, under cap and behind cigarette, as he was arrested in Coaticook, Canada, as a "common gambler," during his unpopular but successful attempt to retrieve Thaw as a fugitive from justice.

Finally freed, Thaw paces the deck of the *Aquatania* just after he had been refused permission to land in England. He went on to France, where he was permitted to spend the summer.

One of the rare moments they spent in each other's company in later years, Jerome and his wife Lavinia posing on the porch of their Lakeville, Connecticut, home with their first grandson, William Travers III.

Three generations of the Jerome family — William Sr., William Jr., and William Travers Jerome III, now dean of the College of Business Administration at Syracuse University.

All this gumshoeing proved fruitless; an iron curtain had been dropped around the district attorney's office.

In desperation, during the fifth week of suspense, the top men at the *World* called one of their star reporters, Irvin S. Cobb, into conference.

Their spokesman told Cobb that reports had reached the executive offices under the World Building's golden dome that he was on friendly terms with District Attorney Jerome, that "we've spent a great deal of time and a great deal of money in efforts to induce Mr. Jerome to state his position . . . we've exhausted practically every expedient . . . a grave emergency exists . . . as a last resort we are asking for your cooperation."

The "gloomy mandarins," Cobb later recalled, wanted him to find out from Jerome what he was going to do about demands for Pulitzer's prosecution; he could approach Jerome, they told him, either as a friend or as a reporter; but whatever his method he must learn what Jerome had in mind or the consequences of waiting might be fatal to his employer.

His expense account for this task, they added, would be "unlimited" — an almost unprecedented challenge to any reporter worthy of his Park Row thirst.

The matter-of-fact Cobb toddled off to the Criminal Courts Building and sent his card in to Jerome. An aide returned with instructions for Cobb to wait for the district attorney in the bar at Pontin's although as Cobb noted, "it was a bit late for before-breakfast drinkers and a bit early for pre-luncheon drinkers." Fifteen minutes later Jerome breezed in. "He had a gusty way of speaking and a rolling, forward-lunging gait almost like a man climbing the slant of a boat deck in half a gale. He ordered cocktails for two as he came through the door . . . There was a quizzical, meaningful twinkle in his eye. Jerome could peer as far into a grindstone as the next one. As the greatest cross-examiner of his time and one of the greatest that ever tried a case, he had reason for being so visioned."

"Well, Kentuck," Jerome said with a grin, "what's on your mind — if anything? Not that I couldn't make a guess."

Cobb allowed that Jerome's guess would probably be correct, his fidgety superiors had sent him over to find out whether Pulitzer would be prosecuted under the laws of the state.

Jerome took a swallow of his drink and then unburdened himself of his feelings about Pulitzer. "I don't like a hair of that man's head. He has attacked me viciously, violently and, as I see it, without due provocation. He never hesitated — or his papers never did — to hit below the belt and gouge in the clinches.

"Even so, I never intended to make either a burnt offering or a martyr out of him. If it had been John K. Jones, ordinary citizen, who was involved in this thing, the *World* would have gone about covering it in an ordinary way. But no. Because it was His Imperial and Sacred Majesty, Pulitzer the First, those damn stuffed shirts down on Park Row couldn't handle it that way. They had to make it terrifically portentous, supremely important. They had to build it up into a breath-taking, world-shaking crisis. They had to turn creation — or their addled part of it — upside down.

"And so, for four weeks they've had their crepe-heeled flunkeys dogging my steps and shadowing my people. Mangy dicks have tried to seduce my clerical force, have tried to pry secrets out of my assistants and my secretaries, have spent dough in great gobs and perspired blood. Whereas, if any properly accredited reporter from the *World* had come to me, as a reporter, and looked me in the face and had asked what my intentions were, I'd have told him — that is, as soon as I made up my mind, which was within twenty-four hours after the complaint was first lodged with me. So, because of all that and for nothing else, I've let King Pulitzer — and his gang of sycophants — stew in their own juice."

With that preamble off his chest, Jerome then briskly informed Cobb that he had never had any intention of prosecuting Mr. Pulitzer to please Mr. Roosevelt and his friends.

Before they parted in Pontin's bar, Cobb offered to buy a round himself, but Jerome turned him down on the grounds that "somebody might claim you'd been corrupting a judicial officer of New York County with a fifteen-cent drink."

Cobb hurried back to the office and delivered the results of his conference with Jerome to the *World's* brass hats. Shortly after word was sent to the Pulitzer mansion that he no longer need fear prosecution by the district attorney's office, the publisher himself got Cobb on the phone and wanted to know how he'd breached Jerome's wall of silence when highly paid agents had failed. Cobb took great pleasure in telling him that all he had to do was ask Jerome a direct question.

"Well," said Pulitzer, "I wish to be God-damned!"

The dismal fate of the libel action instituted by Roosevelt and the others, which was thrown out by the Supreme Court, only confirmed Jerome's judgment in refusing to proceed along similar lines. But if satisfaction was denied the President in the courts, so was the curiosity of the public regarding exactly how the $40,000,000 was split up. Investigators following up details of the transaction in France were balked by the fact that all papers involved, under French law, were sealed and then destroyed after twenty years. A Congressional investigation started in 1912 wound up in a maze of dead-ends, and no satisfactory answer was ever produced to the *World's* waspish inquiry "Who Got the Money?"

10

Scandal and Recrimination

BY 1908 a considerable number of personal and political enemies had combined against Jerome to drive him out of
public life. His reputation (they charged) was built solely on a
flashy series of headlined campaigns against malefactors of small
wealth, the so-called underworld, and on an undeniable talent
for courtroom dramatics. When it came to attacking the major
villains on the metropolitan scene, the men who were looting
the nation's economy from their privileged sanctuary in Wall
Street (which, after all, came under the jurisdiction of New
York County), Jerome balked at the challenge and refused to
employ his forces in the fight against the monopolies and the
"money power." He had failed to measure up to the duties of his
office.

Had Sir Galahad, people were beginning to ask, turned into
Sir Mordred?

The answer was not easy to supply, entangled as it was in the
discretionary nature of a district attorney's powers to prosecute.
It was his duty to proceed against anyone suspected of breaking
the law, of course, but it was also his duty not to prosecute without sufficient evidence, without a reasonable expectation of obtaining a conviction, otherwise he would be wasting time and
the taxpayers' money in fruitless prosecutions. Jerome, furthermore, was handicapped in any determination to proceed against

the predators of Wall Street by inadequate laws supposed to protect the investing public. The Roosevelt administration had pushed through legislation designed to curb the trusts, but the concept that high finance should be hobbled to prevent it from doing as it pleased, from being a law unto itself, was then regarded as untenable, if not anarchistic. The money panic and resulting depression of 1907 aroused a certain amount of argument in respectable circles favoring legislation against Wall Street practices, but the rigors of the Securities and Exchange Commission were far in the future. For a mere district attorney of New York County to declare all-out war on Wall Street would have called for an archangel rather than a civic crusader.

And there was little in Jerome's background or temperament to suggest that his reformist tendencies would take the shape of leading a fight against the Morgans, Whitneys and Harrimans. His father and uncles had, until they were dealt out of the game, reveled in the jungle rites of Wall Street. Jerome himself associated after-hours, in Manhattan's clubs and at dinner parties, with the socially and financially elect. "As the years passed," Milton MacKaye wrote of him, "he became more and more an advocate of the freedom of the individual. His radicalism, thus, could be simmered down to a passionate belief in honesty in public office . . . The District Attorney had always had a strong admiration for the men of big finance, and his true economic conservatism had begun to assert itself . . . His own changing ideas, too, embittered many of his old reform allies."

Obviously, unless they committed the most overt acts of larceny, Jerome was not the man to needlessly harass the gentry of Wall Street or wield an ax against the topless towers of lower Manhattan.

He viewed with contempt the circulation-catching and politically motivated harangues of William Randolph Hearst against the financial titans. The storms of public opinion, which he believed were fabricated in the Hearst and Pulitzer shops in the interests of journalistic demagoguery, drew only his disdain. Likewise the trust-busting flourishes of Theodore Roosevelt. And likewise the clamor of the muckrakers. It was all too cheap and easy to blame the nation's current economic ills on a few men in Wall Street.

His attitude toward reformers of this type was summed up in one sentence, flung out in a public address during March, 1906, when he was already under journalistic fire for advocating "two kinds of law — one for the rich and one for the poor."

"I feel bitterly," he said, "that educated men should bark down the pike like half-bred curs, led away by a Hearst and other unspeakables."

Criticism of Jerome's laxness in prosecuting the transgressions of the high and mighty began, in a minor key, during his first term in office, when it was charged that he had not been vigorous enough in pursuing those responsible for a series of railway tunnel accidents. Hearst, in particular, regarding Jerome as his most serious stumbling block on the road to Albany and Washington, seized on everything his reporters could find to label him as "the brass-buttoned bellboy of the trusts." Pulitzer joined in the chorus when he judged that Jerome was not quite quick and eager enough in pressing for indictments during the insurance scandals of 1905, an extravaganza largely produced through the efforts of Pulitzer's *World*. By that time Hearst proclaimed himself so appalled by Jerome's lassitude that his *Journal* and *American* began demanding that the district attorney be removed from office for malfeasance.

The insurance business had become nothing better than a high-toned racket out of which a few insiders were reaping a tremendous harvest. Immoral and unethical and dastardly it was, undoubtedly, but under the laws then in effect it was not quite illegal. Towering figures of finance who controlled the insurance companies and their treasuries, totaling hundreds of millions of dollars, were using those funds to speculate in securities, engage in vast forays and bribe state legislatures and influence Congress

against passing remedial legislation. The life insurance treasuries
financed great enterprises and made gigantic coups possible, but
none of the profits from these speculations, not a dime of them,
was ever returned to the companies. Wielding those insurance
assets as a weapon in corporate wars gave certain banking houses
a tremendous amount of power, political as well as economic.
Heavy contributions from the Big Three of the insurance business, Equitable, New York Life and Mutual, to Republican campaign funds in 1896, 1900 and 1904 helped to kill off William
Jennings Bryan's "menacing" attempts to reach the White House.
J. P. Morgan and Co. increased its stature in investment banking
through the use of insurance company funds, which also enabled
it to branch out in steel and railroads. And Equitable, for instance, allowed the banking firm of Kuhn, Loeb the use of millions of dollars, which it loaned to E. H. Harriman, who was
thus enabled to build up a railroad empire, take over the Southern
Pacific and snatch away the immense holdings of Jay Gould's
heirs.

There was nothing that the insurance companies' policy hold-
ers or small stockholders, unorganized and unaware as they were,
could do to prevent this misuse of the money they had painfully
invested against the future. How could they pit themselves
against, or even dare to question, the activities of men who were
regarded as the pillars of society, who shone as members of the
Four Hundred and who sat with their families in the Diamond
Horseshoe? The boards of the Big Three were graced with such
almost sacred names as Astor, Vanderbilt, Cassatt, Depew, Gould,
Schiff, Hill, Frick, Harriman, Morton, Ingalls, Bliss.

The insiders who were making free with insurance funds might
have gone on for many more years, quietly tapping this vein for
all it was worth, except that, like lesser brigands, they fell out
over a division of the spoils.

Early in 1905 the Equitable Life Assurance Society, with
assets of half a billion dollars, was racked by dissension inside and

outside its ramparts at 120 Broadway. A rash of stockholders suits had broken out, basis for which had been supplied by a dissident faction in the company's management. At the top level, the elderly president, James W. Alexander, was bickering with the twenty-nine-year-old James Hazen Hyde, who had inherited fifty-one percent of Equitable's stock from his father, Henry B. Hyde, the company's founder. Alexander was fearful that Hyde would soon replace him — Hyde an overly elegant young bounder, the epitome of the brainless and undeserving heir (in Alexander's opinion), who could say, facetiously perhaps, "I have wealth, beauty, and intellect. What more could I wish?" Young Mr. Hyde played into old Mr. Alexander's hands beautifully one night in January by giving a fancy-dress ball at Sherry's, the extravagance of which, as well as the guest list, including young Franklin D. Roosevelt as an extra man, attracted an enormous amount of publicity. Two floors of Sherry's were transformed into a replica of the gardens of Versailles during the reign of Louis XVI. Powdered wigs and other period finery adorned the beldames, debutantes, tycoons and playboys who attended the rout; Pol Roget flowed the night long, and Mme. Rejane, the famous French actress, consented to make an appearance in a sedan chair and give a brief sample of her acting, at her usual professional fee. There'd been naughtier and more expensive parties, but Hyde's timing was unfortunate. Even more disastrous was the somewhat exaggerated publicity, which insisted the ball had cost up to $200,000 (Hyde later claimed it cost only one-tenth that much).

On February 12, the *World* broke a story that Alexander was demanding Hyde's resignation on charge of "misconduct, incompetence and misuse of funds," alleging that the Equitable treasury had been tapped for the Versailles ball and other extravagances. The story was hotly denied, but the *World* obtained proof of a round robin signed by Alexander and twenty-five other Equitable officials in which they threatened to resign if

Hyde did not agree to quit the vice presidency and yield to a mutualization plan which would greatly diminish his influence over the company's affairs.

Behind the Alexander–Hyde feud, however, existed a much more sinister and important struggle. George W. Perkins, the kingpin of New York Life and a partner in J. P. Morgan and Company, had conceived of a Napoleonic maneuver exceeding in scope even the Morgan take-over of the steel industry. He proposed that the Big Three, along with Metropolitan and Prudential, be merged into one colossus with two billion in total assets. The concentrated power of that combine, which Perkins was confident would be entrusted to his own capable hands, would have been overwhelming.

This coup could be engineered only through the elimination of the inadequate, foppish but unexpectedly courageous young James Hazen Hyde. He held out against it. Ten million dollars were offered Hyde to step aside, it was reported, but he persisted in his opposition. A man of purpose existed side by side with the dilettante; Hyde was determined to stay in the insurance business and furiously resented being bullied; nor would he be swayed by all the adverse publicity secretly planted by Perkins and his associates. He continued to resist even when Alexander threatened to demand a public investigation by the attorney general. And he thoroughly alarmed the Alexander–Perkins faction by suddenly advocating that policyholders be represented in the company's management.

Obviously the issue would have to be settled quickly and *in camera* before it could become a public scandal. A special committee chairmanned by the hard-boiled Henry C. Frick conducted a sort of star chamber inquiry which concluded that both Hyde and Alexander should be ousted and the company's affairs straightened out forthwith. Equitable's board of directors rashly rejected the recommendations, despite the fact that they came from a group formed within the insurance business.

Almost a month before the lid blew off the situation, Jerome unburdened himself regarding the difficulties of coping with a business which, as the subsequent investigation showed, had raised a "yellow dog fund" for years to pay the campaign expenses of friendly state legislators, had dictated the appointment of insurance commissioners and controlled the insurance committees of state legislatures. Anyone who believed that Jerome "went easy" on the insurance companies, as was later charged, should have studied that address he made on June 15, 1905 before a dinner of the Merchants Protective Association. "The actions of some of the eminent gentlemen connected with Equitable," he said, "were no whit less immoral than those of Larry Summerfield," a notorious confidence man whom he had just convicted.

Jerome's rather lengthy remarks before the dinner at Delmonico's* are quoted extensively here largely because they constitute the fullest available answer to charges of laxity in prosecution made later by the press.

Within the past decade or so there has arisen a new class of crime, [he said,] rather subtle crimes which do not come within the pale of the law. In the earlier days of American history when a man wanted to rob his neighbor, he did so by force, and there were laws provided which attended to his case if he should be detected and found guilty.

There are no laws to cover 99 out of 100 cases of the crimes committed every day in this era in the name of high finance. In England, France and the countries of Europe the necessity for safeguarding the people against financial crimes has been recognized and laws have been enacted to this end. The United States has been singularly backward in this regard.

When I went up to Albany . . . I found the assemblymen so busy attempting to carry off everything that wasn't nailed down that they had no time to listen.

The trouble in this country is that the morality of a great many people is governed by what is on the statute books. Thousands of

* As reported in the New York *Times,* June 16, 1905.

New Yorkers are entirely blind on the moral side and only know that an act is immoral when it is written into the law as a felony.

The things that Equitable officials did were not criminal as defined in Section 528 in the Penal Code, which has to do with larceny. I contend, however, that in the moral sense they should come within the purview of this section and I defy them to distinguish their acts from the acts defined in it.

Gracious goodness—this isn't high finance; it's stealing.

He recalled that Summerfield told him he "didn't know he was doing wrong in selling the suckers something that has no value at a high price . . . it's what all the big fellows are doing." His audience laughed, at which Jerome remarked, "You think that is funny, don't you? Well, it is funny and again it isn't."

By now the press, led by the *World*, whose exposures were arousing protests from all over a shocked nation, which had regarded its insurance premiums as something almost as sacred as Holy Writ, was demanding that the whole indemnity business be investigated.

Under unremitting and increasing pressure the State Insurance Superintendent Francis Hendricks conducted an investigation *sotto voce*, but refused to make public the testimony he had taken, let alone any conclusions he might have drawn from it.

Hendricks kept three copies of his report in his office safe, refusing requests from both Governor Higgins and District Attorney Jerome for a look at them. A New York *World* correspondent in Albany, through one of Hendricks's subordinates, managed to get hold of a copy over the weekend, and on July 11 the *World* spread testimony taken in secret before Hendricks over ten pages of the paper.

An intensely frustrated and annoyed Jerome commented that it was "very strange that a newspaper is able to obtain this testimony while the District Attorney, aided by the Governor, is unable to obtain a copy."

Now that the lid had been pried off, the insurance scandal

had to be brought out in the open. Governor Higgins requested the state legislature to appoint a group which became known as the Armstrong Committee to investigate the charges against the insurance companies. Counsel for the committee was a promising young lawyer named Charles Evans Hughes, who was so patient, thorough and gently persistent in conducting the hearings that large and hitherto secret areas of insurance operation were at last thrown open to public scrutiny, and who handled himself with such dignity and assurance that he was elected governor the next year.

The Armstrong Committee hearings, beginning September 6 and ending December 30, unraveled the affairs of the Big Three and other insurance companies and disclosed how their interlocking directorates, their security-buying syndicates and their free-spending lobbies in Albany and other state capitals diverted corporate funds with the efficiency of a cream separator. In addition, their officers paid themselves magnificent salaries. Richard A. McCurdy, president of Mutual, for instance, saw nothing off-color in the fact that he was paid $150,000 annually while dividends to policyholders dropped from one hundred and ten dollars to seven dollars. Furthermore, the $50,000 he spent on office furnishings was defended as "adding dignity to life insurance." Perkins, as head of New York Life, bought $8,000,000 worth of watered International Mercantile Marine bonds from Perkins of Morgan and Company, the issue having been floated by Morgan. Self-righteous James W. Alexander of Equitable was revealed to have joined in a number of profit-taking syndicates himself and had placed six relatives on the Equitable payroll.

Young Mr. Hyde was also shown to have profited from the insiders' manipulation of securities, $60,000 in one year. Two days before the investigation ended he boarded a liner bound for Europe. "I wish to deny emphatically that I am going to live abroad," he told reporters. But somehow he lingered in France for thirty-four years, until he found the Nazi occupation distasteful and repatriated himself. McCurdy of Mutual, described as a "broken man" after completing his testimony, also went into exile and died shortly thereafter.

J. P. Morgan himself, though the prime mover in tapping insurance funds, which he gladly took in exchange for water-logged bond issues, was never called to testify. Immense wealth, after all, still had a few privileges. It was his son's fate, many years later, when summoned before a Congressional hearing in Washington, to have a lady midget dropped in his lap while flash bulbs popped and the image of super-capitalism was touched up with a few strokes of low comedy.

Even more devastating, perhaps, was the revelation that in one year alone (1904) the Big Three spent more than three-quarters of a million dollars on lobbying and corruption. Mutual's lobby-ist in Albany, for instance, maintained what the newspapers called the "House of Mirth," providing entertainment of all kinds for weary legislators. From 1898 to 1904, Mutual spent $2,000,000 on what were listed as "legal expenses," much of it dispensed through the jolly establishment a few doors from the Albany legislature in the form of liquor and female companionship.

The Armstrong Committee soberly noted that the companies "systematically attempted to control legislation" in New York, and also "divided the country, outside of New York and a few other states, so as to avoid a waste of effort, each looking after its chosen district and bearing its appropriate part of the total expenses."

The net result of all these discoveries was that legislation, based on the Armstrong Committee's recommendations, was passed to control the insurance companies' political activity and regulate their use of the funds entrusted to them. Controlling interest in Equitable, feuding over which had brought about the investiga-tion, passed to Thomas Fortune Ryan, much to the distress of E. H. Harriman, who had counted on his carefully fostered friendship with young Hyde to grab that plum for himself. Chief counsel Hughes lost his chance at the Presidency against Woodrow Wilson in 1916 and wound up as Chief Justice of the United States Supreme Court. And J. P. Morgan several years later took over the much-coveted Equitable.

But the same tide which carried Hughes to high office was running against William Travers Jerome. It was easier, as Jerome himself had learned while serving as counsel for the Lexow Committee a decade earlier, to reap the laurel of a spectacular investigation than to obtain convictions, which the public demands as a result of those free-wheeling inquiries, in court and under inadequate laws. Wrongdoing may have been as evident as the large scarlet nose on Morgan's face, but it was another thing to define it, prove it and punish it.

Jerome's attitude toward the manipulation of insurance funds was expressed in a speech (March 23, 1906) in which he pointed out in his usual racy style: "The real evil is that eighteen or twenty men should control $1,500,000,000 of quick-moving assets; eighteen or twenty men who meet every day at lunch . . . who can make of the game of finance a brace game [that is, a crooked gambling game]."

Although Hughes had stolen the political thunder necessary to win the governorship, which Jerome himself coveted, he conceded that Hughes had conducted the Armstrong hearings in "man-like" and "lawyer-like" fashion. He moved deliberately — and much too slowly and reluctantly in the opinion of the Hearst and Pulitzer editorial writers — to bring justice to bear upon a number of insurance executives.

Eventually, between 1906 and 1908, fifty-six indictments were obtained by Jerome and his assistants. All fizzled out. Jerome's critics, of course, charged that they were pressed with insufficient enthusiasm, or that he was so bedazzled by the better-publicized rewards of prosecuting murder cases, including the Thaw trials, that he simply lost interest in the less spectacular insurance cases. There may have been some truth in the latter allegation, for by temperament he preferred the excitement and human drama of a good juicy murder case to the dreary involvements of corporate misdeeds.

Yet it was not true that he "let all the big fish go" in the insurance scandal, as charged; the record shows that more than one gentleman with white piping on his waistcoat had to face the humiliation and distress of being indicted, and that at least one sizable effort demonstrated that it would be more difficult to convict than to indict.

Among the fifty-six indicted were such principal figures as two vice presidents of Mutual on June 11, 1906; George W. Perkins, vice president, and Charles Fairchild, a director, New York Life, in December of that year; John R. Hegeman, president of Metropolitan, and Thomas D. Jordan, comptroller of Equitable, in May, 1907; Mutual's president, Frederick A. Burnham, general manager George Burnham, Sr. and vice president George P. Eldridge, in March, 1906; William A. Brewer, president of Washington Life, in April, 1906, and Foster M. Voorhees, secretary, Washington Life, in January, 1908.

To try out the possibilities of a successful prosecution in these cases, Jerome made a test of the indictment against the ambitious Mr. Perkins, the biggest fish in his net. Perkins admittedly had contributed $50,000 of New York Life's funds to the Republican National Committee in 1904. Jerome charged that this was an unlawful diversion of corporate funds amounting to grand larceny, and proceeded against Perkins on this basis.

By agreement with Perkins's counsel, the validity of the charge was tested in the state's highest courts. The result, however, was negative enough to dishearten the most vigorous of prosecutors. Perkins's counsel applied for a writ of habeas corpus, which was turned down by the Superior Court. The Appellate Division reversed this decision, however, and the Court of Appeals upheld the reversal. As an inquiry conducted at the instance of Governor Hughes later determined, there was simply no existing statute making it illegal for a company officer to hand out campaign contributions from corporate funds.

Jerome could hardly be faulted for not following this line of attack, forestalled as he was by the higher courts, but he was condemned by the *World* and the Hearst papers for not humiliating Perkins to the full extent of his powers. When Perkins appeared for a preliminary hearing, the Pulitzer organ thundered, he should have been hauled into court a manacled felon instead of being permitted to stroll in without escort.

Never a man to turn the other cheek, Jerome struck back at his journalistic critics with all the invective at his command. He paid his respects to what he and many others were calling "yellow journalism" in an address before a banquet held by Delta Upsilon, of which he was a member, on March 23, 1906. Conceded that Pulitzer himself might be a "right-minded man," he denounced his editors as an "unmitigated and unspeakable bunch." Most newspapers try to be "clean and decent," he said, but "two newspapers stand as exponents of the vulture that seeks the carrion — and seeks it with a sense of recognition."*

A former assistant district attorney now in private practice, he charged, was approached by an unnamed newspaper editor who told him, "You represent certain insurance grafters . . . Turn up something on the District Attorney's office, say that these men are being prosecuted because they have not got Wall Street backing, and in our paper we will deal kindly with these men under indictment . . ."

Such remarks only increased the hostility of the press, which closed ranks against him, with the exception of the *Times* and *Globe*. The newspapers had built him up as the great civic crusader; now they were eager, in their professed disillusionment, to tear him down. The anti-Jerome barrage increased to drumfire proportions when the even more malodorous activities of the local traction magnates were thrust upon the public notice.

* Here he undoubtedly referred to Hearst's *Journal* and *American*.

2

EVEN BEFORE Jerome took office for his first term, there were rumblings of complaint against the Metropolitan Street Railway Company and the way it was being operated by the syndicate headed by William C. Whitney and Thomas Fortune Ryan. The traction company, it was charged, issued $260,000,000 worth of stocks and bonds which were so waterlogged that the restless shade of the late Jay Gould, whose manipulation of the elevated railway system twenty years before must have served as a pilot model for Metropolitan, could only have looked upon the operation with the greatest envy. Metropolitan operated surface lines but its masterminds were hardly any more earthbound when it came to corporate financing than the spirit of the departed Mr. Gould.

In his first campaign, Jerome, in fact, had pledged himself to hunt down any wrongdoers "even if their tracks lead straight to the offices" of the Metropolitan, adding that "No one knows better than I do that when I am attacking the Metropolitan Street Railway Company I am arraying myself against the most dangerous, the most vindictive and the most powerful influences at work in this community." His listeners understood that he was referring to the fact that Whitney and Ryan were supposed to be among the chief financial supporters of Boss Croker.

Six years later Metropolitan went into receivership, thousands lost their life savings, and there were loud outcries for Jerome to live up to his campaign promises, belated though their fulfillment would be.

Between that promissory speech in 1901 and Metropolitan's collapse in 1907 there was played out a melodrama of corruption, jury-rigging, stock juggling, thimblerigging and brazen looting seldom seen since the days when Vanderbilt, Drew, Gould and Fisk were engaged in their epic struggle for the Erie Railway. Joseph H. Choate considered it was the city's all-time

financial scandal. "This 'debacle,' this complete collapse," Choate
said in 1910, when he was trying to recover certain funds from a
Metropolitan subsidiary on behalf of its stockholders, "only
occurred in 1907, but the debauchery and corruption which had
preceded it lasted many years. I do not hesitate to say that the
greatest enormity committed in New York was the flotation and
inflation of the Metropolitan Street Railway Company, its securities and those of its subsidiary companies."

The groundwork for this systematic and long-sustained conspiracy against the investing public was laid while Jerome was
still a struggling young attorney. It went back to the horsecars
of the seventies, in fact, when street transportation was in its infancy and people unable to afford their own carriages had to
travel on the "bobtailed" little rattletraps drawn by decrepit
horses and ancient mules. The development of electric power
brought with it the comparatively swift trolleys, which made
large-scale rapid transit systems possible and started the middle-
class migration to the suburbs. It also attracted the attention of
the big financiers. Until then the streetcar business had been in
the hands of small operators, unable to finance the electrification
of their lines and share in the new prosperity. In New York City
Jay Gould had combined the elevated railways but the surface
lines were operated by thirty different companies and anyone
making an extended journey through the city had to pay three
or four different fares.

The big syndicators, with all the necessary financing available,
aimed to eliminate all this small-time competition, combine the
existing lines, and float tremendous security issues not only to
finance the improved systems but to enrich themselves. The
Number one syndicate was composed of six men, William C.
Whitney, Thomas Fortune Ryan, Peter A. B. Widener, William
L. Elkins, Charles T. Yerkes and Thomas Dolan. Together they
consolidated the street railways and often the lighting companies
of New York, Chicago, Philadelphia, Pittsburgh, and a hundred

other cities and towns in Pennsylvania, Connecticut, Ohio, Massachusetts, Rhode Island, Indiana, Maine and New Hampshire. The public benefited from their endeavors in that they provided quick transportation to the outer edges of the cities and freed the working classes from the tenement districts and made it possible for even those who stayed in the slums to get out in the country Sundays and holidays. Trolley-riding, before and after the turn of the century, was one of the few pleasures available to the masses, and the scuttling cars, loaded with singing proletarians bound for picnics and beer busts in the country, became part of the national legend.

Behind the utility and gaiety of all this, the Whitney–Ryan–Widener–Elkins–Yerkes–Dolan syndicate worked almost frantically to extract the last illicit dollar from their enterprises before public indignation and restraining legislation could catch up with them. To obtain and keep their franchises, they spent millions on bribery in their regional fiefs; thus Yerkes, in Chicago, controlled mayors and city councils; Ryan and Whitney were the invisible powers in New York's Tammany Hall, and in Philadelphia Widener and Elkins dominated the City Hall and linked themselves with the state Republican machine.

None of the members of the syndicate could have qualified as an Alger hero, though most had risen from humble circumstances. Yerkes had served time for embezzlement; his formula for success, as he frankly stated it, was to "buy old junk, fix it up a little and unload it upon other fellows." Widener was a German butcher who invaded Philadelphia politics with a jovial bluster, becoming a ward leader and city treasurer before branching out as a traction magnate. Once when stockholders demanded discussion of a proposed lease, he blandly advised them, "You can vote first and discuss afterward." Elkins, a former butter-and-egg man who made his stake in the oil strike at Titusville prospered largely through his close friendship with the more imaginative and expansive Widener. Dolan was also a Philadelphian, adept at combining municipal politics with grabbing off street railway franchises.

By far the ablest and supplest of these financiers were the two men who operated the New York branch of the syndicate, the well-bred and well-educated Mr. Whitney and the reticent and dogged Mr. Ryan, whose talents dovetailed so beautifully.

William C. Whitney came of a distinguished Massachusetts family and was graduated from Yale with high honors. He forged ahead rapidly as a New York lawyer and a power in national politics. Handsome, polished, brilliant, he seemed to be headed for a career of the greatest distinction; but he was also greedy for money and power and had a Medici's taste for luxury and magnificence. He was an anti-Tammany Democrat originally and helped to bring down the Tweed dictatorship. One of the rewards for his early idealism was his appointment as Secretary of the Navy in President Cleveland's cabinet, and one of his larger achievements in that post was modernizing the fleet and creating the Navy which, built up from the hulks of the Civil War, demonstrated such power in the Spanish–American War. Still in his forties, he quit the ranks of public servants, turned his back on political idealism and made his peace with Tammany Hall, a pragmatic gesture which enabled him to start buying up the old horsecar lines, obtaining their franchises from the Tammany-dominated city government, and which eventually installed him in one of the lordliest mansions on Fifth Avenue, stocked with art treasures and furnished with carvings, panelings, staircases and tapestries stripped from European castles. He had discovered that virtue was not, sufficiently, its own reward.

One reward of its opposite was his happy meeting of minds with Thomas Fortune Ryan. Two men could hardly, on the surface, have been less similar; it was an intellectual mating of a New England Puritan and a Virginia-born Irish Catholic, of the elegant Whitney and the rather flashily-dressed, ruddy-faced Ryan. Ryan began his career as a clerk, married the boss's daughter and made his way upward in Wall Street, gaining a reputation for such smooth operation that Jay Gould used him in some of his maneuvers on the Stock Exchange. He had two valuable traits: an unrivaled appetite for hard work and a striking ability, much admired in the necessarily conspiratorial atmosphere of Wall Street, of being able to keep his mouth shut, but politely rather than grimly. In other men these traits might have added up to a close-mouthed drudge, but Ryan had a priceless overlay of Irish geniality. Whitney said that Ryan was "the most adroit, suave and noiseless" man he had ever known. The combination of Whitney's political and Ryan's financial aptitudes was unbeatable.

With the other members of the traction syndicate Whitney and Ryan worked in collaboration, cooperating and coordinating whenever possible, rather than as a unit with a single head. Their interests interlocked. Thus Widener and Elkins were officers in various corporations formed by Whitney and Ryan, just as the latter pair were involved in traction enterprises operated by the syndicate in other cities.

Metropolitan was organized in 1893, along with a holding company, the Metropolitan Traction Company, which Ryan once described as "a great big tin box."* The most valuable franchise lying around was Jacob Sharp's lower Broadway line, which Sharp had obtained by bribing aldermen. When Sharp refused to sell out, the syndicate promoted an investigation by the state legislature which uncovered the fact that Sharp had paid various aldermen $500,000 for voting him the franchise. Among the results of the inquiry were the indictment of several aldermen, the flight of others to Mexico, and the conviction of Sharp for wholesale bribery. Just before he died in Ludlow Street jail, to which he had been sentenced to four years at hard

---

* Financial historians say Metropolitan was the first holding company ever organized, an institution which flourished most amazingly when the late Samuel Insull built his ultimately collapsible pyramids of power.

labor, Sharp saw the light and sold out to the syndicate.

Whitney, Ryan and their collaborators made the most of their ruthless bargain. Using their political influence, they obtained the necessary franchises, with the lower Broadway line as the foundation stone of their system, and replaced the horsecars with trolleys. Through subsidiaries they awarded themselves huge blocks of stock. The syndicate built the Lexington line for an estimated $2,500,000 and turned it over to Metropolitan for $10,000,000 of Metropolitan stock; the Columbus Avenue line for an estimated $500,000 in exchange for $6,000,000 worth of Metropolitan stock. It bought the Fulton horsecar line, whose assets consisted of one-third of a mile of track, ten rickety little cars and thirty spavined horses, worth possibly $15,000, and turned it over to Metropolitan for $1,000,000 worth of securities. The insiders spent about $50,000 electrifying the line running along Twenty-eighth Street and awarded themselves $3,000,000 in Metropolitan stock. In addition they leased much more valuable lines along Third, Fourth, Sixth, Eighth and Ninth Avenues which had been held for many years by various old families and their estates, for which they paid exorbitant annual rentals.* This may have seemed like bad business, but only if the syndicate members were interested in running an honest and efficient transit system. Their real interest, of course, was draining off premature profits through inflated construction costs — and later in dumping the watered stock issued by Metropolitan on the basis of these inflated costs and ruinous leases on the investing public.

Metropolitan Street Railway was capitalized at $260,000,000, a grossly exaggerated view of its worth. To the investing public, unaware as it was of the syndicate's methods, the stock seemed a good buy. It seemed even better when Metropolitan began to pay regular seven percent dividends.

Immediately after Metropolitan was listed on the big board in 1897 it was subjected to a speculative joy ride, propelled both

* According to testimony before the Public Service Commission in 1907.

by the insiders' manipulations and the innocent enthusiasm of the public at large. Eventually it was selling at $269 a share. And all the time it was driving toward this peak, the members of the syndicate secretly unloaded as fast as discretion allowed.

Just how much the insiders thought of Metropolitan's worth was indicated in 1904, when William C. Whitney died and his estate came up for probate. He'd left an estate valued at $40,000,-000. Not a single share of Metropolitan was found among its assets.

Then came the panic of 1907, and the dry rot in the corporation's foundation was clearly revealed. Its thousands of stockholders found their holdings were worth no more than shares in a salted gold mine out West. Metropolitan went into receivership; its affairs were being investigated, at least seven years too late, by the Public Service Commission; and there was an uproar of demands that members of the syndicate be brought to justice.

By this time two men in particular were making themselves heard in the thunder of denunciation. One was William N. Amory, a former street railway executive, who had been demanding an investigation for several years; the other, William F. King, who had been one of District Attorney Jerome's chief supporters for re-election in 1905, and who was now chairman of the Metropolitan stockholders' committee.

Amory charged that Metropolitan had been looted for a total of $90,000,000, of which $30,000,000 had been drained off through inflated construction costs, another $60,000,000 through various stock-rigging and stock-juggling devices. (A broker, Grant B. Schley, testified before the Public Service Commission, for instance, that Whitney had unloaded $1,092,747 worth of Electric Storage Battery stock on Metropolitan's treasury.)

In a pamphlet (*The Truth About Metropolitan*) Amory, who once had been secretary of the company which operated the Third Avenue line, declared that:

the Metropolitan Managers have engaged in a deliberate scheme of stealing trust funds, their own stockholders' money. Their crimes comprise conspiracy, intimidation, bribery, corrupt court practices, subornation of perjury, false reporting, the payment of unearned dividends year after year, the persistent thefts of stockholders' money, carried on over a long period by a System constituting the basest kind of robbery . . . and finally, as a result, the wreck and ruin of a great corporation. All these offenses have been committed that a few men might become multimillionaires easily and quickly, and be able to hold onto their graft . . . It was the genius of William C. Whitney that conceived the possibilities of the Metropolitan railways, and erected this monument of infamous graft. It was the skill and unscrupulousness of Thomas F. Ryan to which many of the completed deals owe their success.

Amory further charged that the district attorney had "deliberately whitewashed" Metropolitan's chief looters in his investigation.

For months, intermittently, Jerome had been presenting evidence on Metropolitan's downfall to various grand juries. But nothing had been produced to implicate Ryan or any of the other Metropolitan bigwigs in any criminal acts under the laws then on the statute books. As one grand jury reported, it "could not but feel that the physical and financial destruction of these properties was due in no inconsiderable degree to dishonest and probably criminal acts, rather than mistakes of judgment and lavish and reckless financiering," that "disbursements deserving severe condemnation" had been made, but it was unable to obtain any evidence upon which it could return indictments.

Not only the inadequacy of the existing laws but the thoroughness with which Metropolitan's masterminds covered their tracks impeded the investigation. All documentary evidence of how the corporation's finances were managed had been destroyed. Investigators learned that all the ledgers, journals, checks, vouchers and other records dating back to the company's formation in 1893 had been sold to a junkman for one hundred and seventeen dollars on the written pledge that they would be ground into pulp and kept safe from "prying eyes." Thus Isidor Kresel, Jerome's "digger-in-chief," upon whom he relied completely in such matters, had little or nothing to work on.

For such handicaps, Jerome found scant sympathy among the Metropolitan stockholders and the New York newspapers. They wanted action, not excuses; and if Thomas Fortune Ryan's scalp was out of reach, William Travers Jerome's would do nicely in compensation. Mr. King's committee filed a demand with Governor Hughes for Jerome's removal from office.

Worse yet, on January 27, 1908, General Sessions Judge Otto A. Rosalsky, who had worked for Jerome's nomination in 1901 and his renomination in 1905, severely criticized him for his methods in handling the Metropolitan investigation. Judge Rosalsky complained in particular of Jerome's tactics before the grand jury.

The District Attorney conducted his examination of Thomas Fortune Ryan before the grand jury so as to invalidate any indictments which might have been found against him, had they been found . . .

The investigation was further impeded by the fact that the District Attorney, in open court, stated that there was no evidence at hand to show that one Thomas Fortune Ryan, a witness before you, had violated the law . . .

While this witness was not actually in custody, he was the person who, if not in legal form a defendant, was, nevertheless, in point of fact, directly accused by the District Attorney of committing a crime and therefore the District Attorney had no right to question him on any matter relative to the charge in view of the constitutional inhibition . . . which provides that no person shall be compelled to testify against himself. The privilege of permitting an accused person to appear before the grand jury should be accorded very sparingly and when accorded it should be surrounded with the utmost care and caution. If it is not done, the indictment found is liable to be set aside by the court.

Judge Rosalsky concluded by ordering that the whole case against Metropolitan and its surviving manipulators be resubmitted to another grand jury.

"No opinion of Judge Rosalsky," Jerome snapped to a *Times* reporter, "would be sufficient to make me do anything."

Nevertheless he proceeded, as ordered, to resubmit the matter to a special grand jury impaneled before Justice Dowling in Supreme Court. Some of his verbal indiscretion may have been due to the fact that, while being attacked regarding Metropolitan, he was in the midst of final argument in the second Thaw trial — a matter which, as events proved, was an enduring obsession with him. He had to rush from the Thaw trial to the grand jury chamber, and back again, trailing reporters firing questions he regarded as impertinent. A *World* reporter noted that there was "blood in Jerome's eye" when he brushed by William F. King, and he seethed when King offered to procure evidence against Metropolitan officials at his committee's expense "provided the District Attorney will allow this committee to present said evidence to said grand jury through their counsel." Jerome, said King, "has no heart for this prosecution." Two days later Jerome was further enraged by a statement made by Amory and published in the New York *Herald* that he had information incriminating the top dogs at Metropolitan but "I do not intend to present this information to Mr. Jerome or any of his assistants for the reason that I would just as soon give it to Thomas Fortune Ryan or Paul D. Cravath [Ryan's attorney and a former law partner of Governor Hughes]."

And now the journalistic tom-toms began to beat in compelling rhythm for Jerome's impeachment.

3

"Now," noted the *Literary Digest,* the news magazine of its day, in its March 7, 1908 issue, "there is scarcely one journal left to do him reverence."

Jerome-baiting had become the chief occupation of New York's editorial writers. His attacks on the newspapers naturally encouraged them to whet their scalping knives and attempt to prove once again that no public figure could get away with blackguarding the press.

After Judge Rosalsky's rebuke from the bench, demanded the *World*, "what further reason can Governor Hughes give why a special prosecutor should not be appointed to enforce the law against criminals of power?"

Governor Hughes, however, did not propose to let the editorial council under Pulitzer's golden dome make up his mind for him.

Instead of removing Jerome or replacing him with a special prosecutor in the Metropolitan investigation, the governor appointed a special commissioner, Richard L. Hand, to hold hearings on why Jerome should or should not be removed from office. Then Hand was to make his recommendations, and Governor Hughes would decide whether Jerome was fit to keep his place.

The *World* was ready to write his political obituary. "Mr. Jerome is one of the tragedies of American politics," a Pulitzer editorial writer declaimed. "No man of his generation ever had more brilliant opportunities. No man of his training and talents ever rendered a sorrier account of his stewardship . . . By the manner in which he has conducted his office he has given stability to the Socialist charge that there is one kind of justice for the poor and another kind for the rich."

The New York *Globe*, however, came vigorously to the district attorney's defense:

Many of those most clamorous in shouting against Mr. Jerome apparently forget that he would show himself a most despicable character if he should consent to insincere and unjust indictments in order to save himself from criticism . . . his conduct at all times has been singularly open, and never has created the impression of a man who had sold out or was deliberately playing a part. Mr. Jerome, often-times indulging veritable paroxysms of self-revelation, has moved in and out of this community for many years. Abundant have been the oportunities to study him, and despite the attacks of the King Committee, and despite the fact that he might not be elected again if a candidate, there is no falling away in the belief in his integrity. His has not been the demeanor of the scheming villain, and if he is not such a villain, if it is not assumed that he has been controlled by base motives, the King charges shrivel to nothingness.

Jerome could also take comfort in a number of letters he received from prominent members of the New York bar, offering help and sympathy. B. F. Tracy, himself a former district attorney, offered to defend Jerome at Commissioner Hand's hearings without charge. The distinguished Joseph H. Choate wrote, "I hope you don't feel disturbed by these charges . . . They seem to me to be preposterous." "I sincerely trust," wrote Elbridge T. Gerry, "that you will pay no attention to these attacks." And the highly respected John L. Cadwalader wrote:

In the unadulterated democracy in which we live no one is content to mind his own business and there appears to be no escape from self-constituted bodies — generally without experience — who propose to conduct public affairs over the heads of the constituted authorities. I see one of these bodies is proposing to run your office, and because there is not room for two district attorneys at the same time, propose to put you out. I hope you will not seriously mind.

But Jerome minded very much. He was embittered enough by the King–Amory attacks, but they were understandable, coming from bilked stockholders. It was the journalistic criticism that enraged him, all the more, perhaps, because he had positively basked in favorable publicity in the days when he was smashing down the doors of gambling joints and buckling on the armor for assaults on the more easily identified villains of metropolitan life. He took his fall from journalistic grace very hard, much as the spoiled darling resents a withdrawal of any of his privileges.

Giving the address of the evening before the annual dinner of St. George's Society, he once again used the public platform to assail the "corrupt" press of New York City. He had discovered, he told the banqueters on April 27, three days before the hearings into his conduct began, that newspapers worshiped the commercial gods and the leading advertisers controlled their editorial policy. "The leading publications of this city are dictated to by the counting rooms." He also accused them of a two-faced attitude, one beaming from the editorial page, the other leering from the advertising columns. "A great paper in this city, that on its editorial page pleaded for virtue a year ago, printed eighty percent of the advertisements of an illegal calling." Here he referred to the *Herald*, whose proprietor was that old friend and patron of the Jerome family, James Gordon Bennett, Jr. Through an investigation initiated by Hearst, Bennett was convicted of sending obscene matter through the mails, a charge based on the fact that the *Herald's* personals columns were highly spiced by ads offering the services of "masseuses with highly magnetic manners" and "witty affectionate ladies" who craved the companionship of "jolly sports," which had brought the *Herald* a revenue of $250,000 until the federal government was persuaded to take action.

Jerome's blanket indictment of the press was understandably annoying to the magisterial *Times*, which reproached him in an editorial: "However much Mr. Jerome may hate 'the newspapers' now, he has used them rather often, the yellowest not the least readily, and more than once they have had reason to regret having obliged him." A few days later, having returned from an out-of-town race meeting where he relaxed in preparation for the hearings, Jerome toned down his remarks about the press to the extent of admitting that a few newspapers were still honest and objective.

To all outward appearances, Jerome approached the hearings before Special Commissioner Hand in his usual public mood of bristling self-confidence. The offers of eminent counsellors to undertake his "defense" were turned aside with thanks, Jerome announcing that he would not only act as his own defense counsel but would be his own star witness. It was obvious that he intended to out-argue, out-act, out-storm and out-accuse everyone arrayed against him. A passive defense was not worthy of consideration. As one writer was to comment years later, Jerome was "at his boldest . . . he carried the battle to his accusers."

A week before the hearing began his cause was strongly bolstered by the report of the latest grand jury investigation into the charges against Ryan and other figures in the Metropolitan collapse. Judge Rosalsky had ordered the renewed inquiry in hopes that indictments could finally be returned. If they had been found, after Jerome had previously failed to obtain them and excused himself on the ground that no evidence of crimes had been uncovered, it would have been most embarrassing. Certainly it would have seriously prejudiced his case before Commissioner Hand. But the grand jury found no grounds for indicting Ryan and others. As the *Times* commented on April 21, "The bearing of the grand jury's report upon the proceeding against Mr. Jerome is obvious. It is also obvious that the interests of the community would now be better served by giving attention to the reorganization of the surface railway system rather than by further exploration of its past history."

The specifications in the complaint against Jerome ranged from the reasonable to the ludicrous. He was charged with neglecting his duty in not prosecuting the insurance and street railway officials with sufficient vigor . . . that he had known of a professional juror in the pay of Metropolitan who served in a number of cases affecting that company . . . that he had "shown no respect for the justices of the Supreme Court of the First Department" in a speech delivered before the City Club in November, 1905 . . . that he had conducted himself improperly in certain conferences with an associate of Charles W. Morse

of the American Ice Company . . . even that he had been observed shaking dice in a barroom with Thomas Fortune Ryan's
two sons.

All these accusations were aired before Commissioner Hand
in the hearings running from April 27 to May 9. Forty witnesses
were summoned, and three thousand pages of testimony taken,
much of it rambling, irrelevant, vague and unsupported.

Jerome's manner was alternately scornful and defiant. At times
he yielded to melodrama, as when he shouted at Commissioner
Hand, "I think I can prove, if Your Honor deems it necessary,
that this inquiry is more than a fishing expedition — it is a blackmail excursion." He did not enlarge on who might be trying to
"blackmail" him or for what purpose.

He was a prickly, sometimes impolite and generally unco-
operative subject for Franklin Pierce, attorney for the King
Committee, both as a witness and as his own defense counsel.

Pierce sought to question him on whether he had remarked
before the City Club, as charged, that "I have no reverence for
the justices of the Supreme Court of the First Department."

Turning aside Pierce's questions, he slyly announced that he
had advised himself, "as counsel for the respondent," that "he
should not answer."

One of the local judiciary with whom Jerome had clashed was
Judge Samuel Seabury, who many years later was to conduct
the investigation into Mayor Walker's administration. Seabury,
as a judge of the City Court, had explored the limits of his
authority, in much the same way as Jerome waging his campaign
against the gamblers while on the Special Sessions bench, in
delving into the affairs of the Metropolitan Street Railway. He
found that one William H. Tillinghast, nominally a night watch-
man for the company, had insinuated himself on juries when cases
against the company were being tried; consequently he tried to
force Jerome to widen the investigation, gathering in the
company's officials and attorneys, but the district attorney,

claiming the evidence would not support such charges, had stalked out of his courtroom saying, "In all my experience I never saw such a proceeding!"

That passage at arms had taken place in 1904 but it still rankled in Seabury, who had since advanced to the Supreme Court. Seabury's feelings were hardly soothed, either, by Jerome's public reference to him as a "cad." When he appeared as a witness at the removal hearing, Jerome asked him:

"Mr. Justice, will you be good enough to express your honest opinion of me?"

"I find it impossible," was Seabury's glacial reply, "to raise you to the level of my contempt."

Thus when Pierce cross-examined Jerome on the charge that he had labeled Seabury's investigation into jury-rigging "an indecent exhibition," he bluntly owned up to making the statement and added, "I now repeat it as an express of my mature judgment." The allegations that he was lax in certain prosecutions, he said, were all part of a knavish conspiracy against him, the nature of which he did not exactly define. On May 6, at what the newspapers termed the "liveliest session of the hearings," he stormed at those who accused him of malfeasance in office: "I want to prove that these people have lied and conspired to ruin my reputation. I want to prove that they went to the brother-in-law of a convicted murderer and tried to get contributions from him to ruin my reputation — solicited money from this rich man. Let us have it all out and clear the air!" Anxious though he may have been to clear the air, he did not explain or expand on the "conspiracy" against him, nor did the other side, strangely enough, attempt to pin him down.

Regarding an alleged tardiness in investigating Metropolitan, he described himself as "so engrossed" in campaigning for re-election that he "had no personal knowledge of traction matters until January 22, 1906."

The damning testimony recorded before the Armstrong Committee in its hearings on the insurance business was of little use to him as a public prosecutor, he maintained. "The Armstrong Committee hearings were conducted, not for the purpose of getting any evidence to convict anyone but to get information on which the Legislature might pass laws limiting the income of insurance companies."

On the last day of the hearing, May 9, he admitted under cross-examination that he had rattled the dice cup with Ryan's two sons. It happened during the first Thaw trial, he recalled, when he slipped out of court during Delphin Delmas's summation to recuperate over a drink or two at Pontin's. There he ran into the Ryan boys at the bar, and they shook dice for drinks.

"Furthermore," he added defiantly, "I admit for the purposes of this case that Allen A. Ryan is a close friend."

President Roosevelt had been following accounts of the proceedings with an understandable relish. When he read of the dice-rolling incident confessed to by Jerome, the President professed himself to be shocked and horrified. "He shook dice for drinks!" Roosevelt exclaimed to a White House caller. "How could he so far forget his dignity?"

Commissioner Hand labored over composing his findings for almost three and one-half months, during which time most people gradually lost interest in the sensational charges against Jerome and turned to other matters for diversion. (A female hog-butcher named Belle Gunness was revealed to be the country's Number one murderess, having disposed of twenty-five to thirty lonely-hearts correspondents on her farm outside La Porte, Indiana. There was also much front-page excitement over the great New York-to-Paris automobile race, via Japan, Siberia and eastern Europe, in which various international contestants strived to outdo each other in the dirty-trick department. New York City was shocked by revelations that the Black Hand, as the Mafia was then known, had taken a firm, terroristic grip on the city's 600,000 citizens of Italian descent; it was estimated that $6,000,000 had been extorted from them by their compatriots, with hundreds of stores and tenements bombed.)

Hand's verdict on the charges against Jerome were summed up in one word: Disproven.

On the charge that William H. Tillinghast "had served a number of times as a juror through the connivance of court clerks when he was not upon the panel, and had received money from the Metropolitan Street Railway Company in consideration of his favorable action as a juror," a matter about which Jerome was allegedly cognizant but "took no action," Hand decided the accusation was baseless. He found that Jerome had taken "proper, prompt and thorough action" on January 2, 1906, when Tillinghast was sentenced to three months in prison for "having falsely personated another juror."

Hand declared that Jerome had prosecuted George W. Perkins and a number of other insurance-scandal figures "in good faith," likewise that he had investigated Metropolitan to the full extent of his legal powers.

The commissioner also decided that Jerome's theory of his duties as a public prosecutor was "the correct one," adding that "It is undoubtedly his duty, when an indictment has been found, to assume toward the defendant named therein the attitude of the people's advocate, and present upon the trial such facts and reasons as may fairly result in a verdict of guilty, leaving it to the defense to present facts and reasons which may remove the conviction of guilt or weaken it so far as to give the benefit of a reasonable doubt to the defendant upon the familiar principle that the truth and justice will most certainly be arrived at by adhering to the theory of trials so long accepted in our civilization."

Testimony had shown, Hand said, that Jerome's consultations with E. R. Thomas, an associate of Charles W. Morse in the

American Ice Company, had been solely for the purpose of trying to persuade Thomas to testify against Morse.

As for the charge that Jerome had shown disrespect for the justices of the First Department of the Supreme Court in his public remarks, it was "not within the scope of this investigation."

Hand also dismissed as inconsequential the matter of Jerome's shaking dice with the Ryan brothers. "Mr. Jerome's real attitude toward the vice of gambling . . . is found, I think, in his connection with the 'Canfield Bill' and other official action."

Jerome, he concluded, had brought much of the criticism on himself through his prickly attitude toward outside advice and suggestion, his supreme belief in himself and his abilities. "A certain self-confidence and contempt of the opinions of other men, a certain rashness of expression to the verge of recklessness, a certain delight in the exercise of his astuteness of mind and vigor of expression, and a certain impatience with criticism have combined, I think, to make men far more eager to attack than they would otherwise have been."

Hand's report was forwarded to Governor Hughes, who could accept its verdict of disproven or order Jerome's removal.

Now he found many friends in the journalistic camp who had awaited the outcome of Hand's inquiry before committing themselves to one side or the other. The Baltimore *News*, reflecting nationwide interest, commented that the result was "not unexpected," considering the general faith in Jerome's integrity. The Brooklyn *Standard–Union* said it was "the rightful due of an honest and competent official." The New York *Evening Post* announced that it had always believed in Jerome and his official objectivity. To the New York *Sun*, taking a sideswipe at its more successful rivals on Park Row, the charges against Jerome had been motivated by "malice, mercenary interest and yellow sensationalism." The district attorney, "a public servant of rare ability and energy," had been thwarted in coping with insurance czars and traction magnates because their conspiracies were "so cleverly planned as to be just out of reach of the statutes." If Jerome's political career was doomed despite the fact that Commissioner Hand had found him blameless, it was because of "the unreasonable expectation of the crowd has been impossible of gratification, and therefore . . . many who shouted loudest for Mr. Jerome are now full of bitterness toward him, because he has not done what they desired and imagined he would be able to do." Jerome, in fact, had met with "the common fate of an idol of the people."

Both Hearst's *American* and Pulitzer's *World* announced that they pinned their hopes now on the governor, pointing out that if Hughes accepted the Hand report he would be admitting, in effect, that his much-lauded insurance investigation had really disclosed no wrongdoing and "amounted to nothing."

The *World* was bitter indeed at the outcome of Hand's inquiry, and derided the claim that Jerome had failed to try and convict certain wealthy predators because their schemes were concocted to keep them beyond the reach of the law. "It is to insult the courts," the *World* said, to assume "that they can punish only petty crimes. It is to say that we must ignore the demand of the whole civilized world that the gigantic crimes of craft and cunning unveiled in the community should be visited by retribution. It is to give notice to the West and the South that money invested in New York County lies at the mercy of thieves . . . The people look to Governor Hughes as the court of last resort."

But Governor Hughes let them down, concurring, a short time later, with Hand's opinion that nothing had been proven against Jerome.

Mr. Jerome allowed that he was pleased, but indicated that he had been expecting nothing less than absolution.

11

An Inexorable Friend of the Court

JEROME HAD BEEN cleared of any malfeasance in office, of any neglect of duty which would call for his removal by the governor, but traces of doubt and suspicion linger after the most unqualified of exonerations, the most ringing of acquittals. Certainly they did in Jerome's case. Some of the popularity which had twice swept him into office in defiance of the wishes of both the Republican and Democratic bosses had seeped away. The constant attacks of the Hearst and Pulitzer organs, which were then the most widely read among the city's masses, had resulted in a loss of public confidence; if not in his personal honesty, then in his willingness to consider the crimes of the rich as reprehensible as the crimes of the less privileged.

People could hardly have been blamed for asking themselves whether sterner measures might not have been taken if the district attorney of New York County had felt the same way about George W. Perkins as he did Dick Canfield, the same way about Thomas Fortune Ryan as he did Abe Hummel or Colonel William D'Alton Mann.

The darker mood of the electorate necessarily caused an abandonment of any hopes that Jerome might run for governor, then offer himself as a candidate for the Presidency in 1912 (a maneuver which, if it had succeeded, would have offered the unprecedented possibility of two members of the same family

heading the governments of Great Britain and the United
States, Jerome during World War I, his cousin during World
War II).

Well into the last year of his second term, however, Jerome
apparently consoled himself with the thought of continuing in
the district attorney's office. "Jerome hoped to succeed himself
for a third term," wrote the late Augustin Derby, one of his
assistants. "One day toward the end of his second term, at a
time when my associate Keogh and I were in charge of trials in
the Court of Special Sessions, Jerome came into my office, sitting
down informally with his feet on a chair, as was his practice.
'Derby,' he said, 'I expect to serve another term and I don't
want to make any changes in the office. If you and Alec stay
where you are I can go to sleep on that court.'"

But his own enthusiasm for staying in office was not matched
by that of any of the reform groups which formed the basis of
his political strength, many of them alienated, of course, by the
King and Amory charges and unreconciled by Commissioner
Hand's verdict. There was a humiliating episode at the Cooper
Union Forum, where he appeared to defend his record and was
mercilessly heckled for two hours with bluntly phrased questions
on his attitude toward Metropolitan and its officials. Many of
those who hurled questions had been coached for what was an
"obviously prepared attack," the newspapers said, but he could
detect little sympathy in the audience for his side of the story.

Several days later his admirers gave him what they styled,
somewhat defeatedly, a "grand rehabilitation dinner."

Fusion's leaders were unimpressed, however, and they soon
proceeded to nominate Charles S. Whitman, a Republican, as
their candidate. Jerome considered offering himself as an independent candidate but was finally convinced there would be
no mass rallying around his standard. The electorate obviously
felt that it had no further need for the Jerome brand of crusad-

ing. Whitman was elected district attorney, served one term, and was elected governor.

Jerome always blamed the failure of his political hopes on his refusal to come to terms with Tammany, but this was only part of the reason. His political career withered when he refused to present himself as a crusader against the "malefactors of great wealth." Had he been less honest and more adroit, he might have been able to hitch his wagon to the very distant star of economic reform . . .

Jerome closed the door of the district attorney's office behind him on December 31, 1909 and never sought public office again. He and his staff gathered at a final dinner at Pontin's, and "he spoke with great emotion as he bade us farewell," Derby recalled. "He stressed the quality of loyalty to a superior as a supreme virtue, and stated that he was grateful that he had received it in full measure from us." Like most of Jerome's young disciples, Derby felt that if Jerome had been slightly more flexible in dealing with the political bosses and machines he would have achieved the highest offices. "After all the years he stands out like a mountain peak in personality, and if he missed greatness as a man, it was by a very narrow margin."

Jerome entered private practice immediately on leaving office, but it was characteristic of him to persist in tying up what he regarded as the one loose end of his career as a public prosecutor. He was convinced that Harry K. Thaw was a menace to society and should never be allowed to regain his freedom, despite the continuing efforts of his family to have him released from the asylum for the criminally insane. It was his duty, Jerome believed, to oppose those efforts whenever and wherever they took shape, either officially or as a friend of the court. For the next five years he assumed the highly controversial role as what the newspapers called Thaw's Nemesis, a role he played with undiminished vigor and unquenched thirst for legal combat.

2

ON THE OTHERWISE quiet Sunday morning of August 17, 1913, an all-points bulletin went out from police headquarters in Manhattan:

Arrest Harry K. Thaw, 40, 5 feet 11½ inches, 166 pounds, brown hair and eyes, medium complexion. Escaped from Matteawan State Hospital for the Criminal Insane at 7:45 A.M. in a black taxicab with two men. Taxicab accompanied by a six-cylinder Packard. Watch all railroads, steamships, etc.

If anyone was surprised by Thaw's escape after five years of confinement, it was not anyone familiar with the metropolitan press. The publicity-mad Thaw had kept himself in the headlines by clamoring in and out of court for his release, and the Thaw family's journalistic advocates, paid or unpaid, never let up in their campaign for his "vindication." The Hearst papers were particularly vociferous, depicting Thaw as a martyr kept behind bars through the efforts of the late Stanford White's friends and their legal mercenary, William Travers Jerome. So far, however, all attempts to free him through writs of habeas corpus had been defeated.

Thaw, according to the newspapers (other than Hearst's), was not finding durance too vile. To pacify his sweet-tooth, vanilla éclairs were baked in lots of two hundred and dispatched to Matteawan, where he shared them with favored guards and fellow inmates. Furthermore, in the company of a guard, he was allowed to slip out of the asylum for overnight stays in the surrounding towns, during which he amused himself as any worthy habitué of the Tenderloin would.

Alienists who examined him from time to time reported that symptoms of paranoia persisted, not the least of them being a conviction that Jerome was his personal enemy. It was not himself who should be locked up, Thaw said, but Jerome. The former district attorney, he told Dr. Charles E. Lane, was "erratic" and probably a menace to the community.

Having lost all faith in due process of the law, Thaw and his supporters on the outside proceeded to concoct an escape plan, which, considering the amiable laxness of his guards, should not be too difficult to bring off.

The man elected to spring Thaw was Richard J. (Big Dick) Butler, a Hell's Kitchen politician, saloonkeeper and Tammany handyman. As Butler later told the story, he was approached by Alfred Henry Lewis, a Hearst editorial writer, in Shanley's Broadway restaurant, a hangout favored by the politicians and sporting gentry. "It will do me a world of good," Butler quoted Lewis as telling him, "if you could accomplish the release of a young man who is held illegally . . . This man's mother is wealthy and it's breaking her heart to see him locked up." The prisoner, Lewis added, was Harry K. Thaw.

Lewis had written a series of editorials picturing Thaw as the victim of "a gang of old roués" who were bent on avenging the murder of their fellow orgiast. His participation in the escape plot, Butler believed, was due to the fact he "sincerely believed what he wrote." Surviving journalists of the period who knew Lewis as a corrosively cynical character with a Broadway wise guy's attitude toward the quick dollar find it difficult to imagine him helping to free Thaw out of pure idealism.

Lewis, at any rate, arranged a meeting between Butler and H. A. Hoffman, a former deputy sheriff of Dutchess County, in which the Matteawan State Hospital is located, who had taken Thaw on a number of his excursions outside the asylum's walls. Hoffman told Butler he would be paid $20,000 if he and several helpers would be waiting at the gates of Matteawan with an automobile. Thaw would slip out the gate while the milk was being delivered.

With three Hell's Kitchen characters named Gene Duffy, Tommy Flood and Mike O'Keefe as his assistants, Butler hired a

Packard touring car and engaged one Roger Thompson as its chauffeur. Flood, a cab driver, would also bring his hack along. The whole party then outfitted itself with linen caps and dusters at Macy's and proceeded to Beacon, on the outskirts of which Matteawan is located.

Shortly after dawn Butler and his friends waited at the front gate of Matteawan. The milk wagon entered the gate, and a moment later Thaw slipped out. He jumped into the taxi, which sped off with Butler and Thompson, who hadn't been informed that he was taking part in an escape plot, following in the Packard. A mile down the road Thaw was transferred to the Packard, and with Butler and Duffy as his escorts began his strange flight. No one apparently had any idea what to do with Thaw once he was spirited away. Butler thought he was supposed to be taken to Milford, Connecticut, and deposited on a train for Pittsburgh. Thaw objected to this plan, however, and offered his deliverers more money if they would take him to Canada.

Somewhat confused, still undecided what to do with Thaw, Butler and his group continued on their way through Connecticut. At one point Thaw, peering melodramatically out the rear curtain to see whether they were being followed, asked Butler if there were any tools handy in the car.

"Why?" Butler wanted to know.

"Jerome might come along," Thaw said, "and we could fight him off with the tools."

Thaw, Butler observed, was "obsessed" by two things, Jerome and his clamorous sweet-tooth. Despite his fears that Jerome would somehow be leading the pursuit in person, he insisted on stopping in New Haven to stoke up on a double chocolate soda. He also took the time to write postcards to Mother Thaw in Pittsburgh and to the Associated Press in New York warning that news agency against handling the story of his escape without due regard for his dignity, with the postscript, "Be careful or I will sue."

At New Haven Butler left the group to return to New York, where newsboys were already coursing through the streets with extras telling of Thaw's escape. Thompson and Duffy stayed with Thaw, changing course for the Canadian border. At Rochester, New York, their car broke down and had to be abandoned, the flight continuing in a rented horse and buggy.

Thaw and his companions caught a Maine Central train bound for Quebec. At Colebrook, New Hampshire, Deputy Sheriff Burleigh Kelsea boarded the train on other business. The alarm for Thaw hadn't reached Colebrook as yet, but Deputy Kelsea's attention was attracted when Thaw began showing off boisterously. Kelsea went up to him and asked if he wasn't Harry Thaw. "I am," Harry said with a guffaw, "but don't tell anyone." At the first stop, Coaticook, Quebec, and on his own initiative, Kelsea placed Thaw, Duffy and Thompson under arrest. The Canadian authorities wanted no part of Thaw, even after the bulletin for his arrest arrived, but the deputy insisted that he be kept in jail for the American authorities.

Meanwhile, in New York, a great uproar had erupted, investigations had been set afoot, scalps were demanded, every constable in New England was alerted to be on the watch for Thaw and his companions.

The newspapers immediately contacted Jerome, as Thaw's official Nemesis, at his country home in Lakeville, but for once he was unwilling to discuss the case. Through the years since he had left the district attorney's office, it had become a sort of avocation with him, along with the fascination that abnormal psychology held for him. To keep himself up to date on developments in that growing field, he often consulted with psychologists and neurologists. He had faithfully appeared as a friend of the court each time Thaw sought his release. One sanity hearing had lasted for weeks, and was terminated only after Jerome took over the cross-examination of Thaw. Something about Jerome, aside from the fact that he had been so persistent in prosecuting the case, brought out the worst in Thaw as a witness trying to prove he had recovered mental stability. To Thaw, Jerome, perhaps, embodied the whole censorious world which had tried, since childhood, to curb his inclinations and had viewed him with contempt as "Mad Harry." Thaw became enraged, glaring-eyed and almost incoherent as he tried to disprove the statements of alienists quoted by Jerome and the testimony of Susan Merrill, who had kept the Tenderloin resort in which Thaw had found outlets for his sadism — and once again he only proved to the court that Jerome was right.

Jerome was also present in April, 1912 when Thaw and his family launched another effort to obtain his release on a writ of habeas corpus returnable in a Brooklyn Supreme Court. This time the Thaws mustered five alienists who swore that Thaw had recovered his sanity. They also had engaged highly skillful counsel, headed by Clarence J. Shearn, a bald little man with a booming voice, who fittingly enough also served William Randolph Hearst for almost forty years as guardian of his legal interests. "Powerful interests have long been at work," was Shearn's theme, adapted from Hearst editorials, to prevent the courts from freeing Thaw. The hearings began during the excitement over the sinking of the *Titanic*, relegating newspaper accounts of them to the rear-page province of the patent medicine and truss ads, and irking Harry no end. Possibly this lack of interest encouraged him to plot a sensational escape, and recapture public attention, when Javert–Jerome once again interceded successfully against him.

All that sustained Thaw, aside from a mental self-portrait of himself as a modern Prisoner of Zenda, was his mother's boundless determination that her son should be released. Mary Copley Thaw, resembling the heroine of a Greek tragedy in her heedless and tireless efforts to prove him the victim of injustice, lived only for the day her darling Harry would walk free. The New York *World* reported that she spent $800,000 on the cause up to the summer of 1909, another $200,000 since then, a small part of this expenditure going toward the publication of a pamphlet charging Jerome with maliciously and illegally preventing her son's release.*

Thaw could also take comfort in the fulminations of such publicity-minded figures as the Reverend Dr. Parkhurst, who still looked wistfully back to the days when he was cleansing the Tenderloin. "I think the relentlessness, I might almost say the savagery, with which Jerome has pursued Thaw has created a degree of sympathy in the public mind for Thaw," Dr. Parkhurst told the newspapers. "Sophocles or Euripides," commented another appalled observer, "would have made a great tragedy out of Thaw's career and the pitiful struggle he has had to escape his Nemesis."

Jerome's attitude, as he expressed it, was that "I have no rule in life except to do the thing directly before me the best I know how, then take up the next job . . . In all these different proceedings both while I was in office, and since I have left office, I am not conscious of having done a single thing which it was not my duty to do as an attorney, and I know of nothing that has been done, which if I omitted it, would not have exposed me justly to the criticism of my professional brethren. I am at a loss to understand why the acts of an attorney in the discharge of his professional duty, and strictly within those professional duties, should be characterized either as 'relentless' or 'savagery.' "

The courts so far had sustained Jerome in his contention that two principles were involved: public safety was the paramount consideration, and the rehabilitation of the criminally insane could be certified only after all danger of relapse has been removed. It was Jerome's contention that Thaw was a paranoiac, that paranoia could not be "cured," and that he must be kept behind bars to the end of his life. One judge, in upholding the

* *The Secret Unveiled*, by Mary Copley Thaw, 1909. One of the charges she made was that Jerome proclaimed he would "delay the second trial in the hope that Thaw would go crazy in the Tombs."

views of his *amicus curiae*, pointed out that "Americans are solici-
tous enough concerning the rights of the individual criminal; they
need to cultivate regard for the rights of the community."

One figure in the Thaw case who had come to agree with
Jerome was the prisoner's wife. Evelyn Nesbit Thaw had given
birth to a son in October, 1910 whom she said was conceived during one of Thaw's excursions outside Matteawan (Thaw himself later denied he was the boy's father). Nevertheless the Thaws
had cut off her subsidy, and her life since then had not been
easy. The immigration authorities in England had prevented her
from landing there; she had been evicted from a New York
hotel; she was sued for nonpayment of a clothing bill, and she was
reduced to capitalizing on her notoriety by appearing in the roof
garden of Madison Square Garden, the scene of White's murder,
displaying her incendiary face and figure in a dancing act at
$4,000 a week.

No subsidy from the Thaw treasury, no testimony on Harry's
behalf, had become her credo. When Attorney Shearn tried
to persuade her to testify for her husband, she replied, "I want
it understood here that Harry Thaw hid behind my skirts
through two dirty trials, and I will not stand for it again. I won't
let him or you, Mr. Shearn, throw any more mud at me."

After Thaw escaped, she predicted to reporters, with some
accuracy, "They will catch him, for he cannot resist the tempta-
tion to walk up to some stranger and say 'I am the famous Harry
Thaw.' " Meanwhile she would "take means of protecting myself . . . The great danger with Harry will be that of drinking."
She rejoiced in the fact, she said, that their son was safe in
England, where he was being reared and educated.

Only a few hours after Evelyn received the reporters came
word that Thaw had been taken into custody in Canada. Removed to the more commodious jail at Sherbrooke and comfortably installed in the hospital ward, as befitted so wealthy and
well-connected a guest of the Dominion, Thaw began holding

a practically nonstop press conference with the correspondents who converged on the city from all directions. "I lost all that was dear to me in the world," he said, "when Evelyn went back to her old life on the stage." When he wearied of talking to newspapermen, he could always go to the windows overlooking the street and wave royally at the crowds gathered below to demonstrate their sympathy for the fugitive from "American injustice." It was partly a cousinly dig at the United States and a desire to show the superiority of Canadian justice, perhaps, but the local mob really outdid itself demonstrating solidarity with the fugitive. The provincial courts, possibly reflecting this attitude, indicated at the outset they would be reluctant to turn Thaw over to the American authorities. A New York *Times* correspondent reported that:

Men and women almost trampled upon each other in a mad rush to shake his hand. When he went to the courtroom he rode in an open carriage, acclaimed by the populace, lifting his hat and bowing right and left like an emperor . . . Wherever he goes the cry in French and English of "Here's Thaw!" goes up, followed by the usual cheer for "British justice." Never before has there been seen anything like the demonstation the Province of Quebec has been making over — the soldier, sailor, or statesmen Thaw? — no, the Tenderloin rounder Thaw.

Seventeen lawyers, headed by Clarence J. Shearn and including five distinguished King's Counsels from Toronto and Montreal, gathered in Sherbrooke to help Thaw fight extradition. Together they planned every possible move to prevent their client from being deported and returned to Matteawan. To aid the cause, they imported Dr. Britten D. Evans, the inventor of the "brainstorm" theory which had seemed so impressive (and since had become a standard gag in the repertoire of lesser vaudeville comedians), and three other alienists who were willing to swear up and down that Thaw was as sane and responsible a citizen as could be found.

Thaw and his legal multitude were brimming with confidence, but it was short-lived.

On August 22, in Albany, it was reported that William Travers Jerome was conferring with the Attorney General on the Thaw extradition case.

A few hours later it was announced that he had been appointed a Special Deputy Attorney General and would depart almost immediately for Sherbrooke.

"Let him come! Let him come!" Thaw all but gibbered to reporters. "It is the same band who are pursuing me. A clique of Mr. White's friends have always hounded me."

3

JEROME ARRIVED August 26, having driven up from New York in his touring car. He installed himself at the Hotel Magog, and then went back to the garage to tinker with the engine of his automobile, which had been malfunctioning on the journey north. Reporters interviewed him as he bent over the engine in shirt-sleeves with a monkey wrench. He didn't care to discuss the legal aspects of the case, but he was voluble on the subject of Canadian sympathy for the fugitive.

"Well, I'd like to tell the Canadian people something," the New York *Times* quoted him.

This man Thaw seems to be trying to spread the impression that he is being persecuted. Who wants Thaw? Not New York State!

New York is trying to get Thaw back, not because it wants him, but because of the effect that his escape would have on the great mass of people when Socialistic tendencies are so widespread. If Thaw were to remain free, everyone would say it was Thaw's millions which bought his freedom . . . Why, the very fact that Thaw was at liberty would have a demoralizing effect on the people. Thaw free would be a real menace. That's why New York State wants him back.

It was, if Jerome was quoted correctly, a curious basis for a legal proceeding. His fellow lawyers might have been inclined to argue with him on the point that Thaw's extradition was necessary to demonstrate that the law applied equally to the rich and poor, rather than to recover a fugitive from justice who was also adjudged, thus far, a possible menace to public safety.

Whatever his reasoning, Jerome and his latest pursuit of Thaw attracted much opposition on both sides of the international boundary. The New York *American* published a front-page cartoon by Winsor McCay titled "The Man Hunt," showing Thaw at bay in the Temple of Justice, surrounded by dissolute old vultures in frock coats, silk hats, monocles and spats who were supposed to represent Stanford White's friends. (Considering how that group, as a whole, turned their backs on White when the murder was committed, it seemed odd that they would now be seeking vengeance with all the thirst of feuding hillfolk.) The New York *Journal* again reminded everyone that in killing White Thaw "rendered a considerable service to the community," and maintained that he had been "hounded for years by a crowd of fashionable white slavers." The Boston *American* wailed that Thaw was being "persecuted" and his extradition would be as foul a miscarriage of justice as could be found in the "annals of the Middle Ages."

As for the Canadian populace, Jerome found it almost hysterically opposed to him and he was forced to go around with a bodyguard hastily imported from New York. Thousands of people had come to Sherbrooke to attend the district fair and regarded the Thaw case as an extra added attraction, a sort of real-life sideshow. The magazine *Current Opinion* sardonically observed that:

the populace is gone mad over its mad hero . . . Lawyers opposed to him are threatened with death. Waitresses in the village hotel, touched with the general idiocy, refuse to serve them . . . Every little while the crowd gathers and threatens to rush the jail in the rescue of the maniac, who bows to it and addresses it through his cell window.

The New York *Times* correspondent commented that the outpouring of public sympathy was wasted on Thaw, so cozily
accommodated in a hospital ward with four beds at his disposal
and catered to by "a noble old sheriff who ought to have fought in
the War of 1812."

In his first appearance before the court at Sherbrooke, Jerome
was brushed aside, all but thrown out of the courtroom by the
presiding justice, when he presented his plea for extradition.
"This is an *ex parte* proceeding," Jerome was informed by the
bench and told to be gone. The packed courtroom thereupon
exploded with cheers and applause, which the bench did nothing
to discourage.

Jerome spent a day chain-smoking furiously in the lobby of
the Hotel Magog, plotting his next move and holding court with
the American correspondents. Obviously the opposition could
stall indefinitely in this psychological and juridical climate. He
decided to go over the heads of the local judiciary and present his
case to the Provincial government in Quebec City, which was
embarrassed by the anti-American sentiments stirred up by its
uninvited guest and his attorneys. He also planned another move
in the courts, based on technicalities. "All the time the scheme was
brewing," lamented one newspaperman, "Mr. Jerome sat in the
lobby of the Magog Hotel recounting to correspondents stories
of strategic acts which had marked former cases of great public
interest." Mr. Jerome, it seemed, at last had learned to be wary
with the press.

From officials of the Ministry of Justice, he learned that they
were even more alarmed than he was by the hero-worship accorded Thaw and even more annoyed by the delaying tactics of
his lawyers. Jerome was told, in fact, that if the courts didn't act
favorably on the extradition in a few days the Canadian immigration authorities would simply shove Thaw across the border.

But first Jerome gave the courts their chance, or as the New
York *Times* headlined it August 31, "Coup Puts Thaw in Jerome's

Reach." Jerome himself sought a writ of habeas corpus on the grounds of faulty commitment. Once out of jail, Thaw might more easily be maneuvered across the border. His attorneys, alert to the writ's possibilities, countered that they would appeal to the higher courts, if Thaw was released, to have him put back in jail. The Provincial government, increasingly annoyed by the publicity the case was attracting all over the world, with its citizens depicted as making a national hero out of a murderer, announced that no matter what the outcome in the courts Thaw would be turned over to the immigration authorities.

Thaw, said a representative of the Minister of Justice, "came to Canada illegally and he must go."

On September 3, the courts still having refused to act, Thaw's deportation was ordered. This action only increased the resentment against Jerome personally, and in Coaticook, preparing for Thaw's arrest the moment he crossed the border, he was threatened several times with "being shot on sight." Jerome's nonchalance was undisturbed; he walked the streets, chain-smoked on the porch of the hotel in plain view, and tinkered with his automobile to help pass the time.

One afternoon, waiting for the deportation to take place, he joined a crap-shooting contest with American newspapermen in the waiting room of the Grand Trunk Station. A local constable raided the game. The other players were released, but Jerome was arrested on a charge of gambling on railroad property.

"Hell," he said as he was hauled into court, "I didn't even win!"

"They'd better watch him," Thaw told reporters with malicious delight, "or he'll jump bail."

A few days later Jerome was acquitted on the gambling charge and even received the apologies of the court.

Two days after that, on September 10, Thaw was (as one indignant newspaper put it) "thrown bodily out of the Dominion of Canada on the order of the Minister of Justice and in utter disregard of the highest courts of the Province of Quebec."

Jerome and his detectives were waiting at Norton's Mills, Vermont, to take him into custody, but once again an even dozen Thaw lawyers, leaving their five Canadian colleagues in Quebec, hastened to apply the appropriate counteraction. They persuaded a Federal judge in Concord, New Hampshire, to issue a writ of habeas corpus preventing Thaw's return to Matteawan.

Now the scene shifted to the Eagle Hotel in Concord, where Jerome and his group and Thaw and his lawyers installed themselves. Every day Thaw presided over a strategy conference in one of the hotel's parlors, "in appearance at least," as one correspondent observed, "directing his fight and issuing orders to his attorneys."

The citizenry of Concord proved to be just as addled by sentimentality as the Canadians. Once again Thaw became a local hero, cheered every time he showed himself in public. Presidents Pierce, Hayes, Roosevelt and Taft had visited Concord on occasion but none of them was so enthusiastically greeted as Thaw when he arrived at the railroad station. "Half of those in the crowd were women, and they fought with the men to get a glimpse of Thaw, some of them climbing on the baggage trucks in their eagerness to see the prisoner."

New York State's fight to recover Thaw from New Hampshire was a repetition of the exhausting ordeal on Canadian soil, with infinite variations and ingenious extensions. It lasted, in fact, from September, 1913 to December, 1914. Thaw lived royally and cultivated his popularity around Concord with "many acts of charity."

Jerome stuck to the case month after month, commuting between Concord and New York, to the detriment of his private practice. It wasn't until the closing days of 1914 that Thaw's lawyers exhausted every possibility of delay, and Thaw was finally ordered extradited to New York and less comfortable quarters in the Tombs.

Jerome had spent almost a decade on the Thaw case and both

his patience and his interest were exhausted. Obviously public opinion yearned for Thaw's return to society as a free man. He withdrew from the case, with the result that in July, 1915 a New York jury adjudged Thaw sane and Supreme Court Justice Peter A. Hendrick ordered him released. A crowd of thousands gathered outside to cheer his first confident steps as a free man, causing the New York *Sun* to comment in an editorial headed "How to Be a Hero":

At length, the long ignominious drama is ended. The paranoiac walks forth free, delivered sane by a jury of his intelligent fellow citizens; and he becomes, as he had previously become even in sober New Hampshire, a conquering hero, the idol of "the populace." Cheering crowds crush around him. Women weep over him. Men esteem it an honor to shake the hand crimson with the blood of Stanford White. Washington or Lincoln could not be more deified than this murderer . . . In all this nauseous business we don't know which makes the gorge rise more, the pervert buying his way out, or the perverted idiots that hail him with wild huzzas.

To those who regarded Mrs. Thaw's devotion to her son as the sentimental epic of the time it must have come as something of a shock when Harry sped off to Atlantic City with his cronies immediately after being freed. On the eve of his release, she had told reporters, "We — Harry and I — are going to live very quietly now. He will be home tonight. My happiness is complete." Harry, however, had other ideas about happiness and said he couldn't spare the time to visit his mother.

Jerome publicly "washed his hands of the case," uttering a final prediction that Thaw would be a constant nuisance, if not a menace to society. The headlines of ensuing years bore him out to the last syllable. Thaw and Evelyn were divorced, Harry charging that her son was not his. In 1917, he was arrested on charges of having kidnaped and whipped a teen-aged boy. Again he was committed to an asylum, this time in Pennsylvania, with his mother, finally disillusioned, requesting that he never again be turned loose. But he was released seven years later, just in time to attend the notorious "nude in a bathtub" party given by Broadway producer Earl Carroll, the tabloid sensation of 1924. In the following years Harry was in and out of the courts on breach of promise proceedings, for having started a row in an Atlantic City nightclub operated by Evelyn, for having beaten up a speakeasy hostess and other unsavory activities. His life was troubled, pathetic, sensation-seeking to the day of his death in February, 1947. Evelyn's was equally unquiet; she was the darling of the tabloids during the twenties, constantly involved in disputes over other women's husbands, frequent bankruptcies, speakeasy and nightclub brawls, suicide attempts, charges that she was a drug addict.

Of all the principal figures in the Stanford White murder case she survives (at this writing), a testimony to the durability of her sex, a sweet-faced old lady in a lavender smock laboring over her ceramic statuary in a Los Angeles studio, who refuses with gentle dignity to discuss the years, more than half a century ago, when she was the *femme fatale* of the civilized world.

12

A Long Fade-out—in Technicolor

THERE IS ONE advantage enjoyed by men whose political careers are cut short: they are generally remembered as young men, endowed with a permanent youth. Like Peter Pan they return to a Never-Never Land. This is particularly true if they turn from politics to some unrelated and less publicized field. In time their unfulfilled promise glows brighter by comparison with those who have had their chance and have all too humanly failed.

William Travers Jerome was fifty years old when he left the district attorney's office, never again to present himself as a candidate for office, but in middle age he was so vigorous and youthful, lean and athletic and still possessed of a feline quickness of movement, that most people thought him much younger, forgetting that his career began back in the eighties. The illusion of youth clung to him almost to the end of his days, an unexpected reward for his frustration and disappointments.

More than a score of years remained to him after his retirement from public service, but his returns to the headlines were few and far between. His main concern, now that his active participation in politics was ended, was to provide a reasonable amount of security for himself and his family. No honest man leaves the district attorney's office enriched, and he marched directly from the Criminal Courts Building to a law office on

Broad Street, where he became a partner in the firm of Guthrie, Jerome, Rand and Kresel — William Rand and Isidor J. Kresel having been former assistant district attorneys.

Jerome prospered as a lawyer, though he did not fare so brilliantly as he did as a prosecutor, possibly because his temperament was better suited to the attack. Later on, too, he became deeply involved in the development of a colored motion picture process whose corporate struggles and ultimately resounding success formed an autumnal aura of triumph and rounded off his career with his fair share of material rewards. "My most sanguine dream of financial success," he once said, "is to retire in my old age with a competency such as many a captain of police retires with." He did better than that eventually.

His last abrasive brush with the press, particularly Pulitzer's unfriendly *World*, came shortly after he gave up interceding in the Thaw litigation. Perhaps inadvertently, he became involved in the machinations of agents of the German government then engaged in trying, through propaganda, espionage and sabotage, to keep the United States from aiding the Allies. This presumably innocent involvement must have been quite shocking to his English relatives, particularly since Winston Churchill had risen high in the British government, had served with great vigor and foresight as the First Lord of the Admiralty and had been the prime mover in the ill-fated Gallipoli operation, the failure of which resulted in his reduction to the meaningless post of Chancellor of the Duchy of Lancaster. (In subsequent trips to Europe during the twenties, Jerome sometimes visited with Churchill, according to members of the family, at a time when the political careers of both cousins were in eclipse — Churchill's not at all permanently.)

Jerome's name cropped up in accounts of German plotting in the United States during the summer of 1915, when a United States Secret Service man seated himself next to Dr. Heinrich F. Albert, a particularly energetic but not very discreet minion of the All-Highest in Berlin, on the Third Avenue Elevated. The American switched briefcases with Dr. Albert, who was listed as a "financial agent" of the German government but was actually involved in sabotage and espionage. The contents of Dr. Albert's briefcase were studied with interest in Washington, teetering as it was between neutrality and an Anglo-French military alliance.

Somehow the New York *World* obtained a copy of the drowsy Dr. Albert's correspondence and created widespread embarrassment by publishing it. Early in August it published a rather ambiguous exchange between Arthur von Briesen, a businessman with offices in Broad Street whom Theodore Roosevelt had once termed one of the two "most useful" private citizens in the country, and Jerome. Mentioned in the Jerome–von Briesen correspondence was a possible fee of $10,000 plus a like sum for expenses for handling "a delicate matter," of which no other details were given.

Von Briesen, interviewed by the *Times*, promptly declared that his negotiations with Jerome had nothing to do with his dealings with Dr. Albert. "The correspondence between him and Jerome," the *Times* said it was informed by von Briesen, had been "in no way related to any German activity in this country," adding that von Briesen "had occasion to need the services of a criminal lawyer, and had considered engaging Mr. Jerome." Most people were satisfied with this explanation, but the *Times* on August 21 published a letter from a person signing himself only as "H." inquiring, "If Herr von Briesen is correct in his assertion that his negotiations with William Travers Jerome concerned a purely criminal case, how was the correspondence found in the possession of an official of the German government?"

The question went unanswered; Jerome himself refused to be interviewed on the subject, and his office would only say that "no comment whatsoever" would be forthcoming. In any case the United States's declaration of war against the Central Powers was twenty months in the offing, and there was nothing illegal in a lawyer's corresponding with a potential client, no matter what his presumed sympathies.

That same year Jerome and Kresel engaged in a bitter court fight with a brilliant opponent named Max D. Steuer, known to newspaper readers as The Wonder Worker, The Demon Defender and The World's Greatest Criminal Lawyer, all titles to which he had some legitimate claim. Steuer, like Kresel, came of immigrant Jewish stock, but there wasn't the slightest bond of sympathy between the two men. Most courtroom "feuds" are nine-tenths pretense; between Kresel and Steuer there was a deadly, unremitting and destructive enmity.

Jerome and Kresel represented Abe Erlanger, whom they had once indicted as a leader of the "theater trust" which monopolized Broadway show houses. The firm of Klaw and Erlanger was then the most successful producing company on Broadway. But it was illicit passion, not the box office, that spun this particular plot. Steuer had instituted action against Erlanger on behalf of his alleged paramour, Edith St. Clair, a musical comedy actress of no great luster but, as time and events proved, the possessor of a certain talent for offstage dramatics. Miss St. Clair charged that Erlanger, in breaking off their affair, first had promised to support her for the rest of her life, then had agreed, instead, to pay her $25,000 in ten annual installments. The theatrical magnate responded that he had been "framed" into making the agreement. A jury found for the plaintiff, awarding her $22,500.

Almost as displeased by that verdict as Erlanger himself, Jerome and Kresel pursued the matter with unusual tenacity. Jerome petitioned the court to reopen the case and exploded what the newspapers called a bombshell by submitting an affidavit from Miss St. Clair admitting that she had perjured herself under instructions from Steuer.

Erlanger charged that Steuer had, in fact, been blackmailing him for years. "Steuer didn't go to the Klondike," the producer claimed, "because he had me in Forty-second Street!"

Disbarment proceedings were ordered for Steuer and heard before a referee. And once again Jerome, recalling his unsuccessful attempts to cope with Evelyn Nesbit and Nan Patterson as hostile witnesses, had cause to ponder the advisability of keeping actresses out of court, which they tended to regard, apparently, as a sort of off-Broadway stage set. Much to everyone's surprise, Miss St. Clair began weeping the moment she sank into the witness chair; between sniffles she agreed with Steuer's counsel that "devious means" had been used to induce her to sign the affidavit. Thus she repudiated the repudiation of her testimony at the original trial, and Steuer was cleared.

But that wasn't the end of the Steuer–Kresel feud. Kresel quit Jerome's firm to practice on his own with even greater success, specializing in handling appeals for the gilt-edged corporation lawyers of lower Broadway, and undertaking, as a civic duty, various investigations. One was an inquiry into the magistrates courts, in which he was chief counsel, and Steuer masterminded strategy for Tammany Hall. That same year, 1930, Steuer conducted an investigation into the collapse of the Bank of the United States, in which Kresel was a director. Kresel was indicted and convicted, but the conviction was reversed on appeal.

One of the most satisfying phases of Jerome's post-political career was his continuing relationship with the young men who had staffed the district attorney's office during his two terms. Every year his former assistants gave him a dinner on the occasion of his birthday. He was intensely proud of the fact that they kept demonstrating their regard for their old chief. It was the sole visible vanity in a man noted for his irony, his sardonic humor and profane wit. One of his grandsons, William Travers Jerome, III, recalls attending several of the last dinners — a custom which, in fact, was continued as a sort of commemoration a few years after Jerome's death — and how the old gentleman swelled with a highly uncharacteristic pride.

One of the more sentimental of these gatherings occurred on April 19, 1919 at the Manhattan Club. It was not only Jerome's sixtieth birthday but many of his former assistants had just returned from service overseas — among them Lieutenant Colonel William Rand, one of his law partners; Major Arthur Train, Captain Theodore H. Ward, Lieutenant Edward S. Tinker, Major A. C. Vandiver; also Judges Charles C. Knott, Frederic Kernochan, Francis P. Garvan, Joseph Corrigan and Daniel F. Murphy; and Isidor J. Kresel, George W. Whiteside, Charles W. Appleton, Mason Trowbridge, John F. O'Neill, James W. Osborne, William Dean Embree and Augustin Derby.

By then his domestic arrangements, though highly unconventional, had settled into a happy and peaceful enough routine. Mrs. Jerome was established in a comfortable home in Yonkers, along with her brothers Gus and Nick, which he visited infrequently.

Jerome himself had taken up residence in a brownstone at 125 East Thirty-sixth Street, a household over which Mrs. Elliot presided. His wife in everything but name, Mrs. Elliot entertained his personal and business acquaintants, none of whom, so far as is recalled, objected to his private design for living. Here he had set up another metal-working shop, and in his study he was surrounded by reminders of his political career, including a silver loving cup presented by the grand jury of April, 1909; a bronze statue of Abraham Lincoln (Jerome's political hero, above all others) given him by his staff when he retired; a silk screen presented by residents of Chinatown grateful for his help in settling a dispute between tongs; a framed two-dollar bill sent him in 1901 with the inscription, "I am a poor man. This is all I can afford. Good luck"; a cartoon drawn by C. R. Macaulay showing Jerome with halo and wings, rolling his eyes piously, after Commissioner Hand had cleared him of any misdeeds in office, and another cartoon, by Robert Carter, showing him as a smugly smiling tiger with mustache, *pince-nez* and glowing cigarette. Always facing him on his desk was a bronze plaque he had turned out in his own shop, with the quotation from Emerson by which he sought to guide himself:

> Thy lot or portion of
> life is seeking after thee;
> Therefore be at rest from
> seeking after it.

Although his estrangement from his wife had widened with the years, he finally was drawn closer to their only son, as William Travers, Jr. married, matured and finally succeeded in gradually loosening the maternal bonds. The young man had been very popular with the debutantes and built up a reputation as a Prince Charming of the stag lines, but his father believed he should have been devoting more time to establishing himself in a career. William, Jr., his father feared, was showing signs of taking after the more feckless members of his family.

Then the young man fell in love with a slender, attractive young lady named Hope Colgate, whose family had founded the soap business which still bears its name and contributed heavily to the foundation and maintenance of Colgate University upstate. The Colgates were prominent in Baptist denominational affairs and noted for a much sterner attitude toward life and its responsibilities than the Jeromes. Hope's father, James C. Colgate, operated a Wall Street brokerage, the family having removed itself from the soap business years before.

Jerome's only concern, as he later confessed, was that Hope Colgate, with her strait-laced family background, might be appalled by the somewhat irregular Jerome way of life. What would she think of the haphazard manner in which Mrs. Jerome kept her house, cluttered as it was with two unemployable brothers? Worse yet, what would she think of his own ménage, whose centerpiece was a lady who was not his wife? How would she react to stories of the Jeromes's antics in business and society dating back to the Civil War, and several rather noisy skeletons in the family closet? Already Colonel Mann's *Town Topics*, which was still struggling to maintain its pose as the monitor and catchpole of high society, had run an item hinting that the sedate Colgates were courting trouble if they allowed themselves to be connected with the unconventional Jeromes.

Jerome was determined, when he learned that his son was serious about Hope, to find out if she was "regular." One of the troubles with his own marriage, he believed, was that Lavinia was utterly incapable of enjoying life, in the sense that he knew enjoyment. So he invited Hope and her friend, Kate Chase, of Waterbury, whose father was an old hunting and fishing companion of his, to join a camping trip to northern New England some months before she and William, Jr. were married, in 1917.

She remembers vividly the late afternoon on which Jerome submitted her to his own acid test for feminine compatibility. He paused while making a stew at the campfire and came over to Hope flourishing a raw onion.

"Do you like raw onion?" he demanded.

Intuitively recognizing this as a test, Hope nodded and took a slice of onion, pretending to be delighted with it.

"Now there's a girl after my own heart," said Jerome, beaming. "She likes raw onion!"

Later she confessed to him that she had thrown the onion slice away when he wasn't looking, but Jerome was "tickled because I'd put something over on him."

Hope had cause to wonder whether she'd won him over, however, when she and William, Jr. were married. The only person who wept at that ceremony, to her amazement and consternation, was her reputedly hard-boiled father-in-law. Tears wetted his cheeks as she and his son exchanged their vows, and as quickly thereafter as politely possible Hope cornered him and demanded to know why he was so aggrieved at acquiring her as a daughter-in-law. Did he think she wasn't good enough for his son? On the contrary, Jerome assured her, frankly telling her of the "weaknesses" he suspected were handed down from one generation of Jeromes to the other and of his fears that William, Jr. would turn out to be something of a playboy like his grandfather.

Hope's father, during a subsequent discussion of William, Jr.'s possibilities, bluntly told Jerome: "You don't know your own son," and announced that he was taking the young man into the Colgate brokerage. Though William, Jr. had been educated to follow his father into the legal profession, he detoured to Wall Street, proved his ability and displayed as firm a sense of responsibility as his circumstances required. Professionally, his own son, William Travers Jerome, III, who is Dean of the College of Business Administration at Syracuse University (something seems to have drawn the present generation of Jeromes back to their ancestral ground upstate), believes that William, Jr. was not "a particularly happy man," caught as he was between the millstones of a famous father and a masterful father-in-law. Yet it was William, Jr. whose intelligent and determined efforts saved the Colgate brokerage from disaster during the stock market crash of 1929.

It was only after his marriage, his daughter-in-law has said, that Jerome came to know, respect and value his son. He was further indebted to William, Jr. and particularly to the latter's wife for taking over the major burden of looking after Mrs. Jerome and her brothers. Hope struggled valiantly to keep that household, near their own home in Yonkers, in some kind of order. She recalls that when Nick Howe died suddenly, she called Jerome at his office, as he had instructed her to do in any kind of emergency affecting Mrs. Jerome, and he hurried out to Yonkers . . . and that as she guided him upstairs to where his brother-in-law lay, he glanced into the rooms as he passed and almost groaned, "Oh, no, not such a mess as this!"

When Hope's first child was still a baby, she remembers, Jerome joined a family gathering at Thanksgiving. They were all seated at the table when the infant began wailing in a nearby room.

Hope shrugged and said, "Let him cry," although Mrs. Jerome urged her to go to the baby's side and comfort him.

Jerome beamed and all but broke out in applause when his daughter-in-law refused to follow the tradition of the Jerome wives and mothers, on the grounds that there was no sense in humoring an infant's whims.

He is remembered as an exceedingly affectionate and proud grandfather, who took William, Jr.'s children on frequent camping trips and whose gruffness came to the surface only once that his grandson, William, III, remembers, that being the occasion on which the boy lost his prize fishing rod in a Maine lake. But the only time he showed any trace of the solicitude which he abhorred in the raising of children was when he warned Hope to keep a close watch over her children if she ever heard of Harry K. Thaw's escaping from the asylum in Pennsylvania. "I don't think he would harm me," Jerome explained, "but he might try to get at the ones I love."

For several years after her marriage, Hope kept hearing whispers of his attachment to Mrs. Elliot and of the legally unsanctified house they shared on East Thirty-sixth Street.* She resented hearing of the relationship in this fashion, and the indication that her father-in-law did not consider her grown-up, tolerant and understanding enough to tell her about it himself.

She went to Jerome one day and insisted on being told the truth about his relationship with Mrs. Elliot. He told her that he had loved Mrs. Elliot for many years, and added, "I wish you would get to know Mrs. Elliot because I know you'd love her too."

She wanted to know why he didn't divorce Lavinia, and do the

* The only public notice of that living arrangement could have been found in the fact Jerome gave the house as his Manhattan address (which the obituaries listed as his residence) and a line in the city directory which read: "Elliot E Stewart h [home] 125 E 36th."

honest and forthright thing by marrying the woman he really loved. Perhaps the thing that concerned his daughter-in-law most about the situation was that it placed her father-in-law, whom she greatly admired and respected, in the furtive and hypocritical position of a "back street" romancer. Furthermore it was as unfair to Mrs. Elliot as it was to Mrs. Jerome.

She does not recall the exact words of his reply, but it was both touching and unsentimental, matter-of-fact. He couldn't divorce Lavinia, or ask her to divorce him, because she had done nothing to justify such an action; she had been the best kind of wife she knew how; she had done nothing to betray or belittle him. Their incompatibility was no more her fault than his. No, he could not justify divorcing Lavinia merely because she stood in the way of his happiness.

So Jerome continued to live his double life. From then on, however, Mrs. Elliot was brought into the family circle. Jerome's grandchildren saw almost as much of her as they did of their grandmother, and accorded her a similar respect and affection. William Travers Jerome, III remembers especially the great care she took in buying them Christmas presents given in their grand-father's name. "Mrs. Elliot had two great attractions for Grand-father," as he recalls. "She put him on a pedestal and made a per-fect audience for him. At the same time she would argue with him, on an intellectual plane, and there was nothing he liked better than an argument." By the time he married, Mrs. Elliot was so much a part of the family that Dean Jerome took his bride-to-be to be inspected and approved by her.

Despite the sternness of her Baptist upbringing, his daughter-in-law declares that "Mrs. Elliot gave Mr. Jerome the only happi-ness he ever knew." Hope never learned, close as she was to Mrs. Jerome, whether Lavinia knew of her husband's relationship with Mrs. Elliot. "Mrs. Jerome never mentioned her name," she says, "or gave any indication that she knew of Mrs. Elliot's existence."

If the arrangement was deplorable from the moral standpoint,

Jerome at least managed to carry it off with dignity, and without scandal or recrimination.

Right down to his last days, his life was full of activity, both in his profession and outside it. He dined out frequently, played poker at least once a week at the Union Club and was a familiar figure in the more respectable sectors of Manhattan's night life. Gregarious though he was, he also found time for more private pleasures. An omnivorous reader, he plowed through the Waverley novels at least once a year, and thoroughly explored the works of Freud, Jung, Adler and other pioneers in the field of psychiatry, taking pride in the statements of Drs. Carlos McDonald and Austin Flint, who had testified at the Thaw trials, that he knew more about mental health than "any other lawyer in the country." He golfed, hunted and fished with great enthusiasm, and continued to devote much time to his metal-working (a counterpart of his cousin Winston's passion for brick-laying). His work as a coppersmith, silversmith and goldsmith, practiced as it was over a period of more than thirty years, was said to be of almost a master craftsman's caliber.

One of his more prized efforts in the metal-working line — and a surefire conversation piece — was a silver candlestick he had fashioned from one of the spokes of a roulette wheel seized in the raid on Dick Canfield's gambling house. It was one of the few trophies he kept of his big-game hunting in the underworld.*

Automobiling was also something of a passion with the man who was said to have been the first to employ a motorcar in political campaigning and who had known the open road since the days when driving was an adventure complicated by maddened horses, enraged farmers, unmarked and unpaved roads. He was a fast but careful driver. On a long journey he would stop every hour on the hour, get out of the car, puff on a

* The poker chips taken in the Canfield raid also wound up in Jerome's possession. He used them in poker games at which he was the host. They were also the playthings of his grandchildren, who played tiddlywinks and other games with them.

cigarette and walk around for exactly five minutes before starting out again.

Politics, of course, continued to absorb him; it seems to hold an unbreakable fascination for any who have played the game, the losers as much as the winners. But it was a sort of secret vice. On the surface he appeared to be contemptuous of those who would sacrifice everything, betray their friends and allies and enslave themselves to a fickle and often ill-informed electorate for the dubious rewards of public office. He looked on the ordinary political type, whether it was Warren Gamaliel Harding or the lowliest heeler for a district leader, as someone lacking in wit and imagination.

His interest being rather parochial, he viewed politics as a means of keeping officeholders in line, of throwing out rascals and frightening the political machines into behaving with a certain decent circumspection. A mugwump to the end, his active interest was centered on local politics and the recurring necessity for reform, and Tammany Hall remained the focus of his resentment and suspicion.

He was interviewed fairly frequently by the newspapers, and his aphorisms were generally quotable and carried a sting.

Tammany Hall, as he defined it, was "a quasi-criminal organization that has existed since the days of Aaron Burr on public plunder."

On the difference between graft and corruption at the turn of the century and in the twenties: "The only difference is that the stealing is more refined. In my day they took what they wanted and made no bones about it."

On President Franklin D. Roosevelt and the "vagaries" of the New Deal's first year: "I am reminded of a quack doctor feeding bread pills to a hysterical woman."*

He detested Prohibition in company with most freedom- and

* The quotations are from the New York *Times* for Oct. 25, 1921, Oct. 2, 1933 and June 18, 1933.

whisky-loving Americans, and did not let it stop him from enjoying his daily quota of highballs. What particularly appalled him about the dry laws was the way they encouraged the growth of racketeering and the strengthening of the underworld's grip in many areas of the nation's existence, as well as the public's indifference to the situation. He accurately foresaw that repeal of Prohibition, desirable as it was, would come too late to reduce the underworld's growing power. "Many think that repeal will end rackets," he told reporters as he sailed for a summer on the Brittany coast on June 17, 1933, "but it won't. If the racketeers are not stopped, they will go into other lines of effort after repeal. It is certain they are not going to join the church." Today's headlines bear him out.

Twice he ventured back into the New York political arena, when the trumpets of reform sounded and there was a youthful stirring in his blood and once again he faced the roaring crowds, waving placards and upturned, hopeful faces of his fellow citizens. The first time was in 1921, when he campaigned for Major Henry H. Curran in a hard-fought mayoralty campaign; the second in 1933, during the upsurge of reform led by Fiorello H. La Guardia.

In the first instance, when he was still in his vigorous early sixties, he stumped the city from Brooklyn to the Bronx like the dragon-slayer of twenty years before.

Some of the excitement had gone out of political campaigning — no more torchlights, no more beer busts, no more parades led by brass bands. People had grown more sophisticated, less easily swayed. The microphone and loudspeaker, forerunners of an electronic revolution in campaigning, already had made their appearance. But the chance of turning out the current villain of the civic-minded, Mayor John F. Hylan, a Tammany man, and of raising reform's banners once again exhilarated him. He threw in with the Coalition candidates, headed by Major Curran and including La Guardia, then president of the Board of Aldermen, on October 19, 1921, when the campaign was well under way. It had been ten years since he mounted a political platform, he told reporters, but he was "delighted" to join the fight against "a grotesque mountebank who for four years has made the people of our city ashamed."

Tammany front man he undoubtedly was, but there was little of the "grotesque" about the prosaic Hylan. Jerome's wrath was partly stimulated by the fact that Hylan was a political protégé of William Randolph Hearst. Hearst had made his peace with Tammany but Jerome was not so forgiving. "If I had been willing to kowtow just a little to Tammany Hall," he once told his daughter-in-law, "I could have been governor."

The pungent Robert Moses has characterized Hylan as "a decent political hack . . . dull, plodding and transparent." Whatever the maladministration charged to him during his first term, he had endeared himself to a large section of the electorate by expanding the subway system and pledging himself to defend the five-cent subway fare to his last dying breath. For many years the five-cent fare was the First Article of Faith of any aspiring New York politician.

The night of October 21, addressing a rally of the Seventh Assembly District Republican Club at Broadway and Eightieth Street, he made his reappearance as a political orator. Advance publicity that Jerome would speak, reawakening memories of "Jerome on the Square" and the way he had roused the city, caused quite a flutter on the upper West Side. There was room for only three hundred persons in the clubhouse but two thousand more thronged the streets outside to listen to him over the loudspeakers. One reporter observed that the crowd was "visibly stirred" as he "traced the entire political career of John F. Hylan in the manner of a prosecutor." The city, he told his audience, had been "misgoverned by a gang of abominable grafters for four years." He suggested that Curran's campaign slogan be "Treat 'em rough." He scoffed at Hylan's claim to having had a successful business career, recalling that his first venture was "manufacturing bicycle whistles" and his subsequent enterprises were "not as clean as bicycle whistles." When he was through, the crowd had reached such a pitch of enthusiasm that it took the police half an hour to clear a path to his car for him.*

In subsequent speeches, Jerome ripped into Mayor Hylan's claims to being the defender of the five-cent fare, pointing out that a ten-cent fare would be "confiscatory"; replied to charges that he had been hired by Curran's campaign committee at the rate of $2,000 a speech by labeling them "indications that somebody is getting hurt"; spilled scorn over Hylan's "Honest John" sobriquet, and charged that the Hylan administration had neglected the city's schools to the point that the number of children forced to attend part-time sessions had increased from 36,000 to 122,000 — the old Jerome mixture of fact and invective, hurled at his audiences with great vehemence.

"I'll stick to him [Hylan] until I get my knife under his fifth rib!" he roared at a rally in Washington Heights, using a curious figure of speech for a man celebrated for his prosecution of murderers.

On the lower East Side, his return aroused so much fervor that heckling became a dangerous pastime at any meetings addressed by Jerome. The night of November 5, in a rally at Public School 65, the school auditorium was the scene of violence when Jerome's speech was interrupted by a man who demanded to know why this campaign's reform party was known as the Coalition instead of the familiar Fusion. "The word Coalition is used in England by the party fighting and killing Irishmen," the heckler pointed out. He was quickly surrounded by menacing Coalitionists, despite Jerome's plea that he be allowed to come up on the platform and argue the matter out. In a few moments, he was kicked and beaten insensible and thrown out on the street, regardless of Jerome's attempts to calm the crowd.

* According to the New York *Times*' account, Oct. 22, 1921.

It appeared that Jerome was stirring up a tidal wave of enthusiasm for the Coalition ticket, but when the votes were counted two days later "Honest John" Hylan was re-elected by a 417,000 plurality, the biggest in the city's history. The people, it seemed, were willing to listen to Jerome, to cheer him and be momentarily impressed by his fiery personality, but his attack on the Hylan administration had been too general, too weighted with the clichés of "graft" and "corruption" to sway their votes. The burning issue was simply not there.

On his next and last foray into the bear pit of municipal politics, burning issues abounded. The year was sober and hungover 1933, the city was still recovering from the long binge of the Jimmy Walker years and his carefree antics as the fun-loving "Night Mayor." His successor had been the earnest bumbler, John P. O'Brien, who was no match, politically, ethically or intellectually, for the little firebrand Fiorello La Guardia, the nominee of the reform element once again banded together as the Fusion party.

Jerome was now seventy-four years old, but he could not resist a last fling when he returned from a trip abroad that fall and found the city in a rage for reform, with forlorn apple-sellers on every corner and the streets uneasy with hundreds of thousands of the hopelessly unemployed. "Dire economic pressure," he had said a year ago, "is the only great reformer." That pressure was now frighteningly evident as it had not been in 1921.

He joined the Fusion effort as chairman of the campaign committee for one of his former assistant district attorneys, Chief Justice Frederic Kernochan, Court of General Sessions, who was seeking re-election. "I'll tell you why I'm here," he announced to reporters in Kernochan's Paramount Building headquarters. "I have been messing around in reform and Fusion movements since 1890. The recent Fusion movements have not succeeded in making a political issue out of the Divine Commandment 'Thou

Shalt Not Steal.' New York City has been systematically looted for thirty years by a gang of thieves."

La Guardia was swept into office with a plurality of 260,000 in the first Fusion victory in twenty years, but Jerome's candidate was among the few Fusionists who was not carried along by the general landslide.

More than four decades of intermittent politicking thus were closed out for Jerome with a final defeat, vicarious though it was . . .

In other areas, he was more successful. The last dozen years of his life were devoted, in addition to his law practice, to the development of Technicolor, the pioneer colored motion picture process whose corporate vicissitudes provided one of the minor epics of Hollywood and Wall Street in the early years of their uneasy marriage. A group of Bostonians had developed the process, principally Dr. Herbert T. Kalmus and his wife Natalie, Dr. D. F. Comstock, Professor E. J. Wall, W. B. Wescott, C. A. Willat and J. A. Ball. The first Technicolor film was produced in 1917, an adventure picture titled *The Gulf Between* and filmed in Florida, which stirred little interest except from the technical standpoint. Projecting the film required so many special attachments, as the late Dr. Kalmus recalled,* that the projectionist almost had to be "a cross between a college professor and an acrobat, a phrase which I have since heard repeated many times." In the next two years, however, Dr. Kalmus and his associates managed to develop multi-component processes which eliminated most of the difficulties in the projection booth.

Jerome, who was fascinated by scientific subjects of many kinds, attended a showing of *The Gulf Between* and was convinced of Technicolor's possibilities. A wealthy client asked him to investigate its potential as an investment, and Jerome recommended it. His client turned down the recommendation, but

---

* In a paper read before the Society of Motion Picture Engineers in their Fall, 1938 meeting.

Jerome and several friends raised $40,000 to keep the company going. Without that tinkerer's and hobbyist's fascination of Jerome's, Technicolor would probably never have become one of the industrial giants of Hollywood. Its first and continuing need was for money with which to buy the time and effort required to perfect the process and capture Hollywood's interest. And the money problem became Jerome's principal concern as counsel, propagandist and eventually chairman of the board of directors. In all, he later estimated, he raised $4,000,000 to keep Technicolor in operation during the lean years.

In 1920, he persuaded three of Hollywood's mightiest, Marcus A. Loew, Joseph M. Schenck and his brother Nicholas — who between them were the chief financial powers behind what became Metro–Goldwyn–Mayer and Twentieth Century Fox — that they should make a full-length film in Technicolor. It was *The Toll of the Sea*, starring Anna May Wong and directed by Chester Franklin. Right from the start Technicolor established the rule that any production made with its process must have a Technicolor adviser and a Technicolor cameraman attached to oversee every detail of the photography. *The Toll of the Sea* was a mild success, grossing $250,000, of which Technicolor received $165,000.*

Several other Hollywood productions were filmed in color, including *The Wanderer of the Wasteland* and *Ben Hur*, the latter requiring four different Technicolor cameras to capture the spectacle of pagan Rome. (This was the version in which Ramon Novarro starred.) A greater coup was persuading Douglas Fairbanks, Sr. to shoot his million-dollar film *The Black Pirate* in color. Fairbanks finally admitted that he "could not imagine piracy without color," and the film was a resounding success, but as Dr. Kalmus later recorded "for the Technicolor company it was a terrible headache. Technicolor was still making the double-

* According to *Technicolor Adventures in Cinemaland*, a pamphlet written by Dr. Kalmus.

coated, cemented-together relief prints, so that the red and green images were not quite in the same plane, and the pictures didn't project too sharply on the screen." New prints had to be sent to all the exchanges. When word of these projection difficulties got around, the Hollywood studio heads advised Technicolor they would make no more films in color until the company had developed a sure-fire process which would eliminate blurred and overlapping images.

The only solution, it appeared, was for Technicolor to make a number of short subjects itself to prove the bugs had been eliminated from the process.

By now two and a half million dollars had been spent in half a dozen years. The board of directors, which Jerome now headed, could have decided to cut their losses and give up the struggle. Jerome, however, believed they were on the brink of success, and with his fellow directors firmly in tow went along with the plans of Technicolor's creative and scientific brains.

As Dr. Kalmus put it, they had to "prove that there was nothing mysterious about the operation of Technicolor cameras." Jerome and his fellow directors got the money up, and several two-reelers on patriotic subjects were produced, possibly on the theory that even a hard-boiled Hollywood producer would hesitate to criticize a flag-waver. This time the films were shown without any outcropping of technical difficulties. Technicolor was ready for the next technological revolution in Hollywood — the coming of sound. At first Technicolor inserts of production numbers were made for several of the big musicals filmed in that turbulent period. Then Warner Brothers signed up for twenty films to be made in Technicolor. In 1930 Technicolor signed contracts for thirty-six feature-length films; its laboratory crews were working three shifts, and $3,000,000 was spent for new plants and equipment.

Wall Street was amazed by its success story, most of the experts having written it off years before as unpromising. In a fifteen-month period its stock jumped from one dollar to forty-two dollars on the exchange. At the beginning of 1929 the company owed its creditors $750,000, but four months later all debts were discharged and a cash reserve was being built up.* Technicolor stock boomed even as most other issues were still trying to find bottom on Wall Street. Production slacked off in 1931, but by that time the company had worked out a three-color process much superior to the old two-component system, and a lucrative association was formed with Walt Disney, who began making his cartoons in color.

Technicolor was firmly established, artistically and financially, and Jerome, in the last few years of his life, found himself a man of considerable substance. The New York *Sun* reported that, in addition to his income from Technicolor, he was earning more than $100,000 a year as a lawyer, largely from fees for handling estates. He found this autumnal success no less sweet than the more publicized triumphs of his earlier years; besides it delighted the gambler in him, for he had invested everything he had in Technicolor and it had turned out a royal flush. Now that he was a success in business as his father and uncles had been, he could afford to be "contemptuous of the adulation that once warmed him" in politics, look upon it as "all water over the dam," announce himself "a little bored" with the more celebrated Jerome of twenty-five years ago, as a magazine interviewer observed.**

His life was comfortable, with just enough work to occupy him a day or two a week at his law offices overlooking the harbor, and no more than that in connection with Technicolor's prospering affairs.

To the last few weeks of his life he maintained his interest in public affairs, castigating Jimmy Walker for having "quit under

* Interviews with Jerome in the Yonkers *Statesman*, April 18, 1929; the New York *Evening Post* of the day before.
** Milton MacKaye in *The New Yorker*, Jan. 30, 1932.

fire," proclaiming that what the country needed was "another Grover Cleveland" rather than another Roosevelt, and cynically remarking of an old collective enemy: "Tammany goes out and Tammany comes back in. No Tammany investigation is ever futile. Tammany, by the calendar, must be investigated every fifteen years to keep the boys from stealing the town."

He refused to consider writing his memoirs, telling Samuel T. Williamson of the New York *Times* on October 25, 1932, "When I'm ready to write 'em, I'll be ready to die. That seems to be the only thing left to a man who writes of his past. To write of it he must think it more important than the life to come."

Thus his life was robust and active to the end, which came quickly and relatively painlessly in his seventy-fifth year, when he contracted pneumonia in the damp chill of February in his native Manhattan. He sank into a coma and died on February 13, 1934 in the house he shared with Mrs. Elliot.

"No greater monument to a public official has ever been erected than that every man who served under Mr. Jerome is labeled 'one of the Jerome men,'" said Mayor La Guardia. "We have not had a district attorney since William Travers Jerome held that office."

"No one who lived through those fighting days of Mr. Jerome's," said the *Times* in an editorial reflecting on the "intangibles" of his career, "can forget the sort of thrill which ran through this city, and, indeed, spread to other cities throughout the land."

Though no one said in the outpouring of eulogies, the great value of his career, the great "tangible" which left its mark on countless other men, was the fact that he proved to millions of immigrant Americans, not just in New York but all over the country, that the rule of the law — one of his pet phrases — applied to all.

Private funeral services were conducted by the Reverend Dr. Harry Emerson Fosdick, attended only by members of his family (excepting Lavinia, who was very ill and died less than four months later), his friends (including Mrs. Elliot, who survived him by a quarter of a century), and the now graying men who had served in their youth as members of his staff. He was buried in the family vault at Greenwood Cemetery, Brooklyn, among the kinfolk, playboys and Puritans, who had enlivened the island-borough across the river for almost a century.

One floral tribute would surely have amazed him; just possibly it would have touched him more than any of the others. "Though we have been enemies," the card with it read, "I have always respected you." It was signed by Harry K. Thaw.

A Note on Sources

The author is greatly indebted to several persons for whatever intimacy with the subject has been achieved in this book. Mrs. John Sloane, who was Mrs. William Travers Jerome, Jr. until her first husband's death, demonstrated great insight, intelligence and compassion in reminiscing about her late father-in-law. Likewise her eldest son, Dean William Travers Jerome, III, head of the College of Business Administration, Syracuse University. Their frankness was admirable. Previous attempts at writing a biography of Mr. Jerome were discouraged by his family because of certain phases of his extra-marital life, which they did not want revealed until after the death of the lady involved — and she was a lady — several years ago. On the other hand, they did not want the truth concealed, being not in the least ashamed of it. I am thankful for their trust, and hope it has not been betrayed. They will not have read a line of this until after publication.

I am also greatly, though posthumously, indebted to my late father-in-law, Augustin Derby, former dean of the New York University Law School, who served as an assistant under Jerome, for portions of his unpublished memoirs. And to Horace W. Hewlett, Secretary of Amherst College; Joseph L. Andrews, reference librarian of the Association of the Bar of New York City, and Charles W. Carpenter of the New York office of Technicolor, Inc.

Genealogical data, incidentally, was derived from Jerome family records at the Connecticut State Library, the family itself, Sir Winston Churchill's *Lord Randolph Churchill*, and an article in the spring, 1952 issue of the *Genesee Country Scrapbook*. Further information was obtained from the obituaries of Lawrence Jerome in the New York *Times* and New York *Herald* of August 13, 1888. The family

A Note on Sources

Bible of Isaac and Aurora Jerome, paternal grandparents of William Travers Jerome, was filled in with unrecorded births by their granddaughter, Miss Margaret Middleton, at a later date. It is now in the possession of Mrs. Sloane.

Bibliography

Amory, Cleveland, *Who Killed Society?*, New York, 1960.

Baldwin, Charles C., *Stanford White*, New York, 1931.

Barrett, James W., *Joseph Pulitzer and His World*, New York, 1941.

Butler, Richard J., and Driscoll, Joseph, *Dock Walloper*, New York, 1933.

Cassity, Dr. John Holland, *The Quality of Murder*, New York, 1958.

Chambers, Walter, *Samuel Seabury, A Challenge*, New York, 1932.

Churchill, Allen, *Park Row*, New York, 1958.

Churchill, Winston, *Lord Randolph Churchill*, New York, 1907.

Clews, Henry, *Fifty Years in Wall Street*, New York, 1908.

Cobb, Irvin S., *Exit Laughing*, Indianapolis, 1941.

Collins, Frederick L., *Glamorous Sinners*, New York, 1932.

Dunn, Robert, *World Alive*, New York, 1956.

Fowler, Gene, *Good Night, Sweet Prince*, New York, 1943.

Gardiner, Alexander, *Canfield: The True Story of the Greatest Gambler*, New York, 1930.

Garrett, Charles, *The La Guardia Years*, New Brunswick, 1962.

Golden, Harry, *Only in America*, Cleveland, 1958.

Hand, Richard L., *Report to Governor Hughes*, Albany, 1908.

Hapgood, Norman, *The Changing Years*, New York, 1930.

Hendrick, Burton J., *The Age of Big Business*, New Haven, 1920.

Hodder, A. L., *A Fight for the City*, New York, 1903.

Hoyt, Edwin P., *The Vanderbilts and Their Fortunes*, New York, 1962.

Jerome, Wiliam Travers, *District Attorney Jerome on Yellow Journalism* (a pamphlet), New York, 1906.

Kalmus, H. T., *Technicolor Adventures in Cinemaland* (a pamphlet), New York, 1938.

Leslie, Anita, *The Remarkable Mr. Jerome*, New York, 1954.

Levy, Newman, *The Nan Patterson Case*, New York, 1959.

Lord, Walter, *The Good Years*, New York, 1960.

Low, Benjamin, *Seth Low*, New York, 1925.

MacKaye, Milton, *The Tin Box Parade*, New York, 1934.

Mackenzie, F. A., *The Trial of Harry Thaw*, London, 1928.

Myers, Gustavus, *The History of Tammany Hall*, New York, 1917.

O'Connor, Richard, *The Scandalous Mr. Bennett*, New York, 1962.

Rovere, Richard H., *Howe & Hummel: Their True and Scandalous History*, New York, 1947.

Seitz, Don C., *Joseph Pulitzer: His Life and Letters*, New York, 1924.

Sinclair, Upton, *American Outpost*, New York, 1932.

Steffens, Lincoln, *Autobiography*, Boston, 1931.

Stoddard, Lothrop, *Master of Manhattan*, New York, 1931.

Strong, George Templeton, *The Diary of George Templeton Strong* (edited by Allan Nevins and Milton Halsey Thomas), New York, 1952.

Swanberg, W. A., *Citizen Hearst*, New York, 1961.

Terhune, Albert Payson, *To the Best of My Memory*, New York, 1930.

Thaw, Mary Copley, *The Secret Unveiled* (a pamphlet), New York, 1909.

Train, Arthur, *From the District Attorney's Office*, New York, 1939.
——— *My Day in Court*, New York, 1939.

Wall, E. Berry, *Neither Pest Nor Puritan*, New York, 1940.

Wecter, Dixon, *The Saga of American Society*, New York, 1937.

Werner, M. R., *Tammany Hall*, New York, 1928.

Woollcott, Alexander, *While Rome Burns*, New York, 1935.

PERIODICALS

Amherst Graduates Quarterly (May, 1934)
Collier's Weekly
Current Opinion
Fortnightly Review
Genesee Country Scrapbook (spring, 1952)
Ainslee's Magazine (January, 1902)
Life

The New Yorker (January 30, 1932)
Journal of the Society of Motion Picture Engineers (December, 1938)
Literary Digest
The Nation
Time
World's Work

NEWSPAPERS

Manhattan:
Morning and Evening World
Herald
Tribune
Herald–Tribune
Times
Journal
American
Mail & Express
Globe
Morning and Evening Sun
Commercial Advertiser

Elsewhere:
Yonkers *Statesman*
Boston *American*
Baltimore Post
Brooklyn *Standard–Union*

Index